W9-BZL-667

Neoconservative Criticism:

Norman Podhoretz, Kenneth S. Lynn, and Joseph Epstein

Twayne's United States Authors Series

Frank Day, Editor

Clemson University

TUSAS 571

Neoconservative Criticism:

Norman Podhoretz, Kenneth S. Lynn, and Joseph Epstein

Mark Royden Winchell

Clemson University

Twayne Publishers
A Division of G. K. Hall & Co. • Boston

Neoconservative Criticism: Norman Podhoretz, Kenneth S. Lynn, and Joseph Epstein
Mark Royden Winchell

Copyright 1991 by G. K. Hall & Co.
All rights reserved.
Published by Twayne Publishers
A division of G. K. Hall & Co.
70 Lincoln Street
Boston, Massachusetts 02111

Photograph of Norman Podhoretz by Leslie Jean-Bart.
Photograph of Kenneth S. Lynn courtesy of Kenneth S. Lynn.
Photograph of Joseph Epstein by Fran and Arnold Kapp,
used courtesy Joseph Epstein.

Copyediting supervised by Barbara Sutton.
Book production by Gabrielle B. McDonald.
Typeset in Garamond
by Huron Valley Graphics, Inc., of Ann Arbor, Michigan.

First published 1991.
10 9 8 7 6 5 4 3 2 1

The paper used in this publication meets the minimum requirements
of American National Standard for Information Sciences—Permanence
of Paper for Printed Library Materials, ANSI Z39.48-1984.∞™

Printed and bound in the United States of America.

Library of Congress Cataloging-in-Publication Data

Winchell, Mark Royden, 1948–
    Neoconservative criticism : Norman Podhoretz, Kenneth S. Lynn, and
Joseph Epstein / Mark Royden Winchell.
        p.   cm.—(Twayne's United States authors series ; TUSAS 571)
    Includes bibliographical references and index.
    ISBN 0-8057-7617-6 (alk. paper)
    1. Criticism—United States—History—20th century.   2. American
literature—History and criticism—Theory, etc.   3. Conservatism and
literature—History—20th century.   4. Podhoretz, Norman.   5. Lynn,
Kenneth Schuyler.   6. Epstein, Joseph, 1937–   .   I. Title.
II. Series.
PS78.W56 1991
801'95'09730904—dc20   90-45277

For Christopher and Robin

Contents

Preface

This study was originally conceived as an essay in rebuttal to Sanford Pinsker's 1984 attack on the "neoconservative critics." But I soon realized that nothing short of a book would do justice to what Pinsker, with a flair for alliteration, calls "revisionism with rancor." If anything, I regret having to squeeze my discussion of these three prolific and provocative polemicists (this alliteration bug can be contagious) into the limits of a single slim volume. Because my first chapter attempts to describe neoconservative criticism and to argue for the preeminence of Norman Podhoretz, Kenneth S. Lynn, and Joseph Epstein within that school, I will not anticipate myself here.

I have begun with Podhoretz because he was the first of the three to "make it" in the literary world and because he is the one who has most doggedly positioned himself at the "bloody crossroads" where literature and politics meet. I deal with his autobiographical volumes, move on to his essays on Jewish literature and culture, and conclude with chapter-length discussions of his two collections of literary essays, *Doings and Undoings* and *The Bloody Crossroads*, published over twenty years apart. Because of the nature of this series, I say little about Podhoretz's two books on foreign policy.

Kenneth S. Lynn is the oldest of the trio and the most conventionally academic. Although he arrived at the bloody crossroads much more recently than Podhoretz, his early work merits attention in its own, largely apolitical, right. Lynn's first book, *The Dream of Success*, and the essays collected in *Visions of America* place him firmly in the interdisciplinary American studies tradition of his Harvard mentors F. O. Matthiessen and Perry Miller. In his biographical studies of Mark Twain and William Dean Howells (particularly the latter), Lynn demonstrates an ability to write literary history for both a scholarly and general audience. Not until the essays collected in *The Air-Line to Seattle* (1983) did he begin to show his neoconservative colors. In his 1987 biography of Hemingway, Lynn put all of his talents together to produce a truly remarkable book. I discuss all of these literary studies, while reluctantly passing over Lynn's editorial labors and his important historical volume *A Divided People*.

Joseph Epstein gets the most space here because he has written the most. I have been able to do little more than provide a taste of his three volumes of familiar essays and his two collections of literary criticism. A discussion of his book *Ambition: The Secret Passion* finds a home in the midst of a more general consideration of Epstein as self-appointed culture cop. Because the focus of this volume is literary and cultural criticism, I have reluctantly chosen not to discuss Epstein's short fiction or his sociological study *Divorced in America*. I should note, however, that by the late 1980s the short stories had become numerous enough and good enough to suggest that Epstein might yet achieve distinction as a creative writer. One of his early efforts in the genre, "The Count and the Princess," was selected for *Best American Short Stories of 1982*.

In his 1987 collection *Once More around the Block*, Epstein predicted that literary scholarship would one day reach the point where even he became "a candidate for a book in an author series that has already exhausted such authors for the ages as Kurt Vonnegut and Philip Roth." That day has probably come sooner than Epstein would have imagined, even if he does have to share top billing. Podhoretz, Lynn, and Epstein may not yet be authors for the ages, but they are certainly among the most important voices in contemporary literary criticism.

I am grateful to Norman Podhoretz, Kenneth S. Lynn, and Joseph Epstein for cooperating with this study of their criticism. Particular debts of gratitude are owed to my editors Frank Day and Elizabeth Traynor Fowler, who helped conceive this book and bring it to term, and to Betsy Dendy, who prepared the index. As always, my wife, Donna, has supported me in ways too numerous to mention and too incalculable to repay.

Chronologies

Norman Podhoretz

1930   Born 16 January in Brooklyn, New York; son of Julius and Helen Woliner Podhoretz.

1950   Receives A.B., Columbia University (studies under Lionel Trilling), and B.H.L., Jewish Theological Seminary.

1952   Receives B.A., Cambridge University (studies under F. R. Leavis).

1953–1955   Serves in U.S. Army.

1955–1956   Assistant editor of *Commentary*. Writes for *Partisan Review* and other literary magazines.

1956   Marries Midge Rosenthal Decter on 21 October; they
        have two children, Ruth and John; Decter has two
        children from a previous marriage, Rachel and Naomi.

1956–1958 Associate editor of *Commentary*. Reviews books for the
        New Yorker.

1957   Receives M.A., Cambridge University.

1958   Member of University Seminar of American Civiliza-
        tion, Columbia University.

1958–1960 Editor in chief at Looking Glass Library.

1960   Becomes editor in chief of *Commentary*.

1963   "My Negro Problem—and Ours" published in *Commentary*.

1964   *Doings and Undoings*.

1966   *The Commentary Reader*.

1967   *Making It*.

1968   Supports Eugene McCarthy for president.

1969   Receives L. H. D., Hamilton College.

1976   Supports Scoop Jackson for president and Daniel Pat-
        rick Moynihan for U.S. Senate.

1979   *Breaking Ranks*.

1980   *The Present Danger;* receives D. Litt., Jewish Theologi-
        cal Seminary; supports Ronald Reagan for president.

1981   Appointed chairman of New Directions Advisory Com-
        mittee, U.S. Information Agency.

1982   *Why We Were in Vietnam*.

1983   Committee for the Free World sponsors conference on
        "Our Country and Our Culture" in New York City.

1986   *The Bloody Crossroads*. Quarrels with Gore Vidal over
        Vidal's allegedly anti-Semitic article in the *Nation*.

Kenneth S. Lynn

1923 Born 17 June in Cleveland, Ohio; son of Ernest Lee and Edna Marcey Lynn.

1943–1946 Serves in U.S. Army Air Force.

1947 Receives A.B., Harvard University (studies under F. O. Matthiessen and Perry Miller).

1948 Marries Valerie Ann Roemer on 28 September; they have three children, Andrew, Elisabeth, and Sophia.

1950 Receives M.A., Harvard (studies under Perry Miller and Oscar Handlin).

1954 Receives Ph.D., Harvard. Thesis directed by Oscar Handlin.

1954–1955 Instructor of English at Harvard.

1955 *The Dream of Success.*

1955–1959 Assistant professor at Harvard.

1958 *The Comic Tradition in America;* Fulbright lecturer in Denmark.

1959 *Mark Twain and Southwestern Humor.*

1959–1963 Associate professor at Harvard.

1961 *The Scarlet Letter: Text, Sources, Criticism.*

1963 *The American Society.*

1963–1964 Visiting professor at the University of Madrid.

1963–1968 Professor of English at Harvard.

1964–1968 Chairs Harvard's American Civilization program.

1965 *The Professions in America.*

1968–1969 Professor of American Studies at Federal City College in Washington, D.C.

1969 Becomes professor of history at Johns Hopkins University. Currently Arthur O. Lovejoy Professor.

1971 *William Dean Howells: An American Life.*

1973 *Visions of America.*

1977 *A Divided People.*

1983 *The Air-Line to Seattle.*

1984 Attacked by Malcolm Cowley in the summer issue of the *Georgia Review.*

1987 *Hemingway.*

Joseph Epstein

1937   Born 9 January in Chicago, son of Maurice and Belle Abrams Epstein.

1958–1960   Serves in U.S. Army in Missouri, Texas, and Little Rock, Arkansas. In Texas, works on the Fort Hood weekly newspaper.

1959   Receives A.B., University of Chicago.

1960   Marries Joan Elizabeth Bales; they have two children, Mark and Burton.

1960–1964   Works as a free-lance writer and editor in Chicago. Associate editor of the *New Leader* magazine in New York.

1964   Returns to Arkansas; administrative officer for North Little Rock Urban Renewal Agency.

1965–1966   Directs antipoverty program in Pulaski County, Arkansas.

1966–1970   Returns to Chicago; senior editor at *Encyclopaedia Britannica.*

1970   Divorced from Joan Elizabeth Bales.

1970–1971   Editor for Quadrangle Books in Chicago.

1971–1974   Works as free-lance writer in Chicago.

1974   Joins English Department of Northwestern University as visiting lecturer on literature and writing. *Divorced in America.*

1975   Becomes editor of the *American Scholar.*

1976   Marries Barbara Maher on 27 February.

1979   *Familiar Territory;* "Race Relations" (story) in March issue of *Harper's.*

1980   *Ambition.*

1981   *Masters.*

1982   "The Count and the Princess" (story) in spring issue of the *Hudson Review.*

1983   *The Middle of My Tether;* "The Count and the Princess" in *Best American Short Stories.*

1985   *Plausible Prejudices;* "Schlifkin on My Books" (story) in spring issue of the *Hudson Review.*

1987   *Once More around the Block.*

1988   "No Pulitzer for Pinsker" (story) in March issue of *Commentary.*

1989   *Partial Payments;* three stories in *Commentary:* "Low Anxiety" (January), "Kaplan's Big Deal" (June), and "The Goldin Boys" (October).

Chapter One
Ideas Have Consequences

In the summer 1984 issue of the *Georgia Review*, Sanford Pinsker warned that a gang of right-wing bullies was out to dominate literary criticism in America. He entitled his jeremiad "Revisionism with Rancor: The Threat of the Neoconservative Critics" and prefaced it with Ernest Hemingway's trenchant remark: "If the boys swing to the left in literature you may make a small bet the next swing will be to the right and some of the same yellow bastards will swing both ways."[1] Although neoconservatism had already become a fixture in American politics, this was probably the first time that anyone had applied the term to a school of literary criticism.

The idea that literary study could be a political act was hardly new, but for as long as anyone could remember this had been a left-wing game. For some time feminists and racial minorities had been trying to revise the canon, and the dreary Marxists had never really gone away. To find a genuinely conservative body of American criticism, one had to go back to the Vanderbilt Agrarians of the thirties or, a generation earlier, to the New England neohumanists. Since then, critics of a conservative temperament had shunned the social approach to literature in favor of a more disinterested aesthetic formalism. But Pinsker, in tones befitting an epidemiologist announcing a new black plague, was here to warn us that literary criticism had now entered the age of Ronald Reagan.

Swinging the Other Way

Although the term "neoconservative" was coined by Michael Harrington in the early 1970s, the phenomenon is a good deal older. If a neoconservative is anyone who has moved from left to right politically, William Wordsworth—who admired the French Revolution as a young man but later became a high church Tory—would certainly qualify. In fact, because the term *conservative* first entered the political lexicon around the time of the French Revolution, neoconservatism would seem to be almost as old as conservatism itself. But that is probably reaching back too far. Today's neoconservatives do not resemble the elder Wordsworth any more than Lee Atwater resembles Edmund Burke. We need to look to more recent political history for our frame of reference.

In postwar America there has been no shortage of former leftists swinging the other way. Minor figures such as Will Herberg, Frank Meyer, and Willmoore Kendell made the political pilgrimage from the far left to the far right, as did such heavyweights as James Burnham, Max Eastman, Whittaker Chambers, and John Dos Passos—all to serve on the masthead of *National Review*. (Even Richard Weaver was a member of the Socialist party during his undergraduate days at the University of Kentucky.) To call these men neoconservatives, however, would be to suggest that their political conversions were more gradual and less dramatic than was actually the case. (Chambers even rejected the label "conservative," preferring to call himself a counterrevolutionary or a man of the Right). Seeing what lay at the end of the road down which they were heading, these men slammed on the brakes and reversed course without so much as a pit stop on the anti-Stalinist Left. In contrast, the leading neoconservatives of our day are what the anti-Stalinist Left has become. Although little more than minor figures in the ideological wars of the thirties, such men as Irving Kristol, Nathan Glazer, and Daniel Bell are now the intellectual and spiritual heirs of Lionel Trilling and Sidney Hook.

Since World War II the American Right has been a coalition of three distinct philosophical interest groups: cultural traditionalists, economic libertarians, and militant anti-Communists. Although it is possible to belong to one of these groups without buying into either of the other two, sectarian differences have usually been held in check in the interest of fighting the common enemy on the Left. The intellectuals known as neoconservatives are recent converts to laissez-faire economics and have been cultural traditionalists from the cradle; however, their present commitment to the Right is primarily an outgrowth of the struggle between pro-Communist and anti-Communist intellectuals during the middle decades of this century. It is impossible to understand neoconservatism without knowing something of the history of this struggle.

In the thirties the lines were drawn between the fellow-traveling intellectuals who were determined to support Stalin no matter what (e.g., Lillian Hellman, Dashiell Hammett, Nelson Algren, and Malcolm Cowley) and those who broke with the Soviet Union over the Moscow show trials (e.g., Edmund Wilson, Waldo Frank, and the *Partisan Review* crowd). Those divisions were again apparent in the postwar era when pro-Soviet intellectuals supported the Communist dupe Henry Wallace for president and, despite convincing evidence to the contrary, affirmed the innocence of Soviet spies Alger Hiss and Julius and Ethel Rosenberg. By the time Joseph McCarthy and his various clones were intent on ferreting out suspected Communists from every nook and cranny of American life, the intellectual community was split on the question of who posed the greater threat to personal freedom: international communism or the American government itself. In the sixties, opposition to the war in Vietnam grew so virulently anti-American that those intellectuals who supported the war or who opposed it only on strategic and not moral grounds became an increasingly embattled minority. Finally, as the New Left radicals of the sixties became the Democratic party power brokers of the seventies, the anti-Communist Left ceased to exist as a force in American politics. Thus in the 1980s, cold war liberals, who probably would have preferred voting for Henry Jackson, became Reagan Democrats by default.[2]

Remembering Who They Aren't

Throughout the 1980s much ink, though little blood, was spilled in an attempt to distinguish neoconservatism from the Old Right. Perhaps the sharpest polemical blow for the old guard was struck by Stephen J. Tonsor when he wrote, "It is splendid when the town whore gets religion and joins the church. Now and then she makes a good choir director, but when she begins to tell the minister what he ought to say in his Sunday sermons, matters have been carried too far." Tonsor goes on to speculate that "had Stalin spared Leon Trotsky and not had him murdered in Mexico, he would no doubt have spent his declining years in an office in the Hoover Library writing his memoirs and contributing articles of a faintly neoconservative flavor to *Encounter* and *Commentary.*"[3]

Summing up in more measured terms the popularly understood distinctions between paleoconservatives and neoconservatives, Dan Himmelfarb identified a difference of chronology (old-timers vs. newcomers), mind-set (humanists vs. social scientists), religion (Christians vs. Jews), and intensity of belief (zealots vs. moderates).[4] But each of these distinctions breaks down under closer scrutiny. In neoconservative magazines and think tanks, one can find Christians who have never flirted with the Left, who are primarily literary in outlook, and who are just as uncompromising in their beliefs (particularly in their hostility to communism) as any on the Old Right.

According to Himmelfarb, a far more useful distinction can be found in the different views that neoconservatives and paleoconservatives take toward the American tradition of liberal democracy: "Neoconservatives belong to the tradition of liberal democratic modernity, the tradition of Montesquieu, Madison, and Tocqueville; paleoconservatives are the heirs to the Christian and aristocratic Middle Ages, to Augustine, Aquinas, and Hooker. The principles of neoconservatism are individual liberty, self-government, and equality of opportunity; those of paleoconservatism are religious—particularly Christian—belief, hierarchy, and prescription."[5] These are not just arcane differences in semantics; they have real implications for both interpreting the past and transforming the present.

When neoconservatives look at the American founding fathers, they see authentic liberals—"champions of individual rights, popular government, spiritual equality, and cultural and religious pluralism"; paleoconservatives see "defenders of the 'religious heritage' of Western civilization."[6] Neoconservatives oppose communism because it destroys human freedom, paleoconservatives because it is a godless religion. Adhering to the classical liberal doctrine of equality of opportunity, neoconservatives supported the early civil rights movement but now oppose attempts to achieve equality of outcome through reverse discrimination. Paleoconservatives see the entire civil rights movement as a misguided attempt to use the power of the state to enforce an unnatural social equality. On balance, neoconservatives regard themselves as the true heirs of a liberal tradition abandoned by the radical Left. (Himmelfarb suggests that paleoliberal would be a more accurate term than neoconservative.) Because the Old Right sees the liberal tradition itself as an enemy, it is occasionally willing to make common cause with neoconservatives without ever fully trusting them.

That mistrust is fully reciprocated. Consider, for example, the conflict that erupted when word got around Washington in 1981 that the new president would probably appoint the Southern conservative M. E. Bradford to be head of the National Endowment for the Humanities. A classic paleoconservative, Bradford is an ardent disciple of the rhetorician, social philosopher, and literary critic Richard M. Weaver. (Weaver has been called the Saint Paul of the Vanderbilt Agrarians, too young to have been one of the original twelve but the most effective evangelist for their position.) Unlike most American conservatives, who think that the federal government got too powerful with Franklin Roosevelt (in the case of neoconservatives, with Lyndon Johnson), Mel Bradford has had the temerity to blame an even more revered icon— Honest Abe Lincoln.[7] What's more, Bradford had supported George Wallace for president in 1972. When his appointment to head the NEH was rumored, Jessica Savitch of NBC News was visibly disturbed, George F. Will denounced Bradford on the op-ed page of the *Washington Post,* and the neoconservatives troops rallied for all-out war.

Although their public fire had usually been directed at the liberal Left, the neocons remained privately contemptuous of Old South conservatives, whose distrust of the federal government seemed attributable to lingering racism. It was only when such an individual appeared to be on the verge of assuming political power that their private contempt went public. The anti-Bradford camp closed ranks around a thoroughly respectable neoconservative Democrat, the Brooklyn native William Bennett, who was now director of the National Humanities Center in Research Triangle Park, North Carolina. Bennett had all the right neoconservative connections: he served on the board of directors of Midge Decter's Committee for the Free World, as well as the board of Irving Kristol's Institute for Educational Affairs. Moreover, he had the backing of the Heritage and Olin foundations and of Reagan's chief of staff, Jim Baker. Bradford's supporters included such paleoconservative stalwarts as Russell Kirk and Jeffrey Hart. (He was also backed by the Marxist historian Eugene Genovese, but that's another story.)

When the smoke cleared, Bennett got the nod and went on to become a major figure in American politics. As secretary of education during the second Reagan administration, the outspoken Bennett turned a job that candidate Reagan had promised to abolish into a bully pulpit for traditional values. After making his long-awaited departure from the Democratic party, Bennett was prominently mentioned as a possible Republican presidential candidate in 1988. Although he did not make that race, his position as President George Bush's "drug czar" keeps his name in the news and, as they say, his options open. Mel Bradford is back in the English Department at the University of Dallas, where he is writing a biography of Donald Davidson.

From the Back of the Book

The battle over the chairmanship of the NEH is evidence of the political importance that neoconservatives attach to high culture. As far as federal programs go, the NEH has a relatively modest budget, but in deciding which projects to fund, it exerts considerable influence on America's intellectual climate. (The even more recent debate over the willingness of the National Endowment for the Arts to fund projects many Americans regard as blasphemous and obscene suggests that the culture wars have just begun.) And, as paleoconservative godfather Richard Weaver always maintained, ideas do have consequences. William Bennett's political prominence is the result of the traditional cultural values he espouses, not of any policies he has instituted. If there was ever any doubt that a huge market for such values existed in this country, it was dispelled when, in 1987, Allan Bloom's *The Closing of the American Mind* and E. D. Hirsch's *Cultural Literacy* became two of the decade's top nonfiction best-sellers. That Bloom's book in particular, written in the erudite and scholarly style of the professional philosopher, should have enjoyed such popular success is nothing short of amazing. (How many of the people who bought the book actually read it is another matter.) As a Jewish intellectual whose view of American culture was profoundly affected by the excesses of the sixties (which he witnessed firsthand as a professor at Cornell University), Bloom himself is almost the paradigm of the academic neoconservative.

Now that the political opinions of the neoconservatives have been extensively studied, it is only a matter of time before cultural neoconservatism comes under critical scrutiny. (If scholarly articles are already being written about Bennett, Hirsch, and Bloom as educational reformers, can the dissertations and books be far behind?) Because the focus of this series is literature, it is an appropriate forum for examining what neoconservative intellectuals have to say about the books we read and teach. Unquestionably, the three neoconservative critics who have had the most to say about American literary culture are Norman Podhoretz, Kenneth S. Lynn, and Joseph Epstein. These men are generally not studied in the academy, where the new gnosticism of deconstruction, structuralism, and semiotics is now the rage. They are, however, among the few practicing critics of any persuasion who are still writing for the educated general reader. In that respect, they are clearly carrying on the tradition of literary intellectuals such as Edmund Wilson, Lionel Trilling, Philip Rahv, and Alfred Kazin.

Of the three figures treated in this book, Norman Podhoretz is the best known and the most influential. As editor of *Commentary,* he has done more than any other individual to bring neoconservative thought before the broad intellectual community. Moreover, his political memoir *Breaking Ranks*[8] offers personal testimony of how the sixties could transform a fifties' radical into a man of the Right. Some would argue, however, that because of his involvement with foreign policy, Podhoretz has let his interest in literature wane. (Sanford Pinsker made just such a charge in his *Georgia Review* article.) While it is true that Podhoretz does not do nearly as much book reviewing now as he did early in his career, his 1986 volume *The Bloody Crossroads: Where Literature and Politics Meet*[9] is a work of uncommon critical discernment and ideological passion. He not only encourages neoconservative literary criticism as an editor but continues to show the way as a writer.

Because Kenneth S. Lynn has no magazine of his own, he is not as widely known as Podhoretz and has no editorial patronage to distribute. His work, however, is familiar to readers of *Commentary,* the *American Scholar,* and other magazines of the Right (along with general-interest periodicals that pursue a multipartisan editorial policy). Since the mid-1970s, he has used those forums to revise American literary history along solidly neoconservative lines. As Pinsker points out and Lynn himself readily admits, much of this revision involves revising his own previous opinions—most notably about Mark Twain's *Adventures of Huckleberry Finn.* Lynn is the most conventionally academic of the three critics we are considering (he is the only one with a Ph.D.), and his early writing was in the scholarly tradition of his two most important mentors, Perry Miller and F. O. Matthiessen. In moving right politically, he also became a much livelier and crankier writer.

Although Joseph Epstein teaches in the English Department at Northwestern University, he has never been as academic as Lynn. He seems more like the writer-in-residence who is in the university without really being of it. He is an incredibly stylish and productive writer who publishes a familiar essay in each quarterly issue of the *American Scholar* (which he edits) along with a considerable volume of literary and social criticism in such magazines as *Commentary,* the *New Criterion, Harper's,* the *Times Literary Supplement,* and the *New York Times Book Review.* The two published collections of his literary essays (which are by no means complete) total 820 pages.[10] Like Podhoretz and Lynn, Epstein has undergone a political conversion. Partisans of the Left are quick to point out that as recently as 1973 he published a critical essay entitled "The New Conservatives: Intellectuals in Retreat" in the far-left magazine *Dissent*.[11] Although he has since joined that retreat, Epstein is not nearly as political as Podhoretz or Lynn, and his literary opinions are generally less predictable.

During the question-and-answer session at the end of a talk to the San Diego City Club—"there I am again speaking to the rich," he notes in a characteristically self-deprecating tone—Epstein was asked why his ideas had begun to change. Without resorting to ideology or geopolitics, he gave a very commonsense explanation of the phenomenon known as neoconservatism:

Once I dropped the belief that America was the foremost menace in the world, once I slipped free from the notion that further "programs" (more of the same, without any radical change in perspective or orientation) would alleviate domestic problems, I discovered that the United States, for all its faults, for all that still needed to be made better, was nonetheless a most impressive country—and I couldn't think of any other I should rather be living in. Now here is a startling confession for an intellectual to make: I like it here.[12]

Chapter Two
Culture and Anarchy

Emerson may have been overstating the case when he said that history is the lengthened shadow of a man; however, the history of the great cultural magazines of the twentieth century is largely the story of inspired editors who have fashioned periodicals in their own image. When we think of the *Criterion,* we think of T. S. Eliot. Mention *Scrutiny,* and the name of F. R. Leavis comes to mind. The *Kenyon Review* was for many years John Crowe Ransom's magazine. For a quarter century the *New Yorker* was inextricably identified with Harold Ross, and for another thirty-six years with William Shawn. *Partisan Review* was never the same after Philip Rahv left its masthead, and *National Review* is virtually inconceivable without William F. Buckley, Jr. Since he became its editor in 1960, Norman Podhoretz has molded *Commentary* according to his own changing interests and beliefs. It is a tribute to Podhoretz's genius that this magazine has not only weathered the changes in his view of the world but has greatly prospered during his tenure.

The Americanization of Norman Podhoretz

As a senior in high school, Norman Podhoretz was a brilliant student with high grades and a discerning intellect. His ambition was to attend an Ivy League college (preferably Harvard) and eventually become a respected man of letters. Unfortunately, young Podhoretz neither looked nor acted the part of a blue-blood college student. He wore a T-shirt, tightly pegged pants, and the red satin jacket of the Cherokee Social-Athletic Club. In other words, he was a Jewish slum child, proud of his ethnic roots and naive enough to believe that he could join the American intelligentsia on the basis of merit alone. The opening chapter of his fascinating and plainspoken memoir *Making It* tells of the unsuccessful efforts of his most doting high school teacher to turn him into a facsimile WASP who would wear academic tweed, drink dry martinis, and not care whether the entrée was cooked according to kosher dietary laws. No Eliza Doolittle, Podhoretz was positively resentful of his teacher's solicitude. But what she failed to accomplish in the short run, American culture itself achieved over the long haul.

Podhoretz would eventually attend an Ivy League school (Columbia, not Harvard) and win a Fulbright scholarship to Cambridge. He would even become a famous writer and an important intellectual. Along the way, he would pick up the manners and tastes of America's cultural elite. To an extent, his "education" (if we use the term in the same sense Henry Adams did, as meaning the process of adapting to one's environment) consisted not of intellectual achievement but of the painful assimilation required of one making the journey from Brooklyn to Manhattan. Class distinctions do not disappear in an officially egalitarian society; they simply manifest themselves in ways that are all the more sinister for being unacknowledged.

Rather than leaving him bitter at early slights or derisive of his provincial roots, Podhoretz's odyssey has made him philosophical about the nature of success in American society. On the one hand, the ambition to rise to a position of wealth and eminence has been honored as the official American Dream since the time of Benjamin Franklin. To confess to that ambition has always been considered in poor taste, however, especially among those who aspire to a certain intellectual and aesthetic sensitivity. "It is altogether typical," Podhoretz writes, "that in the contest for popular support between Brutus and Mark Antony after the assassination of Julius Caesar, Antony (at least in Shakespeare's version) should have been able to win by refuting Brutus's charge, advanced in justification of the murder, that Caesar had been an ambitious man."[1]

Literary people, in particular, are taught to sneer at ambition. Since the study of literature is supposed to be of intrinsic value, it is vulgar to be overly concerned with extrinsic rewards. Moreover, at least since the time Hawthorne discovered that none of his co-workers at the Salem Custom House had ever heard of him, high-brow literary folk have grown accustomed to modest fame and fortune and have even come to look upon their relative obscurity and penury as a badge of honor. Popular novelists such as Horatio Alger may have glorified the office boy who rises to the presidency of the corporation, but the writers canonized by critics and scholars are almost uniformly contemptuous of the money-grubbing businessman. Better to starve in a garret than to become like George Babbitt. Better to die unknown like Emily Dickinson than to write a nationwide best-seller.

Although Podhoretz would later come to appreciate the value of money, fame, and power, his ambition as a student at Columbia was simply to make good grades and impress his professors. (He accomplished that well enough to generate hostility among those students who thought it pushy to do anything more than just get by.) In the process, he was exposed to the cultural riches of Western civilization and converted to the life of the mind. His heroes and role models were not cowboys, frontiersmen, or robber barons but professors such as Andrew Chiappe, Richard Chase, F. W. Dupee, and, above all, Lionel Trilling. What Podhoretz perceived only dimly at the time was that competition for intellectual preeminence can be just as fierce as the battle for material wealth or worldly fame.

In one of the most amusing chapters in *Making It,* Podhoretz describes his experience as a Fulbright fellow at Clare College, Cambridge. Ironically enough, he found his status anxieties to be considerably less in this officially class-conscious society. As a Cambridge student Podhoretz was assumed to be a gentleman. He need do nothing to prove that he was, and nothing he could do short of flunking out would have caused him to lose his position. As a young "barbarian" from Brooklyn, he found it remarkably easy to become accustomed to "having lots of space to live in and being called 'Sir.' " "It has been said that it takes three generations to make an aristocrat," Podhoretz recalls; "my own experience would suggest that three weeks are about enough" (*MI,* 66).

Even more important for Podhoretz's later vocation as a critic was the example of F. R. Leavis. Although he readily concedes the narrowness of Leavis's mind and the paranoid cast of his personality, Podhoretz was greatly impressed, even intimidated, by the critic's instinctive knowledge of literary traditions. (Leavis was particularly adept at the Cambridge practice of dating an unidentified passage of prose or poetry within ten years of its composition and giving reasons for his surmise.) What impressed him even more was the high seriousness with which Leavis approached the task of criticism. Not even Lionel Trilling saw the judgment of literature and, to use Eliot's phrase, "the correction of taste" as being of such importance to life. In addition to regarding the role of the critic as a sacred duty, Leavis believed that "to waver in its performance, let alone to depart from it altogether at the behest of other considerations, whether personal (to avoid causing hurt, to curry favor) or ideological (notions of the relativism of taste or of the primacy of nonliterary factors over the literary realm itself) was a sin as cardinal as adultery, as foul as idolatry" (*MI,* 79).

Upon returning to the United States, Podhoretz decided against graduate school in favor of a career in magazine writing. In these days when few novelists can make a living independent of the university, it is that much more difficult for a literary critic to keep body and soul together solely on income from his writing. (That Edmund Wilson was able to do so during a long and illustrious career may account in part for the high esteem in which he is held by the current generation of critics.) Fortunately, Podhoretz found what seemed like an ideal niche for his talents in *Commentary*, a magazine founded by the American Jewish Committee immediately after World War II and edited by Elliot Cohen, a man of incredibly diverse interests and a consuming passion for bridging the gap between Jewish culture and mainstream American life without violating the integrity of either.

Cohen could speak with authority about such disparate figures as Casey Stengel and Henry James, and when he first interviewed Podhoretz for a position at *Commentary*, "he jumped from literary criticism to politics, from politics to Jewish scholarship, from Jewish scholarship to the movies, from the movies to sports, and indeed spent a good deal of time trying to find out how much I knew about baseball" (*MI*, 100). At the end of the conversation—the applicant apparently having satisfied his prospective employer—Cohen gave Podhoretz a review copy of Bernard Malamud's first novel, *The Natural*. " 'Well,' he said, 'you seem to know something about symbolism, you know something about Jews, and you know something about baseball. Here's a symbolic novel by a Jewish writer about a baseball player. I guess you're qualified to review it' " (*MI*, 101).

Unlike the uncompromisingly highbrow *Partisan Review*, *Commentary* sought to popularize intellectually complex issues for the sort of intelligent general audience that has always existed in England but only intermittently in this country. Despite its official Jewish sponsorship, the magazine had never been narrowly sectarian. Cohen believed that anything of interest to him would be of interest to others as long as the writing was engaging, polished, and witty. Because many of the specialists who published in *Commentary* possessed none of these literary qualities (many were immigrant Jews with an uncertain but arrogant grasp of the English language), the magazine's editors were constantly performing the alchemy of revision. Cohen, who was not a good writer himself, possessed a knack for fixing the tortured prose of others. So, too, did Norman Podhoretz. This talent, and the considerable authority of his own critical prose, would eventually make Podhoretz one of the most influential and controversial editors in America. But he would have to experience several more years of frustration and discouragement before that happened.

Not too long after he began writing for *Commentary* and such magazines as *Partisan Review*, Podhoretz was drafted into the army, where he experienced a very different kind of class hierarchy than he had known in Brooklyn, Cambridge, or Manhattan. When he returned to civilian life and began officially working for *Commentary*, things had changed dramatically: Elliot Cohen had sunk into a depression that left him unable to function as an editor, and the day-to-day running of the magazine had fallen into the hands of individuals hostile to Podhoretz. The rank and salary Cohen had promised him when he departed for the army were drastically cut, and Podhoretz's influence on editorial policy was much less than he had expected. Only after he threatened to resign did the American Jewish Committee look into the situation and reorganize the magazine's editorial board. When Cohen returned to the editorship, a sick and diminished man, conditions continued to deteriorate. By the time Cohen committed suicide in 1959, Podhoretz had left *Commentary* for a more lucrative part-time job in publishing and a more concerted stab at free-lance writing. Officially outside the magazine and a critic of growing reputation, Podhoretz was now a more attractive successor to Cohen than those who had stayed with *Commentary* and been tainted by its decline.

The only problem was that Podhoretz had no interest in returning to the magazine, even as editor. What he did not realize at the time was that his very reluctance probably enhanced his market value. When he agreed to meet with representatives of the AJC simply to give his views about the future of the magazine, they asked him what it would take to get him to come aboard as editor. Hoping to deflect the offer, he asked for a free editorial hand and the then-staggering salary of $20,000 a year. After some consideration, the committee granted his editorial demands and came much closer than he expected to his requested salary. Thus, at age thirty, Norman Podhoretz was finally in a position to shape an important magazine and help influence the course of American culture. The fact that he recognized this and was frank enough to admit it earned Podhoretz the sort of abuse usually reserved for child molesters and best-selling novelists. The reaction to his confessional memoir *Making It* taught Podhoretz that even among the liberal intelligentsia tolerance has its limits.

Mugged by Reality

During his early years as editor of *Commentary,* Podhoretz considered himself a radical; however, his radicalism was less a party line than an independence of mind and a willingness to challenge the prevailing liberal orthodoxy on a range of controversial issues. Unfortunately, by the late sixties, a kind of doctrinaire radicalism had become the new orthodoxy in the literary salons of Manhattan and among those provincials who aped the latest fashions by subscribing to the *New York Review of Books.* When Podhoretz continued his independent and iconoclastic thinking, it was only a matter of time before he said something that went against the new party line. *Making It* qualified on several counts. For one thing, it argued that literary intellectuals cherished a dream of success that in its own way was not all that different from the bourgeois ambitions of a used-car salesman. What was even more damning was that Podhoretz saw nothing wrong with that. He might have gotten away with condemning the literati for being insufficiently bohemian (much as the Black Panthers got away with condemning them for being insufficiently revolutionary), but it was the ultimate breach in etiquette to tell them they should be more honest about their lust for social position and power.

The negative reaction to *Making It* had the social dynamics of a lynch mob—a few vicious leaders and a herd of cowardly followers. Much the same could be said of the New Left itself, which was then terrorizing college campuses in its opposition to such counterrevolutionary values as civility and free speech. If Podhoretz had no qualms about challenging a stuffy and self-congratulatory liberal political consensus, he remained committed to the humane principles of liberal civilization. For his kind of radical, the term *radical chic* was quite literally an oxymoron. Not even the convulsions of the sixties could turn Podhoretz into a conservative (neo or otherwise) overnight, but the hard Left was almost that quick in branding him a traitor to his class (though, of course, not in those terms). His political memoir *Breaking Ranks* is aptly titled because it indicates that Podhoretz's move to the right began not as an affirmation of conservatism but as a rejection of the illiberal mind-set of much of the American Left.

Breaking Ranks is framed as a letter to Podhoretz's son John, who knew of his father's radical past only by reputation. The comparison to Benjamin Franklin's *Autobiography* (also disguised as a father's letter to his son) is inevitable. In both cases the son is a surrogate for at least his own generation and perhaps for the reading public in general. As Podhoretz begins to address John, he goes into historical explanations that help to establish the political and cultural context of the fifties for one too young to have known it firsthand. His central point here is that the traditional alienation of the intellectual from American society (and all that that entails politically) began to break down after World War II, as both the nation and its intellectuals became more attractive to each other.

If we go back only as far as the twenties and thirties, we find a time when many American intellectuals were impoverished and most were scorned as impractical dreamers who made less of a contribution to society than stockbrokers or auto mechanics. Following the logic that my enemy's enemy must be my friend, intellectuals tended to side with movements antagonistic to the social and economic status quo. By far the most radical of these was the Communist party. For principled intellectuals, however, enchantment with communism did not survive the Moscow show trials and the brutal Stalinist purges of the late thirties. World War II may have made Stalin's Russia an ally of convenience, but no one who had seen the Nazi death camps could be sanguine about the nature of totalitarianism—left or right. While some fellow travelers remained naive about Soviet intentions, the dominant intellectual consensus in postwar America was anti-Communist liberalism. Many American intellectuals had come to the conclusion that, for all its imperfections, their society was superior to the one defeated in the last war and to the opponent currently being faced in the cold war. Moreover, the rising tide of postwar prosperity (which included a dramatic expansion of job opportunities in academia as a result of the GI Bill and the baby boom) lifted intellectuals to a more privileged position than they had enjoyed at any previous time in American history.

If it was virtually impossible for any sensitive and intelligent American to remain pro-Communist in the postwar era, the specter of nuclear annihilation made it imprudent to be too *militantly* anti-Communist. Right-wingers of the *National Review* persuasion might declare themselves sooner dead than Red, but liberal anti-Communists spent most of their time trying to find an alternative to the extremes of capitulation and confrontation. George Kennan developed such an alternative with his strategy of containment. It might be impractical to try to roll back the Soviet frontiers, but we could at least keep them from expanding. This was the liberal consensus of the Harry S. Truman–Dean Acheson years and the basis for a bipartisan foreign policy under

Dwight D. Eisenhower and John Foster Dulles. When Podhoretz initially broke with this consensus, it was not to join the liberationist forces of the hard Right but to argue for peaceful coexistence with post-Stalinist Russia. When Khrushchev publicly denounced Stalin in 1956, it looked as if the Soviet Union was moving from totalitarian intractability to a kind of garden variety authoritarianism. Not even the Soviet invasion of Hungary could dampen the optimism of peaceniks such as Norman Podhoretz.

It was not that Podhoretz and his cohorts regarded communism as a morally acceptable political system; they simply ceased to see it as a threat to America. Not only had the nuclear age made another world war unthinkable and de-Stalinization rendered the Soviet Union less monstrous, but domestic defenders of communism had been so thoroughly discredited that doctrinaire anti-Communists such as Sidney Hook and Lionel and Diana Trilling had only straw men left to argue with. When Podhoretz looked around for the intellectual action in the fifties, he did not find it among those who were still fighting the battles of an earlier generation. Instead, his new heroes were cultural radicals such as Norman Mailer and Norman O. Brown (two-thirds of what Lionel Trilling called the "Norman invasion") and Paul Goodman. These individuals found ways of attacking the complacency and conformity of American life without resorting to Marx and without harboring illusions about the Soviet Union. Podhoretz began publishing these writers in *Commentary* and promoting them in his own criticism.

So what changed? How did Podhoretz go from joining Norman Mailer in defense of the new radicalism in a debate with Arthur Schlesinger, Jr., and Mary McCarthy to teaming up with Richard Viguerie in denouncing the leftward drift of the Reagan administration on the "MacNeil/Lehrer News Hour"? Those looking to *Breaking Ranks* for the answer are likely to be disappointed. Published in 1979, this book effectively ends in 1976 when Podhoretz was still a Democrat, supporting Scoop Jackson for president and Daniel Patrick Moynihan for the U.S. Senate.

Although no Road to Damascus experience had occurred,[2] Podhoretz had become convinced of the barbarism of the New Left and the mendacity of racial quotas. He had also been sickened by the opportunism of liberals who jumped aboard the Students for a Democratic Society bandwagon, the timidity of intellectuals who feared to challenge the social conformity of the Left, and the treachery of former friends who trashed *Making It*. Moreover, on the international front, he had seen the

Khrushchev thaw give way to a new era of Soviet expansion. Such experiences and observations might have been enough to push any thinking American back to the liberal anti-Communist center. Unfortunately, like so much else in American life, that center was one of the casualties of the sixties. As a result, new coalitions were formed to accommodate changing circumstances. In the words of Irving Kristol, "a neoconservative is a liberal who has been mugged by reality."

Shem, Ham, and Bubba

Spending his young manhood as an enlightened liberal, Podhoretz affirmed the liberal line that blacks were innocent victims of white racism and that American society would not be whole until that happy day when integration was not only the law of the land but a social reality as well. Jews, who had been the victims of so much persecution, could do no less than champion the cause of racial equality. In addition, Podhoretz personally went out of his way to promote the reputation of the angry and gifted black writer James Baldwin. When Baldwin's novel *Another Country* was panned by many in the critical establishment, Podhoretz came to its defense, telling timid liberals that their unease with the book was a result of Baldwin's insistence on following the narrative logic of what they claimed to believe about human brotherhood and the unconditional supremacy of love. "By taking these liberal pieties literally," Podhoretz writes, "and by translating them into simple English, [Baldwin] puts the voltage back into them and they burn to the touch."[3] As a result of his association with Baldwin, whom he published in *Commentary,* and of his own radical skepticism about all received wisdom, Podhoretz gradually came to see that the racial problem in the United States was more complex than liberal integrationists cared to believe.

While all "men of good will" shared Martin Luther King's dream of a color-blind society, Baldwin believed that every black had within him the potential to strike out against whites in the manner of Bigger Thomas, protagonist of Richard Wright's *Native Son,* and that many shared the white-bashing venom of the Black Muslims. Baldwin's passionate exposition of black rage in *The Fire Next Time* suggested that, for all the ostensible progress made in civil rights, America was on the brink of race warfare. At least in part, that long essay had grown from conversations Baldwin had with Podhoretz. (*The Fire Next Time* was originally commissioned by *Commentary* but eventually published in the

New Yorker because Baldwin was able to get more money from the wealthier magazine.) What is more, it caused Podhoretz to reflect on the history of his real feelings about blacks. At Baldwin's urging, Podhoretz recounted that history in a brutally honest piece entitled "My Negro Problem—and Ours."

In his own childhood experiences of a racially mixed society, Podhoretz does not recall familiarity breeding harmony and brotherhood. Nor does he recall wealthy and powerful whites oppressing defenseless blacks. If anything, the blacks were the aggressors—beating and robbing white children out of racial malice. Far from seeing ghetto blacks as a jailed race, the young Podhoretz envied them their bravado, their contempt for authority, and their apparent freedom to move in any direction their anarchic impulses led. At the most visceral level, Podhoretz hated and envied blacks. It is a tribute to his basic humanity that he was able to suppress those feelings through an act of will. But how could someone with such a dispiriting personal experience of integration really believe that race mixing was an unambiguous good? No, integration would not succeed unless it led to such wholesale miscegenation that consciousness of color would quite literally cease to exist in America.[4] That was the solution Podhoretz advocated even though he admitted it would take every ounce of liberal conscience for him to allow his daughter to marry a black.

Given Podhoretz's reservations about the desirability of integration, one might expect him to have been sympathetic to Southern conservatives trying to resist the forced implementation of a flawed social vision. If he felt such sympathies, however, he kept them well hidden. Although he got along well with Southerners he knew in the army (in part because they helped him out in barroom brawls with anti-Semites), Podhoretz has almost nothing good to say about the South in his critical and polemical writings. When he mentions Southern critics such as John Crowe Ransom, Allen Tate, and Cleanth Brooks, it is only to accuse them of the sort of clannishness frequently attributed to the much more fratricidal Jewish literati. In *Making It* Podhoretz denigrates two contemporary Southern novelists (one major, the other minor) with the sarcastic remark, "If Eudora Welty is a good writer, so is Elizabeth Spencer" (*MI,* 252). And he cooperated with the successful efforts to keep the Reagan administration from appointing M. E. Bradford director of the National Endowment for the Humanities. But the group of Southerners for whom Podhoretz seems to feel the most contempt are the self-styled redneck liberals he knew in New York during the sixties.

In *Breaking Ranks* Podhoretz paints a maliciously amusing portrait of Willie Morris, the Mississippian—by way of the University of Texas and Oxford—who took over the editorship of *Harper's* in his early thirties. Podhoretz contends that Morris's "air of fecklessness, combined with a deep southern accent that neither Oxford nor New York had moderated in the slightest degree and a 'shit-kicking' country-boy manner to go with it, all concealed the booster-rocket engine of ambition . . . which had carried him from Yazoo City to the 'red-hot center' of the New York literary world in record time and without as much as a minute deviation from the plotted course" (*BR*, 152). If Morris's rise in the republic of letters was even more meteoric than Podhoretz's (*Harper's* being a more prestigious magazine than *Commentary*), the Southerner proved hypocritically coy about his obvious ambition. Whether running *Harper's* by day or holding court at Elaine's by night, "his mind was on higher and sometimes lower things but never on things in the middle" (*BR*, 153).

Podhoretz saw Willie Morris and the good old boys who surrounded him as liberals caught in a time warp (no doubt owing to their roots in a backward part of the country). At home they had won fame fighting the "oil and gas lobby," something that muckraking journalists elsewhere in America had done shortly after the turn of the century. Arriving in New York from dry counties back home, they sought to emulate the legendary drinking of their hero Faulkner. (One Sunday afternoon, when the Podhoretzes were having coffee after a few hours' sleep following an all-night party at their house, Willie stumbled out of one of the maid's rooms, where he had passed out the night before. " 'What time is it?' he asked politely but without the slightest trace of embarrassment. 'Is the party over already?' " [*BR*, 152].)

But in Podhoretz's eyes the Southern liberals' greatest offense was the smug way in which they assumed that their own triumph over racism made them natural moral leaders for the rest of the country. (According to Podhoretz, "A southern liberal was a person who, having struggled his way to a realization that Negroes were human beings, would never have to do anything else in his life to feel virtuous" [*BR*, 157].) Given the emerging evidence of racism in the North, sensitive Southerners no longer needed to feel their home region uniquely evil and the label "Southern liberal" a contradiction in terms. If anything, they were specialists in how to deal with race prejudice. "Having grown up with it, having lived with it, and having learned how to root it out, they provided a pioneering model for northern liberals, who were only just now beginning to realize how pervasively infected they themselves and the surrounding culture were with the same disease" (*BR*, 160). That neoconservatives bear almost precisely the same relationship to the radical Left that Southern liberals do to racism (right down to the sense of moral superiority at having discovered through painful experience what many others have always known) is a connection Podhoretz fails to make. And yet that analogy is implicit in *Breaking Ranks* and in virtually everything else he has written about his own remarkable political odyssey.

Eternal Vigilance

Norman Podhoretz's ambition to influence American society transcends his literary and cultural writings or even his observations on domestic issues—he aspires to being nothing less than a player in world politics. During his first dozen or so years as editor of *Commentary* he pursued that role by urging a policy of peaceful coexistence with the Soviet Union. In the aftermath of Vietnam, however, both Podhoretz and *Commentary* took a noticeable turn to the right in foreign affairs. It is difficult to say precisely how much the intellectual climate of this country was affected by that about-face, but two of our most articulately pro-American ambassadors to the United Nations got their jobs as a result of articles they wrote for Podhoretz. When *Commentary* authors Daniel Patrick Moynihan ("The United States in Opposition," March 1975) and Jeane Kirkpatrick ("Dictatorships and Double Standards," November 1979) were appointed by Republican presidents to represent this country before the community of nations, both were registered Democrats. And when they left their jobs, both were widely regarded as more hard-line than the administrations they served.

The foreign policy Podhoretz has advocated in *Commentary* since the mid-seventies and in two controversial books, *The Present Danger* (1980)[5] and *Why We Were in Vietnam* (1982), is the classic doctrine of containment formulated by George F. Kennan in his historic essay "The Sources of Soviet Conduct" (published under the pseudonym "Mr. X" in the July 1947 issue of *Foreign Affairs*) and implemented with varying degrees of competence by the Truman, Eisenhower, Kennedy, and Johnson administrations. Until the debacle of Vietnam permanently altered

American politics, postwar foreign policy was a Wilsonian internationalism that saw the United States as the prime defender of democracy wherever it was under attack. For persons whose political memory began in the mid-sixties or later, it is hard to imagine that the Democrats were once the more stridently anti-Communist of the two political parties and that the chief obstacle to bipartisanship in foreign policy was the deeply ingrained isolationism of old-line Republicans.

Of those postwar Republicans who were of an internationalist persuasion, none was more closely identified with the struggle against communism than Richard Nixon. (If anything, he did not believe that Truman's doctrine of containment went far enough.) So it is not surprising that Nixon's election as president in 1968 represented a sea change in American foreign policy. What is surprising is that that change was in the direction of peaceful coexistence. Under the rubric of detente, Nixon and his chief foreign policy adviser Henry Kissinger masterminded the withdrawal of American troops from Vietnam and historic diplomatic overtures to both the Soviet Union and the People's Republic of China, while acquiescing to a decline in military spending as a percentage of the federal budget.

In comparison to what was being advocated by the left-wing peace activists who had gained control of the Democratic party, this seemed like a hardheaded—if not hawkish—policy, and in the wake of Vietnam it may have been all that the American people were willing to support. However, detente resulted in the fall of Vietnam and other Southeast Asian dominoes, the diminution of American credibility throughout the world, and the eventual loss of our military superiority to the Soviets. Even the China card, which was supposed to keep the Russians at bay, was played at the price of weakening our moral stance as a principled opponent of *Communist* totalitarianism. (Witness George Bush's tepid reaction to the massacre of Chinese students in June 1989.) By the mid-seventies, isolationist sentiment had grown so strong that it was virtually impossible for the United States to make an overt or even covert stand on behalf of freedom anywhere in the world. Gerald Ford, who was feckless enough in his own right, gave way to Jimmy Carter, who believed that "an inordinate fear of Communism" was more dangerous than communism itself. The seizing of American hostages in Iran and our protracted inability to do anything about it suggested just how impotent United States foreign policy had become.

At the time Podhoretz wrote *The Present Danger* in 1980, the hostages were still in Iran and the Soviets had invaded Afghanistan. These two phenomena—particularly the first—helped revive a basic American nativism that Podhoretz hoped would lead to Carter's defeat and a more assertive world posture for the United States. For many neoconservatives, the party of Pat Moynihan and Scoop Jackson would have been the preferred vehicle of our national deliverance, but that party had become as much a historical anachronism as the Dixiecrats of a generation earlier. In the 1980 election, hordes of anti-Communist Democrats supported Reagan over Carter, and prominent Democrats such as Jeane Kirkpatrick, Max Kampelman, and Elliot Abrams eventually joined the new administration in important policymaking positions. Although the following eight years brought support for the anti-Communist resistance in such countries as Nicaragua and Angola, as well as sharply increased military spending, Podhoretz remained pessimistic about the willingness of the American people to bear the burdens and pay the costs of world leadership.

Perhaps in the eagerness of the electorate to believe in the liberality of Mikhail Gorbachev and the permanence of the reforms he had brought to Soviet life, Podhoretz saw a reflection of his own earlier naivete about the de-Stalinization policies of Nikita Khrushchev. In fact, much of Podhoretz's recent commentary on foreign affairs seems to have been written in atonement for positions he once took; so much so that when *Why We Were in Vietnam* contained no personal soul-searching but only public analysis, some critics accused Podhoretz of duplicity. Of course, these critics conveniently ignored the considerable amount of intellectual autobiography Podhoretz had already written. (Whatever else may be true, no man who opposed the Vietnam War before it was generally acceptable to do so and then regretted that position after it was chic to have been "right from the start" can be accused of running with the herd.) But the most revealing confession is a literary allusion contained in the title of the book itself. When, in 1967, Norman Mailer published a novel about the malaise and cancer of the American spirit he called it *Why Are We in Vietnam?* That book was dedicated to six friends: Roger Donahue, Buzz Farber, Mickey Knox, Cy Rembar, Jose Torres, and Norman Podhoretz.

Chapter Three
All in the Family

In March 1986 the *Nation* published a special issue commemorating its 120th year of existence. Amid the hoopla and self-congratulation was a short article by Gore Vidal entitled "The Empire Lovers Strike Back." Although the title was an allusion to both George Lucas's epic space serial and Vidal's own novel-in-progress about Teddy Roosevelt and the glory days of American imperialism, the article's real targets were Norman Podhoretz, Midge Decter, and the American Israeli lobby. Referring to Mr. and Mrs. Podhoretz as "the Lunts of the right wing (Israeli Fifth Column Division)," Vidal asserts that *Commentary*'s hard line on foreign policy is dictated by the need to frighten the American people into spending hundreds of billions of dollars on defense, "which also means the support of Israel in its never-ending wars against just about everyone."[1] Not content with criticizing the foreign policy views of Midge and "Poddy" (as he insists on calling Podhoretz) and the military posture of Israel, Vidal argues that the Jewish neoconservatives are really agents of a foreign power wrapping themselves in the American flag. In totally unintended ways, this crude anti-Zionist attack and the responses to it tell us a good deal about Norman Podhoretz's identity as an *American Jew* and the function of that identity in shaping his view of the world.

The Chosen People

As Podhoretz points out repeatedly in *Making It,* when he was growing up, assimilation into the respectable world of literary intellectuals meant leaving behind all traces of ethnic provincialism and becoming a "facsimile WASP." Although he strongly resisted this process, he felt a subconscious need to justify that resistance. Thus, when he was attending both Columbia University and the Seminary College of Jewish Studies, Podhoretz was constantly defending his interest in Jewish culture to his Columbia classmates, most of whom were themselves secularized Jews. The two major points he made on behalf of Judaism were that it entertained no dualism of mind and body (consequently avoiding what intellectuals of his generation considered to be one of the ubiquitous flaws of Western thought) and that it revered learning for its own sake. Although those were two powerful arguments, Podhoretz's friends believed they had sufficiently absorbed the attitudes in question from non-Jewish sources (the already canonized great thinkers of Western civilization) and had no need to reabsorb them with a lengthy study of what still seemed an inferior culture. At the time, Podhoretz felt that traveling the six blocks from Columbia to the Seminary was like making "the journey from Paris to the provinces" (*DU*, 118).

If Podhoretz's attempt to bring the seminary to Columbia fell on deaf ears, his attempt to bring Columbia to the seminary was equally unsuccessful. Quite to his surprise, he found that the students and teachers there thought it an impertinence to try to justify Jewish literature according to the standards of the *Kenyon Review*. To make Judah Halevi into the Hebrew Donne was seen not as an elevation but as a trivialization of the Jewish poet. The one overriding theme of Hebrew and Yiddish literature was the meaning of being a Jew. To evaluate this literature in terms defined by any other culture was seen as a virtual betrayal of the martyred six million. Ironically, such an evaluation was finally made in the world of Columbia when the discovery of Hasidism, through Martin Buber and Gershom Scholem, prompted secularized Jews other than Podhoretz to use their cosmopolitan critical theories to reexamine their own cultural roots. (The epitome of this effort was probably an essay in *Commentary* by Lionel Trilling on the subject of "Wordsworth and the Rabbis.")

The fruit of that evaluation, however, was finally the realization that Jewish literature is as distinct from other literatures as Jews themselves are distinct from other people. As the intellectuals Irving Howe and Eliezer Greenberg point out in the introduction to their anthology of Yiddish stories (the paraphrase is Podhoretz's), the "emphasis on national destiny [in Jewish literature] is so tyrannical and ruthless that no room is left for an interest in individual character, . . . [yet] most of us read fiction primarily because we want to see individual character in its eternal struggle with society" (*DU*, 124). Thus, the pleasure Podhoretz gets reading Jewish literature is of a very different kind from that he gets reading English, French, or Russian fiction and has "everything to do with that part of me which still broods on the mystery on my own Jewishness" (*DU*, 124).

The mystery of Podhoretz's Jewishness was engaged even further by

Hannah Arendt's controversial book *Eichmann in Jerusalem*. In what was ostensibly a study of the trial of Nazi war criminal Adolf Eichmann by the state of Israel, Arendt composed something of a sequel to her earlier masterpiece *The Origins of Totalitarianism*. Whereas others had seen the Holocaust as a morality play of unredeemed evil and virtuous suffering, Arendt found it a much more complex story with ambiguities that appealed to the modern sensibility. For one thing, by emphasizing the degree to which highly assimilated Jews cooperated with the Nazis, she replaced the image of the martyr with that of the collaborationist. Not content merely to note the role that the victims played in their own victimization, she argued that Jewish leaders contributed to the destruction of their own people "to a truly extraordinary degree." As one might expect, this interpretation was not received well by much of the Jewish community.

Not only did Arendt's analysis carry the hint that Jews were partially responsible for what happened to them in the death camps, it also understated the irrationality of Nazi anti-Semitism. As Podhoretz points out, the Nazis were so frantically devoted to exterminating the Jews from Europe that they kept the death camps going even at the expense of diverting needed resources from the war effort. The cooperation of Jewish leaders may have made mass murder more convenient for the Nazis, but that murder would have taken place in any event. The cultural solidarity of the Jewish people probably made them a more visible target, but to argue that for their own good they should have been less well organized is, in Podhoretz's opinion, tantamount to saying that "if the Jews had not been Jews, the Nazis would not have been able to kill so many of them" (*DU*, 344–45).

Even more widely debated than her account of Jewish behavior during the Holocaust was Arendt's interpretation of Nazism as essentially an extreme manifestation of technocratic evil in the modern world. Like many of her other critics, Podhoretz felt that in denying Nazism its uniqueness Arendt was robbing it of some of its evil. Eichmann, she contends, was not so much a vicious anti-Semite as the ultimate bureaucrat. The Nazi soldiers who claimed that they were only following orders were telling the truth. Arendt does not believe that this excuses their conduct, but it goes a long way toward explaining the nature of totalitarianism. The machinery of death relied not on subjective hatred but on the efficient performance of many little dispassionate cogs in the machine. This is what Arendt, in an unforgettable phrase, calls the "banality of evil."

Podhoretz finds Arendt's theory brilliant but utterly unconvincing. It provides a paradigmatic description of something we do not know very well—totalitarianism—at the expense of ignoring much of what we do know about something very familiar—human nature. Any person who joined the Nazi party, let alone the SS, in the 1930s must have been at least a vicious anti-Semite, regardless of how banal he may have been in carrying out his duties later. Because the Third Reich did not last long enough to seal itself off from the rest of the world, "the people who participated actively in Nazism *knew* they were being criminal by the standards under which they themselves had been raised and that also still reigned supreme in the 'decadent' culture of the West" (*DU,* 350). (Podhoretz accuses Arendt of challenging an overly naive belief in human perfectibility with an overly cynical conviction of human malleability.) By ascribing blame to a system rather than to individuals, the banality-of-evil rationale applies a less severe moral standard to totalitarian (specifically Nazi) murderers than we would ordinarily apply to garden-variety street criminals. Thus, Podhoretz's brief against Hannah Arendt is that she is at once too tough on the Jews and too soft on the Nazis. Call it the evil of ingenuity.

Dangling Men

At the time Norman Podhoretz was coming to prominence as a literary critic, so many Jewish novelists were establishing reputations in the world of letters that many observers spoke of a Jewish renaissance, just as their predecessors had spoken of a Southern renaissance a generation earlier. (Others, less charitable, spoke of a Jewish Mafia.) In both instances, a previously insular subculture was in the process of being assimilated into the mainstream of American life. This produced the sort of literary introspection that was not possible earlier, when the subculture remained intact, or later, when the assimilation process was complete. For many Jews reaching young adulthood between, say, 1935 and 1955, the one inescapable question was how to be *both* an American and a Jew at the same time. Two Jewish American writers who responded to this challenge in different ways were Saul Bellow and Norman Mailer.

Although Bellow was born in 1913 and his first novel *Dangling Man* published in 1944, his greatest fame as a novelist came in the fifties and after. In fact, by the late fifties most serious critics considered him the leading American novelist (of any ethnic background) writing in the postwar period. However, from the time Podhoretz reviewed Bellow's third novel, *The Adventures of Augie March,* for *Commentary* in 1953, he had begun to suspect that Bellow's vision contained serious flaws most other critics had failed to notice or were too timid to mention. The intellectual's experience of alienation in bourgeois society, essential as it is to the modernist movement in literature, has always been that much more acute for a Jewish intellectual in White Anglo-Saxon Protestant America. Nevertheless, the new wave of liberal pro-American senti-ment that swept the intellectual community after World War II caused even Jews to reevaluate their relationship to American culture.

Having paid his respects to alienation and victimization in his first two novels, Bellow boldly affirmed the compatibility of Jewishness and Americanness in *Augie March.* Even the book's picaresque form repre-sented a departure for Bellow, who for the first time was abandoning the claustrophobic mode of the Jamesian well-made novel. In terms of language, he had "boldly hit upon the idea of following the example of a book which had found the solution to the problem of literary plural-ism at a time when regional cultures stood in the same 'colonial' relation to the genteel tradition of the East as ethnic cultures later came to do" (*MI,* 162–63). Just as "Mark Twain in *Huckleberry Finn* had crossed the regnant 'high' literary language with the 'low' frontier vulgate, . . . Bellow now similarly crossed it with American-Jewish colloquial, thus asserting in the idiom of the novel itself what its opening sentence, in full awareness of what it is saying, makes alto-gether explicit: 'I am an American, Chicago-born' " (*MI,* 163).

As promising as these intentions may have seemed, Podhoretz thought that Bellow had botched his attempt to *realize* them. He found Augie an unconvincing character, largely unaffected by his fantastic adventures. Moreover, the spontaneity and eclecticism of the novel's language (a mixture of high, colloquial, and Jewish idioms) too often appear forced. (In passage after passage, "Bellow seems to be twisting and torturing the language in an attempt to get all the juices out of it" [*DU,* 218–19].) But, at bottom, these technical weaknesses point to an even more fundamental cultural problem—that in the early fifties the pro-Americanism of Jewish intellectuals was "beset by too much doubt, hesitation, and uncertainty to yield much more than a willed and empty affirmation" (*MI,* 165).

Unlike Bellow, Norman Mailer's individualism is so much more evident than his Jewishness that one is tempted to see him not as a Jewish writer but as a Jew who writes. (Family life, the immigrant experience, the indignities of ethnic discrimination, and other staples of Jewish fiction are largely absent from his work.) In addition, his alienation from conventional American society has always been more bohemian, at times even populist (and hence more indigenously *American*), than ethnocentric. But if any one characteristic has marked Mailer's writing, both for good and ill, it is a preoccupation with ideas of the grandest and most cosmic variety. Although this preoccupation is not peculiar to Jews, ethnicity seems to have been an early and strong influence in making Mailer into something rarely found in American literature—a novelist of ideas. It is as a thinking writer that Mailer most appeals to Podhoretz, even when the content of his thinking and the form of his writing are not altogether successful.

When Mailer's volatile literary reputation was at a low point in the late fifties, Podhoretz published a strong defense of him in *Partisan Review*. Praising the novelist's boldness of thought and willingness to move in new directions, Podhoretz asserts that "Norman Mailer is one of the few postwar American writers in whom it is possible to detect the presence of qualities that powerfully suggest a major novelist in the making" (*DU,* 179). As examples of his subject's originality, Podhoretz cites the new departure represented by each of the three novels Mailer had published up to that point. Beginning with the powerfully written but very traditional naturalistic fiction of *The Naked and the Dead* (1948), Mailer had moved on to the Trotskyite fabulism of *Barbary Shore* (1952) and the Fitzgerald-like lyricism of *The Deer Park* (1955).

Philosophically, the first of these novels represented Mailer's disillusionment with liberal idealism; the second, an end to his brief flirtation with revolutionary socialism; and the third, a new fascination with a kind of native American existentialism. Clearly, it was not Mailer's particular doctrines that attracted Podhoretz. By the time the two men first met, Podhoretz had long since become skeptical of liberalism and socialism and thought Mailer "was being simply foolish in constructing a theory of revolution with the psychopath playing the role Marx had assigned to the proletariat." "But," Podhoretz notes, "this very willingness to risk looking foolish in the pursuit of something very large and ambitious was exactly what I admired about Mailer. He was bold and he was daring; and he wanted to be great" (*BR,* 47).

Mailer and Podhoretz were fast friends during the late fifties and early sixties. Podhoretz's *Partisan Review* essay helped Mailer gain respectability among the highbrow literati who had previously dismissed him as a celebrity and had regarded his work as little more than middle-brow fiction. After stabbing his wife at a drunken party in 1961, Mailer was once again shunned by the literary establishment (this time they considered him a dangerous psychotic). During those dark days, Podhoretz was one of the few individuals to whom Mailer turned for comfort and support. Unfortunately, their divergent political views helped to drive the two friends apart during the mid-to-late sixties.

The catalyst to their parting ways, however, was Mailer's tepid review of *Making It* in *Partisan Review*. At a time when the rest of the literary establishment was trashing him, Podhoretz expected his old and dear friend to stand up for him. This was especially true since Podhoretz's meditations on success were in large part inspired by a similar emphasis in Mailer's *Advertisements for Myself*. Moreover, when Mailer had read *Making It* in galleys he had led Podhoretz to believe that he liked the book. It is one of the ironies of literary politics that the reputations of the two Normans had virtually reversed in a decade. In the late fifties, Podhoretz had had to fight the resistance of *Partisan Review* editors Philip Rahv and William Phillips to get his enthusiastic assessment of Mailer into print. By the late sixties, Mailer was the darling of a radicalized literary establishment and the increasingly conservative Podhoretz the pariah. Although Mailer claimed, somewhat disingenuously, that he had simply changed his mind about the merits of *Making It*, Podhoretz felt betrayed. In *Breaking Ranks* he would accuse Mailer of being a rebel-manqué who tweaks the nose of the establishment by shrewdly playing the royal fool. But like the fool, Mailer knows what boundaries must not be transgressed if he is to maintain his favored position at court.

"Poddy" Strikes Back

Gore Vidal's blunderbuss attack on Norman Podhoretz, Midge Decter, and other Jewish supporters of Israel (that there might be Gentile support for the Jewish state seemed not to occur to him) led to a controversy that was covered by at least twenty articles in American newspapers and magazines and nearly half again as many in such countries as England, France, Germany, Australia, and Israel. It seems that not many people had read Vidal's article when it was originally published but rushed to do so when Podhoretz counterattacked in his syndicated newspaper column. If Podhoretz had any qualms about giving Vidal more exposure, he apparently felt that the greater error would have been to let such a blatant example of anti-Semitism go unchallenged. What he discovered was that left-wing tolerance of anti-Semitism had grown so widespread that very few prominent liberals bothered to criticize Vidal, even when Podhoretz urged them to do so. Many obviously felt that branding the entire Jewish community as a fifth column in our midst was a permissible excess when the real target was Norman Podhoretz and the neoconservatives.

This experience confirmed Podhoretz in his belief that much of the left wing in this country was not only anti-American but anti-Jewish as well. Jews had long been the mainstays of American liberalism, and support for Israel was once regarded as a liberal cause. But sympathy for the Palestinians as an oppressed people gradually began to replace the leftover World War II guilt that had generated so much initial support for Israel among the liberal *goyim*. (The fact that the United States was backing Israel while the Soviet Union supported some of its bitterest enemies only made the Left that much more adamant in its opposition to Zionist imperialism, if not to imperialism itself.) Also, on the domestic scene, minority groups considered more oppressed than the Jews were granted the license to be anti-Semitic. Anti-Jewish feeling among certain blacks surfaced during the 1968 New York teachers' strike and has become so acceptable that when a Jew such as Ed Koch criticizes a black anti-Zionist such as Jesse Jackson, it is Koch whom the Left accuses of being racist. Crazies on both the Right and Left have always thought that the world is run by Shylock bankers. The difference is that in recent years the respectable Right has been much less tolerant of anti-Semitism in its ranks than have its counterparts on the Left.[2]

It would be a gross oversimplification to say that left-wing anti-Semitism has pushed Norman Podhoretz to the Right. Like other neoconservatives, he has finally seen the world for what it is. Those who have been mugged by reality can no longer remain naive about the intentions of the Soviet Union abroad or the promise of socialism at home. However, in an earlier era, a Jewish intellectual who contemplated becoming a conservative might have felt like a black joining the Confederate army. It is no easy task to make common cause with those who have historically persecuted you. But if the establishment Left has actually become more lenient toward anti-Semitism than has the establishment Right, the final impediment to Jewish conservatism is gone. In fact, to a large extent, neoconservatives are old-line liberals who never abandoned their principles to ideological fashion. Countless liberal battles have been won because Jews were willing to fight, and even die, for those principles. Andrew Goodman and Michael Schwerner gave their lives so that blacks could vote, not so that their fellow Jews could be called "Hymies."

Chapter Four

Essays in Criticism

Norman Podhoretz remembers the night he was officially initiated into the "family" of New York literary intellectuals. The party at Philip Rahv's Greenwich Village apartment was the functional equivalent of a bar mitzvah. As the initiate, who was then an inexperienced drinker, gulped down glass after glass of bourbon that his attentive hostess kept refilling, his head began to spin. Just before the entire world followed suit, he remembers "Rahv saying ('Today you are a man') that he wanted me to write for *Partisan Review*" (*MI,* 167). Delirious with the prospect of being able to call Kazin "Alfred," Macdonald "Dwight," and McCarthy "Mary," the young Podhoretz had truly *made it.* Years later he recalled, "About one o'clock in the morning, I staggered through the door with the other guest and after a perfunctory and fortunately abortive pass at her, I made my dizzy way toward the subway station on Sixth Avenue where the bourbon and the gossip and everything else my stomach was still too young to digest came pouring out in retching heaves. And yet in the very midst of all that misery, I knew that I had never been so happy in my life" (*MI,* 168).

The Republic of Letters

In his introduction to *Doings and Undoings: The Fifties and After in American Writing,* Norman Podhoretz makes a startling confession: he does not regard literature as an end in itself. Having sent the art-for-art's-sake crowd and assorted New Critics fleeing in horror, he goes on to say that for him literature is "a mode of public discourse that either illuminates or fails to illuminate the common ground on which we live" (*DU,* 2–3). He thus defines his attitude toward literature as agnostic rather than religious. "I do not go to literature for the salvation of my soul," he writes, "but only to enlarge or refine my understanding, and I do not expect it to redeem the age, but only to help the age become less chaotic and confused" (*DU,* 3). (That, of course, is a pretty tall order and a standard to which few books measure up.) For that reason,

Podhoretz does not see the function of criticism as simply passing judgment on the aesthetic merits of a book. Such judgment is necessary but not sufficient. The most important task of the book reviewer (which, after all, is what a critic is) is to use the book he is discussing as a springboard for making his own contribution to public discourse.

Rather than trivializing literature, such an attitude takes books very seriously indeed. (By divorcing literature from life, the total aesthete is the one who makes it of negligible importance.) That is why Podhoretz and the critics he most admires are so suspicious of inflated literary judgments. In discussing the demonstration issue of the *New York Review of Books,* put together during the New York newspaper strike of 1963, Podhoretz says that the most responsible critics (a group coextensive with "everyone I know") consider books guilty until proven innocent. The reason for such a presumption is the belief that "books are enormously important events, far too important to be confronted lightly, and certainly too important to permit of charitable indulgence toward those who presume to write them without sufficient gift or seriousness" (*DU,* 261). Those who regard book reviewing as merely hack work tend to see it as a kind of low-level literary service— rendered either to the potential customer, who wants to know whether he ought to read the book under consideration, or to the author, who wants to know whether he is a success or a flop. The best reviewers, however, perform a service only to consciousness itself. Alexander Pope is long remembered after those he reviewed in *The Dunciad* have been justifiably forgotten.

Closely related to Podhoretz's high regard for the sort of book reviewing done by himself and "everyone I know" is his belief that some of the best writing of the postwar era is in the form of discursive prose. He is able to cite case after case of artists who consider fiction (or, less frequently, poetry) their main vocation but who actually write with greater force, intelligence, and, yes, *creativity* when cranking out literary or social criticism. (Those mentioned by name are James Agee, Mary McCarthy, Elizabeth Hardwick, Randall Jarrell, Leslie Fiedler, and, preeminently, Isaac Rosenfeld and James Baldwin.) Although this proves nothing other than that some writers are better essayists than novelists, it does seem curious that so much good writing about what used to be the province of fiction (manners and morals) is today being done in discursive pieces rather than in novels.

Podhoretz suspects that this development is largely attributable to a specious romantic conception of literature. When the romantics began to push the notion that poetry should be written in a divine inspiration that had nothing to do with reason and the discriminating intelligence, poetry came to be cut off from life and ceased to be of compelling interest to those concerned with the world around them. The novel, which had not yet become an "art" genre and still carried with it the "smell of vulgarity," rushed in to fill the void. As their poetry became increasingly flatulent and prissy, Victorians looked to the novel to "represent their age most vitally and powerfully" (*DU*, 134). Now that the novel itself has gotten insufferably arty, it has lost what Podhoretz regards as "the only species of imagination worth mentioning—the kind that is vitalized by contact with a disciplined intelligence and a restless interest in the life of the times" (*DU*, 136–37).

Where that kind of imagination is most evident today is in magazine articles. Podhoretz makes clear that he is not talking about essays in the traditional sense of the term. Traditional essays presupposed an audience in agreement about the relevant subjects of discussion and so did not need to convince the reader of the importance of the issue under consideration. The magazine article, however, has to sell itself to the reader, "who wants to be told why he should bother pushing his way through it when there are so many other claims on his attention" (*DU*, 137). If this smacks of a utilitarian view of literature, Podhoretz pleads guilty. We live, after all, in a utilitarian age where architecture and home furnishings must prove themselves useful in order to be considered beautiful. To extend this attitude to literature is far from a denigration of what writers do. In fact, Podhoretz turns the tables very nicely by asserting that "the very concept of imagination as a special faculty—and of novels and poetry as mysteriously unique species of discourse subject to strange laws of their own—itself implies that art is of no use to life in the world" (*DU*, 142). With Matthew Arnold, Podhoretz asks whether Dr. Johnson "had better have gone on producing more *Irenes* instead of writing his *Lives of the Poets*" (see *DU*, 132).

An Older Crowd

Although *Doings and Undoings* is subtitled "The Fifties and after in American Writing," some of the figures Podhoretz deals with were approaching the end of long careers in the fifties while others were just getting started. (In two cases he even reevaluates the work of writers who died within hours of each other in 1940: F. Scott Fitzgerald and Nathanael West.) His general stance toward both groups is one of skepticism.

Because new writers have yet to prove themselves, Podhoretz is leery of pronouncing each new book a masterpiece and each young author a genius. With the giants of the immediate past, there is an even more insidious danger. Like our parents, these men and women are imposing authority figures who are also close enough to us to seem familiar. It is for this reason that we should be most suspicious of our reverence for them. The critic must constantly remind himself that our most recent predecessors lived in a time and a place that is not our own and that, classic as they may seem to us, their work has not been around long enough to stand the test of time. They are neither as contemporary nor as eternal as we would like to think.

Since the early fifties the most intimidating presence in the American literary firmament has been William Faulkner. Out of print and largely unread in the aftermath of World War II, he was rediscovered and republished by Malcolm Cowley, honored by the Nobel Prize Committee, and canonized by the church elders of academia. In today's English departments one can find scholars who regard themselves not as specialists in American or modern or even Southern literature, but as "Faulknerians." With such a vested interest in their man's reputation, the Yoknapatawpha specialists are not about to suggest that the literary world is overcompensating for its previous neglect of Faulkner. Instead, it takes someone with the critical chutzpah of Norman Podhoretz to ask some hard and impolite questions about the squire of Rowan Oak. Unfortunately for Faulkner, the appearance of his worst book, *A Fable,* was the occasion for Podhoretz's discussion. Upon reading *A Fable,* Podhoretz wondered whether Faulkner's other novels were also this bad and "some obsolete piety has prevented us from seeing him truly." Going back to the much praised early works, Podhoretz concludes that this is not the case. Faulkner's masterpieces are indeed masterpieces, but the second time around they struck Podhoretz "as the consummation of a minor, and not, as I once thought, a major talent" (*DU,* 13).

Faulkner's work possesses power, vision, and sensitivity—everything except intelligence. What one does not find on his little postage stamp of soil is a concern with ideas. His much-vaunted complexity consists of writing complicated sentences to express simple impulses. In the gothic backwaters of Yoknapatawpha, "the Enlightenment might just as well have never been. The qualities of reasonableness, moderation, compromise, tolerance, sober choice—in short, the anti-apocalyptic style of life brought into the modern world by the middle class—no more exists for Faulkner than plain ordinary folks do (everyone is at

least a demigod to him)" (*DU,* 15). For Faulkner all creatures, including human ones, are possessed, fated, and doomed. Such a view serves
him well enough as long as he can maintain confidence in his own
convictions. But when that confidence begins to falter, eloquence de-
generates into bombast and myth into stereotype. We have not *The
Sound and the Fury* but *A Fable.* And, equally distressing, we have a
writer who believed the latter to have been his finest novel.

Scott Fitzgerald also takes his lumps from Podhoretz. The publication of Andrew Turnbull's biography of Fitzgerald in 1962 prompted
an inevitable reassessment of both the man who wrote *The Great Gatsby*
and what the hagiographers regard as his tragic failure to fulfill the
promise of a great novelist. Podhoretz is all for making a reassessment
of Fitzgerald; he just rejects the romantic terms in which such discussions are usually cast. He points out that Fitzgerald's failure to become
a more important writer was due largely to his having died at age forty-
four. His talent was not destroyed by the twenties, the thirties, Zelda,
alcoholism, the Ritz Bar, St. Paul, Princeton, the Riviera, Hollywood,
or the corruption of the American Dream. At the time he died, Fitzgerald's novel-in-progress (later published as *The Last Tycoon*) gave every
indication of being as good as anything he had previously written. If
those previous writings, despite their obvious charm and fluency, seem
somehow incomplete, it is because they lack the self-awareness that
distinguishes the work of a fully mature artist.

It seems to me that this charge works better against Fitzgerald's
other novels than it does against *The Great Gatsby.* It is not so much
that the charge is inaccurate as it is irrelevant. According to Podhoretz,
Fitzgerald was drawing a self-portrait in the character of Gatsby but
was incapable of making that portrait into more than a symbol. To get
inside Gatsby or to give him flesh and blood (really opposite sides of the
same coin) would have required more self-knowledge than Fitzgerald
could muster. While this may be true, it assumes that *The Great Gatsby*
would have been a better novel had its point of view been closer to
Gatsby's own. What Podhoretz wants, however, is a different novel
from the one Fitzgerald wrote, not just a better version of the same
novel. Even if the moral education of Nick Carraway reveals little about
the private demons of Scott Fitzgerald, it is itself a significant work of
the imagination. To have made Gatsby a figure of less mystery would
have reduced the importance of Nick and everything he learns from his
encounter with Gatsby. Nick is far from omniscient, but his judgments

are certainly more reliable than anything Gatsby might say or think about himself. Seeing oneself from the outside and at a distance may require more artistry than does mere introspection.

If Fitzgerald's particular kind of romanticism is not to Podhoretz's taste, Nathanael West's "particular kind of joking" is. When *The Complete Works of Nathanael West* was published by Farrar, Straus & Giroux in 1957, it seemed high time for the critical establishment to discover this neglected genius of the thirties and give him his posthumous due. If one suspects that knocking down the giants in the pantheon and raising others to take their place is a critic's way of asserting his own power, the only adequate response lies in the cogency of the critic's own arguments.

In making the case for West, Podhoretz argues that the author of *Miss Lonelyhearts* and *The Day of the Locust* easily surpassed Fitzgerald in his "capacity for intelligent self-criticism" and Hemingway in the scope of his philosophical vision. It was simply West's misfortune to come along at a time when the literary scene was dominated by more overtly political writers. Commenting on West, Podhoretz notes: "His 'particular kind of joking' has profoundly unpolitical implications; it is a way of saying that the universe is always rigged against us and that our efforts to contend with it invariably lead to absurdity. This sort of laughter—which, para-doxically, has the most intimate connection with compassion—is rarely heard in American literature, for it is not only anti-'radical' but almost un-American in its refusal to admit the possibility of improvement, amelioration, or cure" (*DU,* 67). What Podhoretz does not say is that this sensibility was well-suited to the literary climate of the fifties, when absurdism in art and existentialism in philosophy were the order of the day. Had West lived to see the publication of his complete works (all of which had long been out of print), he would have been only fifty-three years old.

Of the older generation of writers, Podhoretz devotes the most space in *Doings and Undoings* to a discussion of Edmund Wilson. Given the high regard in which he holds critical and discursive prose, that is not surprising. He sees in Wilson a brilliant mind, uncompromising intel-lectual integrity, and deficient judgment. If Wilson is in many ways the model of what a critic ought to be, his specific attitudes are condi-tioned by his background as a New England patrician shaped by the values of an earlier age. This fact is often obscured by Wilson's political radicalism and his advocacy of the literary avant-garde. It is well known that his first major book of criticism, *Axel's Castle* (1931), helped introduce Eliot, Joyce, Yeats, Valéry, Proust, and other symbolist writers to the American public. What is often forgotten is that that book was a work of popularization, based on the conviction that there was an intelligent general audience "literate enough to understand a complicated exposition and willing to take the trouble to grapple with what must have seemed hopelessly obscure texts" (*DU,* 39). A later generation of critics did not share this confidence. For the early Edmund Wilson, however, the Republic of Letters had "an existence at least as palpable and concrete as the Republic of France" (*DU,* 35).

Wilson's Brahmin highmindedness, which Podhoretz sees as a kind of secularized Puritanism, led him to imagine that he could transport the Russian Revolution to America and, in the process, improve on it. When he eventually became disillusioned with both Marxism and contemporary American culture, Wilson increasingly immersed himself in his own fascinating but esoteric interests. This included everything from the Shalako festival of the Zuni Indians to the life and literature of Haiti to the Dead Sea Scrolls. The major work of Wilson's later years, however, *Patriotic Gore* (1962), was an eccentric excursion into the American past.

Patriotic Gore is subtitled "Studies in the Literature of the American Civil War," but Podhoretz believes it might more accurately have been described as "the spiritual history of American civilization" (*DU,* 51). With the exception of Harriet Beecher Stowe, the writers Wilson considers are of decidedly minor vintage. They include such luminaries as Sidney Lanier, Ambrose Bierce, George W. Cable, Albion W. Tourgee, Thomas Nelson Page, Kate Chopin (before she became a feminist poster girl), and Frederick W. Tuckerman. He even devotes seventy pages to the eminent John William DeForest. Podhoretz believes that in concentrating on such figures Wilson may have been suggesting that in post–Civil War America "it was almost impossible for literary or intellectual talent that was less than major to come to anything very much" (*DU,* 55). (The reason, of course, was that businessmen were ruling the roost.) In this sorry society Wilson's one unmistakable hero was Justice Oliver Wendell Holmes. Like Wilson, Holmes was an old-style patrician who derived great satisfaction from a "single-minded dedication to his work" (*DU,* 55). For Wilson a similar dedication came to mean a withdrawal into pessimism and crankiness. Instead of being a living community, the Republic of Letters had finally become a cult of one.

New Kids on the Block

On the whole Podhoretz was no more enthusiastic about the writers who emerged in the postwar era than he was about their immediate predecessors. As we have seen in previous chapters, he regarded Norman Mailer and James Baldwin somewhat more highly than his fellow critics did and Saul Bellow a bit less so. When we move to writers who made their first major impact in the sixties, the verdict is even less favorable. The sense of rebelliousness and alienation that had given the literature of the early modernist period a kind of iconoclastic vigor had degenerated into moral listlessness. Not only was there no new system of values emerging to replace the old certitudes that had been discarded, but the new generation of novelists didn't even seem to feel that it was missing anything. Whereas an earlier generation had thrown rocks at the windows of old cathedrals, the new kids on the block chose either to worship unconvincingly in some of those same cathedrals or to walk past them without so much as a genuflection or a curse. It was apparent at the time that the literary scene had moved beyond alienation. What was less apparent was that it was moving toward the enervated minimalism of postmodernism.[1]

In an early review of what would become one of the most popular books of the sixties, Joseph Heller's *Catch-22,* Podhoretz gives that novel a conditional pass. He begins by praising Heller's ability to describe and make credible in fiction "the incredible reality of American life in the middle of the 20th century." It is also to Heller's credit that he does not attempt to *understand* this reality. His "success lies precisely in his discovery that any effort to understand the incredible is bound to frustrate the attempt to describe it for what it really is" (*DU,* 229). If his refusal to intellectualize his material is one of Heller's greatest virtues, his greatest vice is the profound inconsistency of his vision. The first four hundred pages of *Catch-22* insistently make the point "that survival is the overriding value and that all else is pretense, lying, cant, and hypocrisy" (*DU,* 233). At the end of the book, however, Heller shrinks from applying that principle to World War II. Instead, we are told that the war is really a noble cause, which has been perverted by the stupidity and venality of the officers running it. By refusing to go all the way and trash World War II as a fraud, Heller contradicts the radical logic on which his novel had been riding.

Nearly twenty years later, Podhoretz would comment on the political implications of the cult status that *Catch-22* achieved among the counterculture of the mid-sixties to early seventies. Along with Kurt Vonnegut's *Slaughterhouse-Five*, Heller's novel represented the literary "Vietnamization" of World War II. In the first instance, *Catch-22* and *Slaughterhouse-Five* were read not as commentary on the war against Hitler but as parables of American involvement in Vietnam. (That Heller's book was written before that involvement took place did not keep it from being adopted for ideological purposes.) But the ultimate effect was to suggest that if America could behave so criminally in Vietnam, none of her past wars could have been all that pure (see *PD*, 62–63). What neither Podhoretz nor the antiwar crowd seemed to consider was that Heller's final statement about World War II (that it was a noble cause pursued in an ignoble manner) might have aptly described America's role in Vietnam. But who can blame them? *Catch-22* is most memorable for its black comic negations not for its final tepid affirmation. Podhoretz may have been right to tell Joseph Heller that "there are more clauses in Catch-22 than even you know about" (*DU*, 235), but the book's admirers have never been inclined to read the fine print.

Although Podhoretz feels particular scorn for politically tendentious writers, he is also capable of lavishing censure on those who have never been accused of having a social conscience. John Updike is a case in point. To dislike Updike in the early sixties required almost as much gall as panning Saul Bellow or praising Norman Mailer. In fact, Updike was revered by so many people Podhoretz admired that he began to wonder whether he or they were crazy. Updike's highly regarded short fiction struck Podhoretz as "all windup and no delivery" (*DU*, 252), and his novels seemed to alternate in spirit between sentimentality and cruelty. (As an example of the latter, he cites the scene in *Rabbit Run* where Rabbit's wife accidentally drowns her newborn baby in the bathtub.) He finds Updike "a writer with very little to say and whose authentic emotional range is so narrow and thin that it may without too much exaggeration be characterized as limited to a rather timid nostalgia for the confusions of youth." To those who drool over Updike's "brilliance as a stylist," Podhoretz replies, "the fact that prose as mandarin and exhibitionistic as Updike's can be universally praised seems to be an alarming sign of confusion in the general conception of how the English language functions best" (*DU*, 257).

The occasion for Podhoretz's estimate of Updike was the publication of his 1963 novel *The Centaur*. This book is a perfect example of literature that is mythological without being mythic. By weighing his story down with awkward parallels to the centaur myth, Updike tries to persuade us that a modern tale lacking inherent interest and plausibility is loaded with archetypal profundity. Had his handling of the myth been somewhat more subtle, Updike would have performed a service for untenured academics, whose career advancement depends on their publishing unreadable articles on literary influence and the like; but Updike foils even the scholarly treasure hunt by appending an index of myth to his novel. This he did at the suggestion of his wife—who, Podhoretz surmises, "was worried lest the full force of her husband's erudition and ingenuity be lost on the reader" (*DU*, 255). *The Centaur,* Podhoretz concludes, "has only confirmed me in my feeling that in the list of the many inflated literary reputations that have been created in recent years, Updike's name belongs somewhere near the top" (*DU,* 257).

If there is any premonition in *Doings and Undoings* of Norman Podhoretz's later conversion to neoconservatism, it is in his denunciation of the Beat writers. This is not to say that one needed to be an incipient conservative to be repelled by the effusions of Kerouac, Ginsberg, and company any more than one needed to be a knee-jerk liberal to think them a positive force in American culture. (Proving that politics was beside the point, Kerouac in his later years became a nativist right-winger who kept urging William F. Buckley to run for president.) But the vices for which Podhoretz condemned the Beats were quite similar to those he would discern in the New Left a decade later. For him both groups were "know-nothing bohemians" whose primary impulses were antithetical to civilization. While the bohemians of the 1920s rejected bourgeois life and their counterparts in the 1930s attacked capitalism, both groups maintained an essentially cosmopolitan and intellectual bias. This was not true of the Beats or the New Left.

Podhoretz argues that the primitivism and worship of instinct one finds in the Beat writers is more insidious than a garden-variety hedonism. For one thing, it distorts social reality. In his adulation of what he calls the "happy, true-hearted, ecstatic Negroes of America," Kerouac paints an idyllic picture of black life that Podhoretz finds similar in effect to the one painted by Southern ideologues trying "to convince the world that things were just as fine as fine could be for the slaves on the old plantation." Quoting Ned Polsky, Podhoretz charges that Kerouac's celebration of Negro spontaneity amounts to " 'an inverted form of keeping the nigger in his place' " (*DU,* 151). As plausible as that indictment might sound, Podhoretz may be reading too much into an attitude that is not that uncommon among certain middle-class whites. If Kerouac is guilty of anything, it is of a naive wish to place himself in what he conceives to be the nigger's place, a wish that Norman Mailer described in a typically baroque manner in his essay "The White Negro" and that even the most inarticulate fans of jazz, blues, and early rock and roll instinctively share.

Far more serious is Podhoretz's charge that the spontaneity and primitivism of the Beats was not just a rebellion against the middle class or capitalism or even respectability itself. It was a form of nihilism that was hostile not only to intelligence but to ordinary human feeling as well. Podhoretz sees the Beats as spiritual kin to the young savages in black leather jackets who were terrorizing the nation's cities. He reminds us that the history of modern times "teaches that there is a close connection between ideologies of primitivistic vitalism and a willingness to look upon cruelty and blood-letting with complacency, if not downright enthusiasm" (DU, 156). As evidence of this connection, Podhoretz cites Mailer's "The White Negro," which praises the courage of two teenage hoodlums who bashed in the brains of a candy store keeper. (They were, after all, violating the institution of private property.) At that time, Podhoretz could not have predicted that a few years later the pathology of the hipster would find political expression in the organized anarchism of the militant Left, or that the "white Negroes" of the sixties would choose for their role models not Miles Davis or Chuck Berry but Huey Newton and H. Rap Brown. Still, none of this should have come as much of a surprise to him. As his analysis of the new barbarism of the fifties makes clear, those who know nothing might do anything.

Chapter Five

The Neoconservative Imagination

It is common wisdom among literary folk that the critical mind loses its virginity when it ceases to be disinterested. It is perilous enough for a creative writer to be animated by religious or political passion (especially of a nonapproved variety), but for the critic it is absolute death. Of course, like so much common wisdom, this cliché works better in theory than in practice. As long as literature deals with life, it will contain ideas and attitudes that matter to flesh-and-blood human beings. What is wrong with so much literature *and* criticism these days is their tendency to divorce the written word from the passions of everyday life. Throughout his career, Norman Podhoretz has resisted that tendency; however, his early essays betray the tentativeness of a critic whose many opinions do not yet add up to a point of view.[1] In *The Bloody Crossroads: Where Literature and Politics Meet,* Podhoretz finally achieved a point of view, giving his opinions a gravity and conviction that is apparent even to those who disagree with virtually everything he has to say.

From the Finland Station

Borrowing both his title and subtitle from Lionel Trilling, Podhoretz explains that there are two important senses in which the intersection of politics and literature can be a bloody crossroads. "Blood," he writes, "has often actually been shed in the clash between literature and politics. Writers have been killed by politicians for expressing certain ideas or writing in certain ways; but (what is less often acknowledged) these same politicians have also been inspired by other writers to shed the blood of their fellow writers, and millions of nonwriters as well" (*BC,* 11). That such consequences are not the inevitable result of the meeting of literature and politics (even under a traditional tyranny) forces Podhoretz to ponder why they do invariably occur under totalitarianism. It is when political ideology attempts to dominate all aspects of life that it poses its greatest threat to literature and, paradoxically, exerts its most seductive appeal to writers. Because nazism was a comparatively short-lived phenomenon and had few writers among its most zealous defenders, communism is the species of totalitarianism that has shed the most literary blood in this century. Thus, the bulk of Podhoretz's book is concerned with the role of writers in the struggle for and against communism.

The opening essay in *The Bloody Crossroads* is a reexamination of *The God That Failed,* a collection of memoirs by six Western intellectuals (Richard Wright, Arthur Koestler, Ignazio Silone, André Gide, Louis Fischer, and Stephen Spender) who had broken with the Communist party. Published in 1950, this book helped to make the moral case for anticommunism among educated people. Each of the book's contributors was highly regarded in the world of literature and ideas, and each spoke with the credibility of personal experience. *The God That Failed* "dazzled and exhilarated" the young Norman Podhoretz and others of his generation. But like so many of the classics of one's youth, this book did not stand the test of time. Rereading it in the 1980s, Podhoretz concludes that *The God That Failed* failed—not in exposing the detestability of communism (which it did quite well) but in perceiving the necessary alternative to the political faith the ex-Communists had renounced.

When *The God That Failed* was published, too many people took the failure of communism to mean only the *practical* failure of the Soviet Union to provide either a decent life for its own citizens or a reliable paradigm for restructuring other societies. Given the long romance of many intellectuals with Soviet communism (even during the darkest days of Stalin) and the friendly feelings produced by Soviet-American cooperation during World War II, anti-Communists did not think it safe to assume that the *moral* case against Soviet totalitarianism had yet been conclusively established. And yet, from the vantage of hindsight, that assumption probably could have been made. From the Russian Revolution in 1917 up through the thirties, hordes of Western intellectuals were deluded into thinking of the Soviet Union as a worker's paradise. Since World War II, hardly anyone with pretensions to intellectual respectability would make such a claim. With the exception of espionage, the free world is really not threatened by the presence of Soviet apologists in its midst. To the extent that *The God That Failed* was a brief against pro-Soviet attitudes, it was a praiseworthy but superfluous venture.

The problem with the former Communists who composed *The God That Failed* is that they tried to hold on to socialism, and even Marxism, while denouncing the barbarism of the Soviet Union. According to such an analysis, the Soviet system was a tragically flawed attempt to realize a noble ideal or perhaps even the cynical exploitation of that ideal for sinister ends. It would therefore follow that, under different circumstances and with different leaders, a Marxist utopia would still be possible—perhaps in China or Cuba or Vietnam or Nicaragua. A more clear-eyed assessment of the situation would hold that Soviet totalitarianism was the inevitable consequence of Marxist ideology. As William Barrett so aptly put it, "you cannot unite political and economic power in one center without opening the door to tyranny" (see *BC,* 28). "In other words," Podhoretz writes, "to reject Communism while trying to hold onto Marxism or socialism in some other form was—and is—intellectually insufficient" (*BC,* 28). This was the grave error of the anti-Communist Left.

If Podhoretz finds left-wing anticommunism to be an incoherent position, those who occupied that slippery ground can still be useful allies of the neoconservative cause. This is particularly true if the individuals in question are highly regarded for their intellectual achievements and have been dead for some time. When one considers how far neoconservatives such as Podhoretz have traveled in their journey from left to right, it is conceivable that an anti-Communist intellectual such as Albert Camus might have traveled the shorter distance necessary to join them on the board of Midge Decter's Committee for the Free World.

Although Camus's writings seemed to be moving away from politics at the time of his death in 1960, his reputation among present-day French intellectuals is largely based on his break with Sartre over support for the Soviet Union. As his biographer Patrick McCarthy notes, with evident disapproval, Camus is lauded in France today "as the man who resisted Communist pressure during the cold war and who attacked the Russian concentration camps in language that Solzhenitsyn would repeat" (see *BC,* 48). Born in Algeria to a working-class French family, Camus was never tempted to romanticize third-world liberation movements. " 'I have always denounced terrorism,' he once said. 'I must also denounce a terrorism which is exercised blindly, in the streets of Algiers for example, and which some day could strike my mother or my family. I believe in justice, but I shall defend my mother above justice' " (*BC,* 37). For making this statement, Camus was accused by Conor Cruise O'Brien of "choosing 'his own tribe' against an abstract ideal of justice." As Podhoretz notes, "a greater heresy against the dogmas of the Left is hard to imagine" (BC, 45).

Critics of Podhoretz have accused him of a heresy against the dogmas of literary criticism for stressing what is most politically congenial in Camus's writings while ignoring or minimizing the apolitical literary qualities that made him an important artist. (In fact, one of Podhoretz's targets, Conor Cruise O'Brien, charged the neoconservative critic with tendentious misreading for interpreting The Fall as Camus's veiled confession of political cowardice for not championing the United States as forthrightly as Sartre championed the Soviet Union.[2]) Podhoretz's point is that those apolitical literary qualities are so slight as to be insignificant when divorced from the ideas that give Camus's work whatever vitality it possesses. Camus was a failed playwright and, at best, a minor novelist. He was awarded the Nobel Prize in literature not for his contributions to the aesthetics of fiction but because—in the words of the Nobel citation—he "illuminates the problems of the human conscience in our time." While those problems cannot be reduced to the struggle between communism and the free world, Podhoretz believes that they cannot be understood apart from that struggle. Camus believed much the same during his lifetime, and nothing that has happened since his death would have been likely to change his mind.

If politics was only a part of Albert Camus's vision of the world, it was the supreme reality for George Orwell. Respected as a journalist and essayist in his own time, Orwell has come to be regarded as a visionary novelist since his death in 1950. His brilliant anti-Stalinist satire Animal Farm invites comparisons with the best work of Jonathan Swift, and his nightmare vision of the future in Nineteen Eighty-four is part of the political consciousness of millions of people who have never even read the book. Irving Howe regards Orwell as "the best English essayist since Hazlitt, perhaps since Dr. Johnson," and "the greatest moral force in English letters during the last several decades." One of his most recent biographers, Bernard Crick, places him beside Thomas Hobbes and Swift as "one of the three greatest political writers in the history of English literature" (BC, 51). As the prophetic year 1984 drew closer, partisans of every political stripe began to claim Orwell for their own. He was, in words that he himself applied to Dickens, "one of those writers who is well worth stealing."

Like Camus and the contributors to The God That Failed, Orwell identified himself as a man of the Left. He was a self-proclaimed socialist who hated the British class system and believed that his country's rule in India was every bit as bad as Hitler's in Europe. And yet Orwell was far more venomous in his criticism of the hypocrisy and fatuousness of the Left than of any abuses of the Right. His disillusionment with the Loyalists in the Spanish Civil War produced such a devastatingly anti-Communist book in *Homage to Catalonia* that his publishers in both Britain and America refused to print it. No one has written with greater force and clarity about the follies of pacifism, neutralism, and anti-Americanism. When Saul Bellow's Mr. Sammler quoted Orwell in an address to student radicals of the sixties, he was shouted down by a heckler who declared, "Orwell was a fink. He was a sick counterrevolutionary. It's good he died when he did."[3] Like Norman Podhoretz, the heckler believed that, were he alive today, George Orwell would have been a neoconservative.

It is easy to understand why not all leftists are so willing to concede Orwell to the Right. *Nineteen Eighty-four* presents such a compelling vision of totalitarianism that anyone with even a pretense to democratic values wants to define himself as the antithesis of Big Brother. Unfortunately, that is not easy for the Left to do. Although there may be elements of nineteen eighty-four in the authoritarian regimes of the Right and in the occasional excesses of the democracies, no one with any historical sense could believe that Orwell's novel was an even-handed condemnation of East and West. To steal the Orwell of *Nineteen Eighty-four* away from the anti-Communists would be akin to making Harriet Beecher Stowe into an apologist for antebellum slavery. Whether Orwell would have perceived democratic capitalism as the only coherent alternative to communism and adjusted his domestic politics accordingly is another matter. Podhoretz detects the seeds of just such a conversion, however, in the favorable review Orwell gave to F. A. Hayek's *The Road to Serfdom.* Any man who could see " 'a great deal of truth' in Hayek's thesis that 'socialism inevitably leads to despotism,' and that the collectivism entailed by socialism brings with it 'concentration camps, leader worship, and war' " (*BC,* 66) might well have become a neoconservative by, say, 1984.[4]

Impudent Snobs

Although most of the essays in *The Bloody Crossroads* are concerned with the Manichaean conflict between communism and democracy, those grouped in a section called "The Adversary Culture" reveal other

nuances of the neoconservative imagination. Here Podhoretz's overriding preoccupation is with the intellectual's relationship to social and
political power. Because that issue is not as important as he might
think to the career of every intellectual he writes about, some of
Podhoretz's analyses seem thesis-ridden, with his most perceptive observations often appearing at the margins of his discussion. For example,
the real value of his piece on F. R. Leavis is that it identifies the peculiar
strengths (a breadth of knowledge and courage of conviction) that made
Leavis an indispensable critic and the one paralyzing weakness (a narrowness of taste) that made his judgments less than totally reliable. If
Leavis was a bit too dogmatic in his likes and dislikes, he at least
realized that the evaluation of literature was the central vocation of the
critic. Moreover, his opinions—even if they began as prejudices—were
eventually supported by an encyclopedic knowledge and discriminating
understanding of the English canon. What seems carping are the
grounds on which Podhoretz finds the eminently civilized Leavis politically suspect.

It seems that, like so many paleoconservatives, Frank Raymond
Leavis was an unreconstructed Luddite. He harbored an aristocratic
disdain for industry and technology and, therefore, greatly overrated
the primitive and instinctual D. H. Lawrence. Perhaps Leavis did allow
his social views to cloud his literary judgment while preaching an
Olympian disinterestedness. But his enthusiasm for Lawrence hardly
seems conclusive proof of this charge. Rightly or wrongly, the vast
majority of twentieth-century writers are fonder of nature than of machines. There may be a good deal of disingenuousness and hypocrisy in
this attitude, but romantic or sentimental primitivism is hardly a
characteristic peculiar to Lawrence. Since Leavis was not as high on
other modern-day Luddites, his inflated opinion of Lawrence must have
been based on more than ideological affinity.

But when Podhoretz gets his neoconservative juices flowing, subtle
distinctions are ignored. He chides Leavis for failing to realize that
the greatest threat to civilization in our time comes not from the
much-maligned captains of industry but from the neobarbarism of the
counterculture. To make his case, he cites the following passage from
Norman O. Brown's *Life Against Death:* "We are in bondage to authority outside ourselves: most obviously . . . in bondage to the authority
of books. . . . This bondage to books compels us not to see with our
own eyes; compels us to see with the eyes of the dead, with dead
eyes. . . . There is a hex on us, the specters in books, the authority of

the past; and to exorcise those ghosts is the great work of magical self-liberation" (see *BC,* 90–91). As reprehensible as that passage might be, it expresses a sentiment that is no more unique to the contemporary counterculture than a celebration of the primitive is to the novels of D. H. Lawrence. In fact, the passage in question could have come word-for-word from Emerson's lecture "The American Scholar." To the extent that Norman O. Brown is responsible for loosening the moorings of Western civilization, at least part of the blame must go to his early sponsor Norman Podhoretz. But that is a bit of news one would not glean from reading *The Bloody Crossroads.*

What Podhoretz finds politically objectionable in Leavis is much more strikingly evident in a whole class of intellectuals who have come to prominence since World War II. Confining his focus to the United States (although he claims that the phenomenon is international), Podhoretz calls this class the adversary culture. What it opposes are the bourgeois values of life under democratic capitalism. In other words, we have here another instance of alienated intellectuals spurning a society in which they feel underappreciated. The difference is that in contemporary American society intellectuals enjoy an unprecedented degree of wealth, power, and prestige. If they've never had it so good, one might ask, why are they complaining so bitterly? Podhoretz suggests that the answer may lie in the phenomenon of rising expectations. Having come so far, the adversary culture will not settle for anything less than total victory.

But, of course, not all intellectuals wear black hats. Those who are known as neoconservatives have seen the error of their leftist ways and are now vigorously championing everything that the silent majority holds dear but is too inarticulate to defend against those pointy-heads who do wear black hats. Although Podhoretz does not say that the salvation of the free world depended on *Commentary*'s turning to the Right, he does contend that the support of neoconservative intellectuals helped put Reagan in the White House. Such a claim, in addition to inviting hoots of derision from those who find the neoconservatives a bit self-important,[5] badly misstates the power actually wielded by Podhoretz and his cohorts. Just as the Pope commands no troops, *Commentary* can deliver few votes. Nevertheless, a disproportionate amount of the intellectual energy in the Reagan administration did come from neoconservatives, many of whom read and even write for *Commentary.* Certainly, traditional Republicans feel that the neocons got more than their share of the spoils under Reagan. (One is reminded of the older brother complaining about his father's favoritism to the prodigal son.) It is true that neoconservative intellectuals can caucus in a phone booth, but that phone is frequently a direct line to those who control elections and shape the destiny of nations.

Power in the Word

If the deracinated American intellectual has a patron saint, one who has mythologized the plight of the cultivated man in a crass and materialistic society, it is Henry Adams. The great-grandson of America's second president and the grandson of its sixth, Adams was born into a family that seemed destined always to be at the cutting edge of American history. And yet his intellectual autobiography, *The Education of Henry Adams,* is conceived as a tale of failure. It is the continuous, interminable whine of an eighteenth-century man tragically unfit for a world hurtling toward the twentieth century. With minor qualifications, scholars and general readers alike have tended to take Adams's evaluation of himself and his society at face value (perhaps chiding him gently for being too self-critical). Podhoretz, however, regards Adams as a poseur who has had a baneful influence on American culture. Adams's life may have been paradigmatic, but Podhoretz sees in it a different lesson from the one Adams and his cult of admirers have tried to foist on the reading public.

To begin with, Henry Adams had aspirations no more refined than those of his compatriots. He, too, coveted wealth, power, and fame. However, he was sufficiently self-aware to realize that his aloofness and arrogance ruled out a career in politics. (Despite what Adams would have us believe, this had nothing to do with superior breeding; John Hay and Henry Cabot Lodge, whose backgrounds were every bit as patrician as his, enjoyed distinguished careers in government.) In fact, Adams was so indifferent to the culture and life of his own time that his historical research, particularly of the Middle Ages, seems a sophisticated form of escapism, the work of a kind of highbrow Miniver Cheevy. Although he complained of powerlessness in his own time, Adams's writing has remained a force in ours, "when the names of Rutherford B. Hayes or Chester Arthur are scarcely even remembered." While this "demonstrates how much more powerful intellectuals can be in the long run than even the most successful politicians," we should not take it to "mean that Adams is a force for good." "On the contrary," Podhoretz concludes, "in encouraging a bigoted contempt for this country and in subtly denigrating and devaluing the life of the mind, he has exerted so malignant an influence that . . . I see little of value that would be lost by allowing him to slip into the obscurity he so often boasted of wishing to achieve" (*BC,* 114).

One looking for the antithesis of Henry Adams could hardly do better than Henry Kissinger. No descendant of the American aristocracy, Kissinger was an immigrant German Jew. Although he and Adams were both on the Harvard faculty (nearly a century apart), they went from there in very different directions. Adams ended up an embittered curmudgeon, looking with scorn upon the White House from his residence in Lafayette Square. From an office in the basement of that same White House, Kissinger orchestrated American foreign policy. It is difficult for any intellectual who has lusted for power not to look on Henry Kissinger with a measure of envy. Since Norman Podhoretz has never hid his ambitions under a bushel, one might expect his view of Kissinger to be similar to what a minor league ballplayer thinks of the resident superstar. To his credit, Podhoretz has crafted a judicious and perceptive assessment of Kissinger as both diplomat and writer.

Although Podhoretz fundamentally disagrees with the policy of détente fashioned by Kissinger and Nixon, he is impressed with the way Kissinger carried out that policy. With no previous diplomatic experience, Kissinger flawlessly executed the most delicate negotiations between the world's superpowers. Perhaps just as remarkable is that he writes about his experiences so persuasively that even a hawk of Podhoretz's feather is swept along by the force of his rhetoric. Podhoretz praises Kissinger for the strength of his intellect and for a writing style "that is equally at ease in portraiture and abstract analysis; that can shape a narrative as skillfully as it can paint a scene; that can achieve marvels of compression while moving at an expansive and leisurely pace" (*BC,* 145). His only criticisms of Kissinger as writer are that, in an effort to be self-effacing, he is insufficiently introspective and he has yet to publish a reassessment of the policies he helped to form. But if Kissinger has not yet written his version of *Making It* and *Breaking Ranks,* Podhoretz nevertheless ranks *White House Years* and *Years of Upheaval* "among the great books of their kind and among the great works of our time" (*BC,* 166).

The Bloody Crossroads concludes with a look at two dissident writers from the Communist bloc who pose interesting problems for the politically committed literary critic. Podhoretz responds to this challenge by finding Milan Kundera a greater artist but a lesser visionary than

Aleksandr Solzhenitsyn. Cast in the form of an open letter, Podhoretz's discussion of Kundera praises the Czech émigré for not having written another sincere but redundant account of the horrors of life under communism. Podhoretz believes that in *The Book of Laughter and Forgetting*, Kundera "discovered" communism for the novel by showing "the distinctive things Communism does to the life—most notably the spiritual or cultural life—of a society" (*BC*, 170).

Like all good novels, *The Book of Laughter and Forgetting* is rooted in a specific time and place (post–World War II Czechoslovakia), but it achieves its originality by abandoning realism for a kind of neofabulism that actually reveals more about the inner nature of totalitarianism than could be accomplished in yet another conventional tale of jack-booted slave masters and arrests in the night. (Podhoretz draws a useful comparison between the form of Kundera's book and the practice of "the tonal modernist composers who, no matter how dissonant and difficult they may be, . . . are still intelligible to the ear in a way that the atonal and serial composers are not" [*BC*, 174–75].) As a committed artist, Kundera opposes totalitarianism and its efforts to subsume all life into politics. While strongly agreeing with him in principle, Podhoretz warns Kundera that left-wing literary critics in the West are already using his aestheticism to blunt the anti-Communist witness of his novels. Only by being political in the face of totalitarianism can one win the luxury of being apolitical in a free society. (One suspects that Kundera's fellow artist Vaclav Havel would agree.)

If the political message of Kundera's books has been minimized by the anti-anti-Communist literary establishment of the West, such a fate would never befall the blunt-spoken works of Aleksandr Solzhenitsyn. While he was still a persecuted dissident in the Soviet Union, Solzhenitsyn was lionized by the Western intelligentsia and even awarded the Nobel Prize in literature in 1970. Because he fought against censorship in his own country, he was assumed to be a liberal. But once Solzhenitsyn was exiled from his homeland and began speaking freely about world politics, he had the temerity to denounce the West for its cultural decadence and its timidity in facing the Communist threat. Far from being a liberal, he was a czarist authoritarian with little appreciation for democratic capitalism. The one-time media darling was now dismissed as a crank.

Not surprisingly, Podhoretz believes that Solzhenitsyn's heroic struggle against Communist oppression and his prophetic zeal in urging the free world to replicate that struggle redeem all of his ideological eccentricities. Podhoretz doesn't even seem to be bothered by Solzhenitsyn's alleged anti-Semitism, since he believes that the novelist's support for Israel renders that accusation moot. Where he does criticize Solzhenitsyn, and this is where Podhoretz's integrity as a literary critic is most evident, is for his inability to breathe life into his fiction. Paradoxically, Solzhenitsyn's art fails when he is most serious about being an artist— in his novels. When he is simply witnessing to the truth—as in *The Gulag Archipelago* or *The Oak and the Calf*—his narrative skills are most evident. Podhoretz believes that in these nonfiction works Solzhenitsyn transcends the purely personal to "become a vessel through which 'the millions who had not lived to scrawl or gasp or croak the truth about their lot' find voices and tongues and are at last able to tell what they know" (*BC*, 204).

One unmistakable conclusion we can draw from *The Bloody Crossroads* is that the ideas expressed in literature frequently have political consequences. That this is something we need to be reminded of is evidence of how successful such movements as deconstruction and postmodernism have been in obscuring the vital connection between the word and the flesh. Podhoretz has tried to respect the aesthetic integrity of literature (e.g., in praising Henry Adams's historical writing and criticizing Solzhenitsyn's novels), even when doing so runs counter to his own political interests. Nevertheless, political judgments must finally be made in assessing the social and intellectual significance of a book. To be both a literary *and* social critic is somewhat unfashionable these days. In taking his stand at that bloody crossroads, however, Norman Podhoretz asserts a belief in the beauty of politics, the power of literature, and the central importance of both to civilization. These are opinions that add up to a point of view.

Chapter Six
American Studies

In literary studies, as in most things, whatever goes around comes around. Wait long enough, and an approach that seemed dead will be resurrected in slightly different form, quite often by persons convinced they are on to something new. From the mid-1930s until the mid-1950s aesthetic formalism (then known as New Criticism) was the received orthodoxy in college classrooms and literary quarterlies. Imaginative texts were analyzed and evaluated as verbal artifacts rather than as evidence of their author's psyche or manifestations of their historical milieu. Given the excesses of Marxist and Freudian criticism, it is no wonder that John Crowe Ransom would write an essay in 1941 entitled "Wanted: An Ontological Critic." After a generation or more of graduate students had answered Mr. Ransom's ad, however, New Criticism itself began to seem old hat. It was now time to put away the Thomas and Brown reader, which printed poems without their authors or dates for fear that the student might bring too much context to the act of literary analysis. Context was back in, and close reading was dismissed as a kind of sterile intellectual bead game.

One of the reactions to the perceived narrowness of New Criticism was a boom in interdisciplinary studies. If culture itself is intraconnected, why split our study of it into such arbitrary categories as history, sociology, economics, political science, and literature? Looking back to the early years of this century, we find that some of the most provocative writers on American culture (V. L. Parrington, Van Wyck Brooks, Charles Beard, Frederick Jackson Turner, and others) were always wandering off the disciplinary reservation. And even when New Criticism was in its heyday, figures such as Perry Miller and F. O. Matthiessen at Harvard, Lionel Trilling at Columbia, and Henry Nash Smith at Texas and Minnesota consistently stressed the relations between literature and the culture of which it is a part. Kenneth S. Lynn (Ph.D. Harvard, 1954) is very much a part of the postwar renaissance in American Studies.

The Legacy

In his tribute to F. O. Matthiessen, published in Joseph Epstein's *Masters: Portraits of Great Teachers,* [1] Lynn argues that American literary study went through several distinct stages during the first half of the twentieth century (which was almost exactly Matthiessen's own life span). What Lynn calls the Era of Rediscovery began with the work of Van Wyck Brooks and H. L. Mencken around 1908. It picked up momentum in the twenties and thirties with the writings of Lewis Mumford, V. L. Parrington, Granville Hicks, Constance Roarke, and Newton Arvin and peaked between 1939 and 1942, with the publication in rapid succession of Perry Miller's *The New England Mind,* Matthiessen's *American Renaissance,* and Alfred Kazin's *On Native Ground.* Then the whole tradition was magisterially brought together in 1948 in Robert Spiller's three-volume *Literary History of the United States,* with its "all-star cast of contributors" (*Masters,* 103).

The process of rediscovery, expansion, and consolidation that Lynn sketches here covers a period of forty years; now, however, more than forty years have passed since the publication of Spiller's *History* brought the first great era of American literary study to an end. If any trend has characterized the past forty years it has been one of dissipation. Once American literature won academic respectability and ceased to be a special cause in itself, it was enlisted on behalf of all the other special causes running rampant in the academy. In the fifties it was captured by myth criticism. (R. W. B. Lewis's *The American Adam* [1955] and Leslie Fiedler's *Love and Death in the American Novel* [1960] were unquestionably the two most important studies of American literature to appear in the twelve years after Spiller.) Throughout the sixties and much of the seventies, racial and sexual politics carried the day. More recently, Lynn tells us, American literary scholars have invested in "such promising growth stocks as structuralism, women's studies, and film" (*Masters,* 106).

F. O. Matthiessen committed suicide in 1950, just as American literary study and the national optimism of the postwar era were both beginning to run out of steam. Whether or not he was willing to admit it, it must have been clear to him that the deep divisions that had always plagued American culture would doom any attempt at synthesis in either scholarship or social relations. Like Van Wyck Brooks (who suffered a nervous breakdown at his prime and retreated, in his declining years, from cultural analysis to cultural nostalgia), Matthiessen

knew that "American culture was split across the brow," divided between antagonistic traditions (what Philip Rahv identified as the dichot-
omy between the Paleface and the Indian). "Some Americans were the
products of a tradition of learning and knowledge that went back
through nineteenth-century Harvard to the Puritans, but other Americans were the children of a radical, know-nothing tradition born on the
raucous and lusty frontier" (*Masters,* 11). The original legacy, exempli-
fied by Henry Adams, eventually lost its vitality and self-confidence,
while the insurgency, typified by Mark Twain, was plagued with status
anxiety and a sense of dread.

Even as Matthiessen tried personally (and unsuccessfully) to reconcile
the warring American traditions by being both a Christian and a socialist, he could see the handwriting (some would say the graffiti) on the
wall. Before his death "the failure of belief had become the central
problem of American culture. Novelists were turning in on themselves
because there was nothing else to believe in. Meter, rhyme, and other
outside controls were being abandoned by poets in consequence of the
view that poetry was now an end in itself, rather than a means to an
end" (*Masters,* 111). Although Lynn is convinced that Matthiessen took
his life out of personal rather than cultural disillusionment, there is
little doubt that, were he alive today, he would be distressed if not
entirely surprised by the direction that American literature and American scholarship have taken. Lynn does not share Matthiessen's particular philosophical commitments (as a neoconservative, he would probably see variants of socialism as part of the problem rather than the
solution). He does, however, share his former teacher's humanistic
concern for the fate of American culture. Lynn's own career can be seen
as a testament to the strength and ambiguity, not the anxiety, of
influence.

Horatio's Children

The name of Horatio Alger is probably known to millions of Americans who could not tell you the title of a single one of the 120 books he
published during the final third of the nineteenth century. Between the
appearance of his first novel, *Ragged Dick: or Street Life in New York with
the Boot-blacks,* in 1868 and the Great Depression, ten million copies of
his books were sold, making him the most widely read author in the
world. Today, those books are regarded more as sociological curiosities
than as works of literature, to be read not in English classes but in

courses in the history of ideas. His art would never pass muster with New Critics. But to the millions who have read his books and the tens of millions who know them only by reputation, Horatio Alger is synonymous with the American Dream. That dream has particularly fascinated the neoconservative critics, as we saw with Norman Podhoretz's *Making It* and will see with Joseph Epstein's *Ambition: The Secret Passion.*[2] Kenneth S. Lynn's *The Dream of Success: A Study of the Modern American Imagination*[3] preceded both of those works by more than a decade. Appearing in 1955, it was Lynn's first published book and as such lacks both the bias and the verve of his later polemical writings.

The Dream of Success is not so much "A Study of the Modern American Imagination" as it is a series of discussions of the careers of Theodore Dreiser, Jack London, David Graham Phillips, Frank Norris, and Robert Herrick. All five of these men came to maturity during Alger's period of greatest popularity. All five lived in an America very different from the one Alger mythologized. Like others of their generation, "they discovered that America's spectacular growth had also spawned a host of problems too big to be ignored. Industrial warfare, political explosions in the farm belt, rising popular bitterness about monopolies and outbursts of xenophobic hatred were simply the most sensational signs of social trouble. The soaring divorce rate and the increased concern of the medical profession with nervous disorders and mental breakdowns were evidence that the maladjustments generated by the great race of American life were personal as well as public" (*DS,* 9). What differentiates these men from the bulk of their fellow citizens is that, when they saw a gap between the American Dream and the American reality, they responded by writing novels.

More than other novelists of his day Theodore Dreiser realized that success in America was measured in terms of sex and money. For most of his early years he was deprived of both but lived long enough to discover that the good life isn't what he thought it would be on the other side of the candy store window. Having grown up in poverty and been pushed to the brink of suicide by the suppression of his first and greatest novel, *Sister Carrie,* Dreiser was always more captivated by failure than by success. (Carrie's rise in the world is not nearly so gripping a story as Hurstwood's fall.) It was one thing to show a poor boy climbing the ladder of success, it was quite another to show the successful man as a happy and deserving human being. In the world of Horatio Alger, success was achieved by possessing mediocre virtues to a superior degree. No Nietzschean supermen need apply. Consequently,

when Dreiser had elevated Frank Cowperwood to the top of the economic heap, he didn't know what to do with him. So, he returned to
the more manageable theme of failure and wrote *An American Tragedy*.
It was not the impossibility, or even the difficulty, but the banality of
success that bedeviled Dreiser.

The same was true to an even greater degree of Jack London. Like
Dreiser, London was a poor boy who eventually became wealthy
through his writing. In fact, he was the first American author to
become a millionaire. (Horatio Alger sold the rights to his books to
their publishers for lump sums much smaller than what he could have
made in royalties.) Although an avowed socialist whose works have
always been vastly popular in the Soviet Union, London was at heart
more an individualist than a collectivist. There was an element of
calculation in his political sympathies (he correctly predicted that he
would be the first writer to make socialism pay) and a deep-seated
misanthropy that made any permanent alliance with the common man
out of the question.

London's political radicalism consisted primarily of a hatred of the
effete upper classes who he was certain owed their success more to luck
than to genuine ability. Where Dreiser could not imagine an American
capitalist who was both successful and admirable, London was incapable of even imagining a possible world in which he would like to live.
(His political fiction tends toward nihilism, while his most enduring
works celebrate the individual's effort to transcend his environment.)
Thus, on the evening of 21 November 1916, at the height of his
personal success, he took a lethal dose of morphine, turned out the
light, and went to bed. It was, according to Lynn, "Jack London's last
dream of escape" (*DS*, 118).

The second section of Lynn's book is concerned with the generation
of Americans who came of age during the first two decades of this
century (between the election of McKinley and the reelection of Wilson). Horatio Alger was dead, and the robber barons had already
achieved their greatest success. The rags-to-riches dream was still very
much alive for the sizable immigrant population that had invaded
America's shores, but many citizens whose roots went back more than
one generation despaired of making a better life for themselves than
their parents had enjoyed. It was a time of great economic volatility,
when opportunity seemed more limited than before and many middle
Americans were convinced that their best days were behind them.

Such a culture produced an audience for "inspirational essays on getting ahead, reminiscences by famous men of their boyhoods, editorials denouncing unrestricted immigration or spanking the knuckles of the trusts, colored covers depicting George Washington, Independence Hall, the family doctor, or a man priming a frozen pump on a winter morning" (*DS,* 126). This audience was ably served by the *Saturday Evening Post* and its most prolific contributor, David Graham Phillips. In addition to writing most of the *Post*'s editorials between 1902 and his death in 1911, Phillips produced twenty-five books and hundreds of articles and short stories. The villains in his fiction were invariably decadent East Coast aristocrats (frequently the attenuated offspring of hardier frontier stock), and his heroes were salt of the midwestern earth, bent on exposing the corruption of the Atlantic seaboard. It was a populist mythology that would never permanently disappear from American life.

The novels of Frank Norris pandered to many of the same prejudices and stereotypes found in the works of Phillips. What Norris added was a virulent anti-Semitism and a fascination with sex and violence not found in the family-oriented fiction of Phillips and the *Post*. Benjamin Franklin Norris, Jr., was unlike both his father and their common historical namesake. The pampered son of a wealthy family, young Norris was plagued by a sense of personal inadequacy. Unlike the rags-to-riches hero, he seemed to have nowhere to go but down. Living a life of dissipation and idleness, he would never be a source of pride for his father, a successful businessman who greatly admired the evangelist Dwight L. Moody. Lynn shows us that Norris's rebellion against his father was punctuated by feelings of guilt and self-recrimination. He lived hard and died young, leaving behind some strangely powerful, even moralistic, tales of human bestiality.

Reaction against what the Alger myth had become reached its apogee in the work of Robert Herrick. None of the writers Lynn discusses can match Herrick's contempt for the "second generation" of successful Americans, those whose wealth was inherited from fathers who actually lived the Alger dream. He regarded the men of this generation as polo-playing dilettantes and their women as status-conscious, money-hungry vampires, "sucking at the souls of men" (see *DS,* 215). Despairing of any political solution to this sorry state of affairs, Herrick believed that salvation lay in the emergence of a class of altruistic professional men. His "new church was the university, its priest was the professionally trained student" (*DS,* 220).

Not surprisingly, Herrick entered the professional class himself by becoming a university teacher of English, first at the Massachusetts Institute of Technology and later at the University of Chicago. One of Herrick's colleagues at the latter school was the noted economist Thorstein Veblen, whose classic work *The Theory of the Leisure Class* "became the most celebrated indictment of the 'second generation' of success ever to be written by an American" (*DS, 222*). Like Herrick, Veblen apotheosized the professional man as the salvation of us all. But in imagining that man an alternative to the conventional success hero, he ran up against the reality that economic success was usually a reward for professional accomplishment in America.

How to keep his hero untainted by the commercial ethic was an even more vexing problem for Herrick, whose role as a novelist meant that he had to imagine his characters as human beings rather than as mere sociological abstractions. The closest Herrick came to solving that problem was to transport the hero of his novel *The Real World* into the American West. In the West, "he steps across the threshold into the past; moving westward in space has taken him backward in time. . . . In the West, Herrick's lawyer hero is in effect a member of the first, not the second, generation, a representative of the best aristocracy, not the worst, in sum, an Alger hero moving up the ladder in the golden dawn-age of the success myth" (*DS, 230*).

Taken on its terms, *The Dream of Success* is a competent and suggestive treatment of the influence of the Alger myth on the work of five different, yet representative, American writers. Like most of Lynn's later work, this book relies heavily on biography and plot summary. That is the nature of historical criticism. Add wit, style, and ideological passion, and you have compelling reading. These three qualities, however, are found far more often in Lynn's neoconservative work than in his earlier writing. Reading *The Dream of Success* over thirty years after its original publication, I can't help thinking how much better the book would be were Lynn writing it today.

Even in the context of 1955, some questions can be raised. Lynn never makes clear why he chose to discuss the work of these particular five writers. Of the lot, only Dreiser is a major figure; London and Norris are still included in the anthologies but are rarely studied outside upper-division courses in American naturalism; and Phillips and Herrick are virtually unknown except to specialists in turn-of-the-century American culture. In 1955 we could have used a good study of the dream of success in the work of Sinclair Lewis and F. Scott Fitzgerald. For that matter, an extended treatment of Alger himself would have been fascinating.

Lynn might also have mentioned the fact that the first Horatio Alger hero was born over 120 years before Alger himself. It was Benjamin Franklin who first equated the rise from rags to riches with the American Dream. Lynn might have speculated as to why it took nearly a century for that dream to become the central American mythology. (It may have been that Franklin was ahead of his time in writing for an Atlantic seaboard community whose imagination would soon be consumed by the myth of the West, while Alger was writing for a postfrontier nation looking for a new paradigm to replace the now obsolete pioneer and cowboy.) Also, it seems that a cultural and literary historian wishing to examine the dynamics of success and failure in American life during the later nineteenth and early twentieth centuries might have had something to say about *The Education of Henry Adams*. But then the dream of success is such a pervasive and complex phenomenon in American life that any attempt to study it is likely to be riddled with glaring omissions. From Ben Franklin to Lee Iacocca to Sydney Biddle Barrows, Americans have drawn inspiration from people with their eyes on the main chance.

The Novel as History

One would think that the best way of measuring the evolution of Kenneth S. Lynn's sensibility during the twenty-eight years separating *The Dream of Success* and *The Air-Line to Seattle*[4] would be to read the "Eleven Literary Historical Essays," collected in 1973 under the title *Visions of America*[5] and dedicated "To the Memory of F. O. Matthiessen." The earliest of these essays were originally published only a few years after *The Dream of Success,* and the latest ones only a few years before the earliest ones in *Air-Line*. By all rights, we should expect to see a gradual flowering or sudden shift in style by reading these pieces in the order of their first publication. Instead, the most striking differences seem to owe more to subject matter and audience than to any identifiable watershed in Lynn's intellectual history.

Visions of America begins with a lengthy discussion of *Walden* that was first published in Perry Miller's *Major Writers of America* (1962). No student could want a more intelligent and lucid introduction to Thoreau's masterpiece. Structure, imagery, symbolism, and historical context are all here. What is lacking is critical bite. To the extent that there is any moral evaluation of Thoreau and his alternative life-style, it is in the reverential terms one associates with the genteel professors Lynn would castigate so brilliantly in *The Air-Line to Seattle*. Does Thoreau cook the books in his chapter "Economy"? Was his tax resistance a derivative bit of moral posturing? Have socialist critics willfully ignored the libertarian Thoreau's opposition to governmental regulation of commerce? The answers to these and other questions must be found somewhere other than in Kenneth S. Lynn's essay on *Walden*.

Another essay from 1962 constitutes a far more impressive achievement. In his introduction to a Harvard University Press edition of *Uncle Tom's Cabin,* Lynn does much to restore the reputation of a novel maligned by many highbrow critics. As Lynn points out, the novelists generally thought to comprise the pre–Civil War canon of American literature (Cooper, Irving, Hawthorne, Melville, et al.) failed to confront the great moral issue of slavery. When the popular sentimental novelists dealt with race relations, they were apt to be exploiting a prurient fascination with the quadroon slave girl or actually defending the benign paternalism of slavery. It took Harriet Beecher Stowe, a relatively inexperienced writer, to capture the human drama of slavery for a mass audience. What is remarkable from a strictly literary standpoint is her blending of sentimental conventions with a narrative realism not previously seen in the American novel.

Lynn is particularly good at identifying the qualities that make Stowe's novel a much more complex work of art than the myriad of Tom plays it spawned. The neurotic Southern belle, the Byronic aristocrat, and the uptight New England spinster are all familiar figures in American literature, but rarely have they been as effectively realized as in the characters of Marie and Augustine St. Clare and Miss Ophelia. It has long been recognized that Augustine reflects Stowe's mixed feelings of attraction and repulsion to Lord Byron; however, Lynn shows how those feelings were tied up with the author's more personal sense of ambivalence about her Calvinist upbringing. Theologically, the greatest triumph of *Uncle Tom's Cabin* lies in Stowe's substitution of an all-inclusive gospel of Christian love for the more severe strictures of New England Calvinism. The bearers of that new gospel are almost exclusively women. The one notable exception is the title character himself, a man who succeeds in being feminine without being effeminate, who in short is a blackface embodiment of the Protestant Christ.

An even more influential critic who did much to restore *Uncle Tom's*

Cabin to critical favor was Edmund Wilson. According to Lynn, Wilson's book *Patriotic Gore: Studies in the Literature of the American Civil War* tells us as much about the famous critic as it does about Harriet Beecher Stowe or any of the other mid-nineteenth-century authors it purports to discuss. This is fitting, considering the political motives behind Wilson's book. What is scandalous is Lynn's revelation that Wilson was more a patriot than he intended. *Patriotic Gore* was supposed to have been an exposé of the jingoist attitudes—North and South—that made the war between the states inevitable. The result was to be a cautionary tale for the cold war era in which Wilson was writing (after fifteen years' labor, his book was published in 1962). Instead, it turned time and again into a respectful (if critical) meditation on political idealism.

Several other essays deal with figures about whom Lynn has already written extensively. (Because his piece on *Adventures of Huckleberry Finn* and his "Howells in the Nineties" are also part of Lynn's biographies of Twain and Howells, we will pass over them here.) An example is his long introduction to the Riverside edition of Frank Norris's *The Octopus*. What sets this discussion apart from what Lynn has already said in *The Dream of Success* is that nearly half of the essay deals not with Norris at all but with three of his most significant literary predecessors: Mark Twain, Henry Adams, and Henry James.

Lynn begins by citing W. H. Auden's observation that loneliness is the central quality of American writing. In the period before the Civil War, Lynn notes, "loneliness wore the mask of human pride; isolation was tied up with the mad temptations of the unbridled ego, with the fear of being overwhelmed from without or betrayed from within—in a word, with death" (*VA*, 115). By the last few decades of the nineteenth century, however, "the horror of death had given way, by and large, to the chilling despair at not having lived at all" (*VA*, 115). Twain and Adams responded to this trauma by resurrecting, or reinventing, very different forms of the past. For Twain it was the idyllic personal past of his boyhood along the Mississippi River; for Adams it was the culturally homogenous past of medieval Europe. That childhood in the happy valley was not as ideal as Twain remembered nor life in the thirteenth century as elevated as Adams imagined goes without saying. In manufacturing a usable past, however, these writers tell us a good deal about the intolerability of their present.

For Henry James there was no simple escape from the feeling that life had passed him by. In a sense his fiction is a compendium of the inadequacy of the various escapes people might try. In "The Beast in the Jungle," the fatuous John Marcher, who waits all his life for the great thing that will happen to him only to discover that he is the man of his generation to whom nothing is to happen, is but an extreme example of a common plight in the world of Henry James. The only dignified response to such a situation is stoic acceptance. (When James failed to achieve success in the theater, he resigned himself to writing for an audience of one.) In the character of Strether in *The Ambassadors,* however, he urged the next generation to profit from his failure and live life to the fullest. (The climactic scene in which Strether gives such advice to Little Bilham was based on an actual encounter between William Dean Howells and a young associate.) As Lynn showed in *The Dream of Success* and redemonstrates in *Visions of America,* Frank Norris was one member of that generation who took James's advice all too much to heart.

Lynn's discussion of *Sister Carrie* is not only a sound introduction to that great novel but also a shrewd analysis of those qualities that distinguish Theodore Dreiser from his contemporaries. Dreiser's great heresy was not that he dealt with sex in his fiction but that he had the temerity to demythologize it. According to conventions that have persisted in the English speaking novel from the time of Samuel Richardson, a woman wronged is as good as dead. Carrie Meeber, however, is no Clarissa Harlowe. If men temporarily take advantage of her, she always ends up more the victimizer than the victim.

By becoming Drouet's mistress, Carrie is rescued from a life of working-class poverty. But when the more elegant Hurstwood appears on the scene, she has few qualms about leaving Drouet in the lurch. Similarly, when she begins to succeed through her own theatrical talents as Hurstwood is becoming a financial and emotional wreck, she cuts him loose as so much excess baggage. There is no sense of revenge here, only calculated self-interest. Because Carrie is the way she is, we cannot feel properly indignant toward her seducers. When Hurstwood takes his life, we see him as a broken man worthy of pity, not a jaded Lovelace getting his just deserts. (Lynn even suggests that in Hurstwood's suicide there is a tragic dignity that finally makes him a deeper and more complex person than Carrie.) Carrie herself is a case of neither virtue rewarded nor innocence violated. Had Dreiser had the good taste to drown her in the East River, as Crane did Maggie, all might have been forgiven. Instead, he depicts the awful truth that in life there is no poetic justice. For Dreiser's day and age, that was carrying realism a bit too far.

Not content to infuriate the prudish, Dreiser was also scornful of social reformers. Rather than deplore the social conditions that helped make Carrie what she was, Dreiser takes those conditions as a given and admires individuals tough and resourceful enough to succeed within them. It is possible to rise above poverty but not to eliminate it. (To the extent that the Soviet Union had managed to minimize class distinctions, Dreiser found it to be a boring society.) According to Lynn, Dreiser's "attitude toward the poor varied between scorn for the class he had successfully struggled to escape and a sympathy for human suffering that was based directly on his fear that he might someday slide back into the poverty he had known in his youth" (*VA*, 143).

Persons examining *Visions of America* for hints of inchoate neoconservatism might note that the only essay Lynn devotes to an American writer who came to prominence after World War I is "The Achievement of John Dos Passos." Although Lynn concentrates on the technical innovations of his subject's fiction, there is little question that he admires Dos Passos for his independence of thought. "In the era of laissez-faire capitalism," Lynn writes of Dos Passos, "his fictional spokesmen drank champagne toasts to 'Revolution, to Anarchy, to the Socialist State'; with the dawn of the welfare economy they switched to the individualistic insistence that 'if we want to straighten the people out we've got to start with number one' " (*VA*, 177).

Lynn challenges the conventional belief (held not only by card-carrying leftists but by Joseph Epstein as well) that Dos Passos lost his ability to write at about the time that he became disillusioned with radical politics. He even questions the notion that that disillusionment was primarily the result of the novelist's discovery of the ruthlessness of the Communist forces during the Spanish Civil War. Instead, Lynn believes that Dos Passos's political education was the result of his labors on the *USA* trilogy throughout the 1930s. In writing this saga, its author gained a new appreciation for American traditions and American values, for what he called "the ground we stand on." It is not clear from Lynn's essay why this experience should eventually lead a radical leftist to the masthead of *National Review,* but the example of John Dos Passos has an obvious relevance for a later generation of literary folk who have found a new home on the political Right.

Visions of America concludes with an essay whose provenance was explicitly political. Throughout the 1960s the United States experienced an alarming incidence of civil unrest. Racial turmoil erupted into ghetto riots in a host of major cities; on campuses across the nation students were expressing their political idealism by taking over buildings or, in some cases, burning them down; and ordinary street crime seemed to be on the rise everywhere. In response, President Lyndon Johnson appointed a national commission to study the causes and prevention of violence. Kenneth S. Lynn contributed to that project by examining the theme of violence in American literature and folklore.

For the most part a remarkably judicious and balanced discussion, Lynn's essay argues that the mere presence of violence in our storytelling tradition is not necessarily a reflection of violence in American life. Violence (like sex?) is a way of getting and holding the reader's attention. Simpleminded observers who are unaware of certain narrative conventions might read more sociological significance into literary violence than is actually there. (Without offering any supporting evidence, the essay accuses certain critics who should know better—for instance, Leslie Fiedler—of doing this in a messianic attempt to reform American society.) Lynn illustrates his point by restoring the frequently bloody tales of the Southwest humorists to their original historical and political context. What he finds less funny and more ominous is the tragic hopelessness that permeates much of the best literature dealing with the plight of American blacks. Citing Melville's "Benito Cereno," Twain's *Pudd'nhead Wilson,* and Wright's *Native Son,* Lynn notes, "it is significant that these three extraordinarily gifted writers, two white, one black, agree so completely about the insolubility of American race hatred" (*VA,* 205).

Although this report says comparatively little about twentieth-century American literature, one comment made in passing should be of particular interest to close watchers of Kenneth S. Lynn. Speaking of Ernest Hemingway, Lynn writes, "When fragments of an Austrian mortar shell hit him in the legs, and he was hit twice more in the body by machinegun fire, he found his materials with a vengeance. Thereafter a wound was to become the central symbol of nearly all his work and the consequenes of a wound his recurrent theme. In many ways a highly personal testament, Hemingway's work also captures, in hauntingly symbolic terms, the permanently scarring effects of World War I on American society" (*VA,* 203). Within a dozen years, Lynn would not only be changing his tune on Hemingway and the consequences of his wound for American literature, but also attacking anyone jejune enough to hold the views he himself so solemnly presented to the councils of government. But then, who wasn't a little crazy in the 1960s?

Chapter Seven

Lives of the Poets

Prior to the triumph he achieved in his book on Hemingway,[1] Kenneth Lynn had twice tried his hand at literary biography. Anyone who reads *Mark Twain and Southwestern Humor* (1959) and *William Dean Howells: An American Life* (1971)[2] close together cannot help being struck by the superior grace, maturity, and scope of the latter volume. The book on Twain is a conventional, if problematic, contribution to academic discourse. The Howells biography is itself a work of narrative art. (The difference may be due in part to the fact that *Mark Twain and Southwestern Humor* is less a biography than a study of literary influence; however, that alone cannot account for Lynn's growth as a writer in the dozen years separating the two books.) Nevertheless, in choosing to study these particular figures, Lynn tells us a good deal about the continuity of his interests. For him the authentic voice of American fiction apparently speaks in the vernacular tones of realism. However, what he hears in that voice is not altogether familiar.

Send in the Clowns

Hemingway's assertion that "all modern American literature comes from one book by Mark Twain" seems both undeniable and implausible. In style and point of view, *Adventures of Huckleberry Finn* seems closer to the main body of subsequent American fiction than it does to anything written by Nathaniel Hawthorne or James Fenimore Cooper.[3] And yet, common sense tells us that there is no such thing as total originality. As influential as Mark Twain has been on later generations of writers, there must have been predecessors who influenced him. ("Daddy, who made God?," every child has asked.) Kenneth S. Lynn is telling us nothing new in saying that the legacy of Southwest humor helped make Sam Clemens into "Mark Twain." His analysis of that phenomenon, however, is more comprehensive and more dogmatic than what had been previously written on the subject. In fact, the schematic way in which Lynn states and develops his thesis is his book's main virtue and its principal vulnerability.

Reviewers and general readers alike have complained that Lynn's book is long on Southwest humor and short on Mark Twain. (In fact, it is divided about evenly between the two topics.) It begins more than a hundred years before Twain with a discussion of William Byrd of Westover, the eighteenth-century Virginia planter who was the first Southern writer of note. In his *History of the Dividing Line,* Byrd created the myth of the Southern aristocrat living among poor white barbarians. Although selections from this work would eventually appear in standard anthologies of American and Southern literature, Byrd's "memoir" remained unpublished for nearly a century after his death. In 1841 it was rescued from obscurity by Edmund Ruffin, who, like Byrd, was also a Virginia planter and Southern propagandist. But unlike Byrd, who was trying to impress the cultural elite of London, Ruffin was interested in celebrating the higher civilization of the slave states and the nobility of the cavalier myth for a primarily American audience. (Twenty years later, he was granted the honor of pulling the lanyard on the first gun fired on Fort Sumter.) The image remained the same; only the audience and political situation had changed.

Lynn discerns a conservative political agenda behind the Southwest humor published in the first four decades of the nineteenth century. Like William Byrd, the humorists were men of aristocratic sympathies who affirmed the virtues of restraint, order, and social hierarchy as a check against vulgarity, violence, and mob rule. It is no accident that Augustus Baldwin Longstreet, Thomas Bangs Thorpe, Johnson Jones Hooper, and company were passionate Whigs who detested the leveling effects of Jacksonian democracy. Their views were expressed in humorous sketches, usually by a gentleman narrator who observed and described the boorish behavior of backwoods (Jacksonian) clowns. On occasion, a real-life frontier buffoon such as Davy Crockett could be converted to the anti-Jacksonian party and used for partisan purposes. But, for the most part, early Southwest humor was a bourbon response to the rising tide of sansculottism in American society.

The one major figure who does not fit this pattern, and the humorist who serves as the missing link between Twain and his Whig forebears, is George Washington Harris. A fervid Democrat and rabid secessionist, Harris had no use for the conciliatory politics of the Whigs. Beginning in the 1850s the brand of Southern nationalism Harris represented found its paradigmatic spokesman not in the refined and moderate gentleman but in the plainspoken clown himself. Far from being a rejection of the South, this populist distrust of the gentleman represented a new Southern myth, one based more on frontier than cavalier values. Davy Crockett may have originated this trend, but it received its fullest embodiment in Harris's child hero Sut Lovingood. According to Lynn, "what differentiates Harris from Longstreet and the earlier humorists, and makes him the forerunner of Mark Twain and Hemingway and Salinger, is that he negotiates the crucial transition from regarding the child with the patronizing attitude of the fond adult, who 'knows better' about everything in life, to looking at the adult world through the eyes of a child and judging it by the standard of values of a child" (*MI*, 134).

Sut's most obvious and celebrated literary descendant is of course Huck Finn. The standard interpretation of Huck's character, especially during Lynn's formative years as a critic, holds that this child of nature was pronouncing an implicit judgment on a hypocritical and racist society. As Lynn himself put it in an article in the *Yale Review*, "The panoramic sweep of Huck's journey . . . opens to view a whole civilization, and the wrath of Twain's judgment of that civilization is the novel's most biblical quality. Entering many houses in his quest for truth and love, Huck calls only the raft his home, a fact which symbolizes at the broadest reach of social implication Twain's massive condemnation of the society of the Great Valley as he knew it in the tragic quarter of a century before the Civil War" (*VA*, 56–57). Lynn's discussion of *Huckleberry Finn* in *Mark Twain and Southwestern Humor* is largely in this vein.

With careful attention to the text, Lynn shows how Twain's seemingly lighthearted treatment of two biblical stories introduces themes that are crucial to Huck's story. We will recall that at the beginning of the novel, Huck dismisses the story of Moses and the Bullrushes as having no relevance to his life (he takes no truck in dead people). And yet, like Huck, Moses is a lower-class child who floats on a river, is adopted into the most respectable family in town, and escapes to lead slaves to freedom. The similarities between his story and Huck's seem too striking to be accidental.

As if to emphasize these similarities, Twain himself incorporated a story about a floating baby in the original version of *Huckleberry Finn*. This tall tale about a dead baby in a barrel who follows and haunts the father who murdered him was used instead in Twain's memoir *Life on the Mississippi*. (It has since been restored in some more recent versions

of *Adventures of Huckleberry Finn*.) The search for a father, which is
treated ghoulishly in this story, is near to the heart of Huck's experience. In fact, when he is discovered by the raftsmen who are telling the
tale, Huck scares them witless by identifying himself as (the dead baby)
Charles William Allbright.

The question of parenthood also figures prominently in another biblical story Huck knows. Twain used to delight lecture audiences by
reading aloud the chapter in which Huck and Jim debate whether
Solomon was wise in offering to settle a custody dispute by chopping a
baby in two. But, as Lynn astutely points out, this story also bears
directly on Huck's situation. In leaving St. Petersburg for the Mississippi, Huck is himself fleeing a custody battle. On the one side is his
abusive biological father, on the other the well-intentioned but overly
refined Widow Douglas. Only on the river does Huck find the love of a
father and the companionship of a true friend. Nigger Jim is the only
adult in Huck's life who neither mistreats nor tries to civilize him.

Even if the Mark Twain of *Huckleberry Finn* was no cheerleader for the
slaveholding South, his debt to George Washington Harris and Sut
Lovingood seems indisputable. Considerably more problematic are
Twain's ties with the aristocratic Whig humorists. While his depiction
of Pap Finn is reminiscent of the way in which the Whigs portrayed the
backwoods clown, one searches *Huckleberry Finn* in vain for an aristocratic role model. Taken on its own, Colonel Sherburn's speech to the
mob in Bricksville is an affirmation of the courage and dignity of the
Southern gentleman, but the colonel is also a cold-blooded murderer.
(His confrontation with Boggs can hardly be read as a parable of the
moral superiority of the gentleman to the bum.) From Lynn's analysis,
it would seem that while Twain may have learned the effectiveness of
vernacular language from the Whig humorists, his social values were
fundamentally different from theirs.

By the late 1970s, however, even that qualification would be
dropped from Lynn's interpretation of Mark Twain. Writing in the
American Scholar in 1977, Lynn confessed, "Critics like myself wanted
to believe that Huck was renouncing membership in a society that
condoned slavery because they themselves did not wish to live in a
segregationist nation" (*AS*, 48). Now that segregation was a thing of
the past and neoconservative intellectuals had found America to be a
swell place to live after all, Lynn was uncomfortable with the notion
that Huck might actually be discontented with "sivilization" and that
his story might be a radical attack on American society. The essay in

which Lynn expounds on this change of mind is entitled "Welcome Back from the Raft, Huck Honey!"

As anyone well versed in American literary criticism will recognize, his target is an interpretation of *Adventures of Huckleberry Finn* popularized by Leslie Fiedler in his famous *Partisan Review* essay "Come Back to the Raft Again, Huck Honey!" Because the broad outlines of this interpretation have gone largely unchallenged since the early 1950s and Fiedler's essay itself has long since passed into the canon of pop literature (or at least pop criticism), Lynn has his work cut out for him. In the late fifties, he reminds us, Henry Nash Smith had tried to counter the more radical reading of Huck's decision to light out for the Territory by pointing out that Tom Sawyer had wanted to "go for howling adventures amongst the Injuns, over in the Territory, for a couple of weeks or two." When Huck says he means to set out ahead of the others, Smith argues, "there is nothing in the text to indicate that his intention is more serious than Tom's" (see *AS,* 41). Putting the matter bluntly, Lynn concludes, "For decades, students who have finished reading *Huckleberry Finn* have been encouraged by their teachers to entertain misleading fantasies about a young boy's continuing search for freedom and self-realization in the tabula rasa of the Territory. In more properly conducted classes, they would be encouraged to speculate about what sort of life Huck will lead when he returns to St. Petersburg" (*AS,* 42).

Although Lynn provides a bracing antidote to the pervasive misreading of *Huck Finn,* he gives too much credit to what he calls the Dropoursville critics and too little blame to Twain for the present state of affairs. Beneath Mark Twain's public persona of rebel and misogynist was the reality of Samuel Clemens, a man extravagantly devoted to the women in his life and an author whose favorite book among his works was a saccharine tribute to Joan of Arc—the tomboy as saint. Like Tom Sawyer, Twain was adept at imagining a life of adventure and at tweaking middle-class notions of propriety. But Tom, on his most adventurous day, never got farther than Jackson's Island before returning to his long-suffering Aunt Polly, who waited by the hearth until he was done playing pirates.

Lynn seems to believe that Huck Finn represents a difference only in degree not kind. In the Widow Douglas, who is "the most interesting female character Mark Twain ever introduced" (*AS,* 42), Huck has been given a potential Aunt Polly (except that she is richer, younger, and better looking than Tom's aunt). Perhaps sensing that the widow is *too*

attractive an exemplar of domestic values, Twain conjures up the caricatured old crone Miss Watson (a sort of Dame Van Winkle as spinster)
and injects the issue of slavery in the person of Jim. Thus, what "could
have become an extraordinarily interesting study of acculturation, cen-
tering on a contest of wills between an emotionally deprived juvenile
outcast and a smart, attractive, still youthful woman" (*AS*, 45), became
instead the mythically powerful tale of two fugitives on a raft. By the
end of the novel the black man gains his legal freedom (what that may
mean in terms of his future life is an issue Twain is apparently unwilling to confront). But what of his white companion, whom the runaway
boy in all of us dreams of being?

Lynn's argument that Huck will surely return to St. Petersburg
seems to be based on little more than the fact that the Widow Douglas
is a nice lady. There is, however, stronger evidence in the novel to
support Lynn's position. To begin with, if Twain's god on a machine
has saved Jim by transporting Miss Watson to the "Good Place," he has
rendered nearly as great a service to Huck by dispatching Pap to the
bad one. Huck's flight downriver was primarily to get away from Pap,
not the widow. Had he been confident that Pap could not steal him
away and had he not run into Jim, it is entirely conceivable that Huck
would have returned to the widow's in the first place. (Lynn is right in
contending that Twain stacks the deck in order to get his hero on the
raft.) Now that both Pap and Miss Watson are dead, the widow's home
will be a safer and more pleasant place than ever before. Moreover, were
Huck not to return to St. Petersburg he would be turning his back on
both Jim and Tom, two friends whom he has earlier expressed a willingness to go to Hell for.

In an era when the faces of "missing children" stare at us from
billboards and the sides of milk cartons, the reality of dropping out has
lost much of its romance. In the urban jungles of the 1980s it is far too
easy to imagine Huck as a male prostitute and Jim as a drug dealer. No
doubt, if Twain had been a more thoroughgoing realist, he could have
imagined a grimmer fate for a vagrant white boy and a runaway slave in
the antebellum South. What Twain was "remembering," however, was
not the dark and bloody ground of history but the happy valley of
myth. In that happy valley boys and men will always dream of running
away from home, but the boys will never stay away past suppertime nor
the men stray farther than the corner bar. It is a rebellion no Whig need
fear and that even a neoconservative can endorse.

Crossing Martins Ferry

One summer in the early 1870s William Dean Howells, who had been recently appointed editor of the *Atlantic,* and his father were staying overnight with their longtime friend Ohio Congressman James A. Garfield, a former professor of ancient languages and literature at Hiram College and future U.S. president. Sitting with the Garfield family on their veranda, young Howells began to talk about the famous poets he knew. "Suddenly, Garfield stopped him, and ran down into the grassy space, calling and waving to the neighbors who were sitting on their back porches. 'Come over here!' he shouted. 'He's telling about Holmes, and Longfellow, and Lowell, and Whittier!' Soon dim forms climbed over the fences and followed the Congressman to his veranda. 'Now go on!' Garfield called to Howells, and Howells did, while the whippoorwills soared about in the cool of the evening and the hour hand of the town clock drew toward midnight" (*WDH,* 253).

This story is remarkable for several reasons. For one thing, it plays havoc with our historical stereotypes by reminding us that a classics professor was president during part of the Gilded Age. It also tells us something about what has happened to the popular acceptance of literature in this country that graybeard poets with three names were once revered by the masses as only the likes of Bruce Springsteen and Vanna White are in our own time. But what concerns us here is that in the eyes of the people of that northern Ohio neighborhood cracking the eastern literary establishment meant that one of their own had truly made it. Neither Will Howells nor American literature would ever be the same again.

As a country with a huge geography and a short history, America has always tended to mythologize itself more in terms of space than of time. Until well after the Civil War, American literature was a wholly owned subsidiary of the northeastern cultural elite. The rise of realism was due in large measure to the influx of writers from the nation's heartland. Although most of their available literary models belonged to the older genteel tradition, their personal experiences were quite different from those of writers who grew up in Boston and New York.

This was certainly true of William Dean Howells, who was born in the rough Ohio Valley town of Martinsville (later Martins Ferry) and spent the bulk of his childhood in the frontier community of Hamilton, Ohio.[4] Growing up in this environment, it was more important to know how to fight than how to read. To be well educated meant being self-taught. Dropping out of school at an early age to work in his father's print shop and later paying his dues as a statehouse reporter in Columbus, Ohio, young Will Howells knew an area of the country and a side of life never dreamed of by the autocrat of the breakfast table or the author of *Hiawatha.* If H. L. Mencken, Sinclair Lewis, and other young Turks of the twenties were able to caricature Howells as stuffy and complacent, it was largely because he had been overtaken by a revolution he had helped to launch.

In literature as in politics, nothing seems quite so passé as yesterday's revolution. And to make matters duller, the toppling of the old guard by Howells and his fellow bolsheviks from west of Boston was a bloodless, even friendly, coup. (It wasn't his literary genius but his background as a printer that enabled Will Howells to get his foot in the door at the *Atlantic.*) When Howells first had lunch at the Parker House with James Russell Lowell and Oliver Wendell Holmes, the latter turned to the former and said, "Well James, this is something like the apostolic succession; this is the laying on of hands" (*WDH,* 96). The point, of course, is that these aging bishops of the one true church felt so secure in their faith that they could not imagine any serious pretender to literary prominence entertaining heresy. Howells recalls that when he made the mistake of asking Emerson what he thought of Poe's criticism, the sage of Concord at first didn't recognize the upstart's name. Then Howells repeated the question to him. " 'Oh,' he cried out, after a moment, as if he had returned from a far search for my meaning, *'you mean the jingle man!'* " (quoted in *WDH,* 100).

Even after Howells assumed editorship of the *Atlantic* he demonstrated a woolly haired butler's deference toward the old regime. He continued to write respectfully of the worn-out romanticism of his predecessors, while cautiously beginning to publish and review the heartland realists. Only once was he guilty of a serious gaffe in dealing with the graybeards. This was when he invited Mark Twain, the good bad boy of American realism, to deliver the after-dinner address on the occasion of John Greenleaf Whittier's seventieth birthday. Twain's remarks consisted of an outlandish tale lampooning Longfellow, Holmes, and Emerson as low-rent gasbags, who show up at a western miner's shack and proceed to get falling-down drunk while reciting poetry and playing euchre.

It is doubtful that any comedian before or since has ever bombed as badly as Twain did that night. Howells was so embarrassed that he could only stare at his plate. Years later, he would recall, "from a first glance at the three whom [Twain's] jest had made its theme, I was aware of Longfellow sitting upright, and regarding the humorist with an air of pensive puzzle, of Holmes busily writing on his menu, with a well-feigned effect of preoccupation, and of Emerson holding his elbows, and listening with a sort of Jovian oblivion of this nether world in that lapse of memory which saved him in those later years from so much bother" (quoted in *WDH,* 172).

It is altogether too easy to interpret Twain's monologue as evidence of his fearless iconoclasm and Howells's discomfort as a sign of his gutless sycophancy. The truth is that Twain was shrewd enough to know that he was poking fun at names from the past who no longer controlled the literary turf. (His only mistake was in overestimating their capacity to laugh at themselves.) Howells's reaction, on the other hand, was a product more of social sensitivity than of status anxiety. Twain might engage in safe nose tweaking, but he always played the fawning clown for the American public. One searches in vain for a controversial stand that Mark Twain ever took on a public issue. In contrast Howells, that midwestern pillar of the Republican party, put his popularity on the line when he became the only major literary figure to plead for clemency for the Haymarket anarchists. The more one knows of the real William Dean Howells the more complex and admirable a figure he becomes.

Speaking of Howells's frequently overlooked contributions to literary modernism, John Seelye writes, "*Huckleberry Finn* and *The Ambassadors* may mark the extremes of the kind of art possible in America, but neither book, quite literally, would have been possible without William Dean Howells."[5] This statement is true of *Huckleberry Finn* in the general sense that Howells did more than any other individual to promote realism and advance the careers of western and midwestern writers. In the case of *The Ambassadors,* there is an even more direct connection, one that reveals a different Howells from the one we thought we knew. The climactic scene in James's great novel, when Lambert Strether urges a young man not to let life pass him by, is based on an incident in Howells's life.

While vacationing in Paris in the summer of 1895, Howells received a cable informing him that his father was dying. On the eve of his departure for home, he encountered a young Princetonian named Jonathan Sturges in the garden of James McNeil Whistler's home. Reminded forcefully of his own mortality by his father's imminent death, and perhaps emboldened by the fact that Sturges was a cripple, although an unusually handsome and vigorous one, Howells walked up to this comparative stranger, laid his hand on his shoulder, and made a remarkable speech. According to what Sturges later told Henry James, Howells said of his life: "It has gone past me. I've lost it. It couldn't, no doubt, have been different for me—for one's life takes a form and holds one; one lives as one can. But the point is that *you* have time. That's the great thing. You're, as I say, damn you, so luckily, so happily, so hatefully young. . . . Don't . . . make *my* mistake. Live!" (quoted in *WDH,* 306).

This outburst is difficult to square with the cartoon image of Howells as the self-satisfied "Dean" of American letters. Much of the originality of Kenneth Lynn's *William Dean Howells: An American Life* lies in Lynn's insistence that the anguished figure in Whistler's garden, not the corpulent eminence in a fur-lined overcoat, was the real Howells. On the first page of his book, Lynn dismisses Leslie Fiedler's criticism of Howells as "resolutely cheerful, progressive, and sane" and argues instead that by the end of the nineteenth century Howells suffered from "a personal and artistic despair that was every inch as profound as the more celebrated glooms that gripped Henry Adams, Henry James, and Mark Twain during the same period" (*WDH,* 3).

Lynn informs us of the many nervous breakdowns Howells suffered, of the continuing mental illness of his daughter Winny, and of the constant ill health of his wife, Elinor. (If Howells made a lot of money, he had to just to pay the family medical bills.) It may be that his reputation in the twentieth century has suffered in part from his reluctance to parade his personal anxieties on the printed page. Part of the macho code he learned as a youth in Hamilton (and never totally unlearned) was to take a beating with a stiff upper lip. Moreover, Lynn convincingly demonstrates that Howells found work to be the most effective therapy for his emotional problems. Like the wife in Frost's "Home Burial," the harshest critics of Howells have mistaken a flurry of activity for shallowness and insensitivity rather than seeing it as a brave man's way of coping with what amounts to existential dread.

The New Critics are surely right in arguing that we need know nothing about an author's life in order to evaluate the quality of his work. Except in the case of anonymous writing, however, something is always known about the author's life. When the things we "know" are incorrect or incomplete, a particularly pernicious form of the biographical fallacy is at work. A revisionist biographer such as Kenneth Lynn helps us to see familiar figures in a new light. In the process, he forces us to reexamine prejudices we may not even have realized we had. The virtues of William Dean Howells—industry, heroic optimism, and a sense of obligation to family, friends, and country—may seem hopelessly bourgeois and philistine to a literary culture shaped by the convulsions of modernism, but that may be as much an indictment of modernism as it is of Howells. As in other areas of our communal life, America's literary history tells us as much about the needs of the present as about the facts of the past. When Lynn tells us that America's writers were not necessarily as we imagine them to have been, he is telling us something profoundly unsettling about ourselves.

Chapter Eight
Revisions of America

Up through the mid-1970s Kenneth S. Lynn was widely respected as a literary biographer and scholar in American studies. Although he had not attained the prominence of his mentors F. O. Matthiessen and Perry Miller, no one with a serious interest in American literary culture (especially the period between the Civil War and World War I) could afford to be ignorant of his work. Beginning in the mid-1970s, however, Lynn started to publish controversial and polemical essays in magazines such as *Commentary* and the *American Scholar* (edited by Norman Podhoretz and Joseph Epstein, respectively). These pieces were far more lively and interesting than anything he had written before, and they gained him a wide new audience of admirers. At the same time, many in the literary establishment felt that Lynn's defection to neoconservatism was an act of intellectual treason. But then, such a reaction only confirms Lynn's indictment of the genuine illiberality of much of what passes for liberal culture in America today.

In 1983 the battle lines were drawn when a decade's worth of Lynn's neoconservative essays appeared under the title *The Air-Line to Seattle*. The allusion is not to fare wars or frequent flyer bonuses but to a satirical poem written by George Santayana in 1900. This poem, "Young Sammy's First Wild Oats," ridicules an effete and cloistered community that remains oblivious to the outside world. The inhabitants of this secluded glade are Santayana's colleagues on the Harvard faculty. Not only does their ivory tower existence insulate them from the real world of commerce and technology and whizzing west-bound trains (the "air-line to Seattle"), but it also gives them a sense of moral and intellectual superiority to the rest of humanity. Santayana regarded this phenomenon as a secularized vestige of New England Puritanism, and eleven years later he gave a famous lecture labeling the elitist mindset "the genteel tradition in American philosophy." As the saying goes, "the more things change, the more they remain the same." Or, as Kenneth S. Lynn puts it, "Seventy years after Santayana first pinned a brilliantly derogatory label upon the hermetic mentality of the nation's intelligentsia, the spirit of the genteel tradition is triumphantly alive in American thought" (*AS*, 8).

The Liberal Arts

Subtitled "Studies in Literary and Historical Writing about America," *The Air-Line to Seattle* attacks some of the sacred cows of American culture. Of these probably none is more sacrosanct than Ralph Waldo Emerson. As Cleanth Brooks, R. W. B. Lewis, and Robert Penn Warren have noted, "Emerson is, somehow, the *indispensable* figure in American literary history. . . . [T]he themes he sounded most frequently will always be found close to the center of any fair account of the continuity and development of American literature."[1] Emerson is, according to Harold Bloom, the founder of "the actual American religion, which is Protestant without being Christian."[2] As such, he is one of the patriarchs of the genteel tradition.

Over the years, Emerson has proved to be a remarkably inviting but elusive target. He was an orator who violated every rule of public speaking, a philosopher with no gift for systematic thought, a theologian too heterodox to remain even in the Unitarian Church, and a literary giant whose reputation rests on a handful of essays that are little more than a series of lofty aphorisms. Emerson is like the balloon punching bag that keeps popping back up regardless of how many times it has been knocked down. Anyone looking to Kenneth S. Lynn for an explanation of Emerson's durability will go away disappointed. Instead, Lynn gives us (in the context of a review of Gay Wilson Allen's *Waldo Emerson*) yet another reason for hating Ralph Waldo Emerson.

By examining Emerson's life more critically than his hagiographers have been wont to do, Lynn argues that the young Emerson proved himself a callous fortune hunter when he married a seventeen-year-old heiress dying of tuberculosis. From the very moment of their engagement, Emerson insisted that his fiancée Ellen Tucker draw up a will with himself as the beneficiary. Less than a year and a half after their wedding, Ellen was dead and Emerson financially independent. According to Lynn, it was this financial independence that enabled Emerson to resign his position as a Unitarian minister and devote himself to the more ethereal concerns he would laud in "The American Scholar" and similar meditations. The fact that no one before Lynn has made this obvious case against Emerson tells us as much about our literary intelligentsia as it does about Emerson himself. According to Lynn, "The American Scholar" has always been "a holy text for American intellectuals who like to believe that they are morally superior beings who have risen above their countrymen's worship of money." It is thus in their vested interest to conceal the fact that their spiritual godfather "was in no less hot pursuit of vulgar prosperity than the most barbaric businessman of the age" (*AS*, 32).

If our genteel literary scholars are capable of covering up inconvenient information about their idols, they are equally capable of distorting the known facts to fit their ideological preconceptions. A case in point is Justin Kaplan's *Walt Whitman: A Life*. Lynn's major brief against this book is that it interprets Whitman's life and art not in the context of nineteenth-century America but in terms of the received wisdom of late twentieth-century liberalism. For that reason, Kaplan is incapable of understanding Whitman's obvious anxieties about his homosexuality. Living as we do in an age where homophobia is considered déclassé, Kaplan blithely regards what Whitman himself referred to as his sexual "perturbations" as being no big scandal. Not to admit that they were a scandal for Whitman in his day and age is a form of historical shortsightedness that makes much of his life and poetry incomprehensible.

Despite the homoerotic nature of much of his poetry, Whitman spent most of his life trying to deny or suppress his true nature. Referring to his sexual predilections, Whitman wrote in his notebook, "It is an excess—making life a torment . . . diseased feverish disproportionate adhesiveness" (quoted in *AS*, 37). When the British writer (and homosexual) John Addington Symonds wrote to ask him "whether the poems of male companionship that had appeared in the 1860 edition of the *Leaves* had not been calculated to 'encourage ardent and *physical* intimacies,' Whitman disavowed the question as 'damnable' " (*AS*, 37). Apparently the only period in his life when Whitman was able to transcend his sexual anxieties was when he served as a male nurse during the Civil War. This role made intimate male companionship acceptable, even praiseworthy. Lynn speculates that Whitman welcomed the onset of old age because it enabled him "to deny that his relations with young men had ever been anything but fatherly" (*AS*, 37).

Present-day liberals also have difficulty rationalizing Whitman's celebration of technology and his Yankee Doodle patriotism. In particular, opponents of the Vietnam War and other examples of American "imperialism" don't know quite what to make of Whitman's wholehearted endorsement of Manifest Destiny. Although they can read his poem "Passage to India" as a metaphor for the spirit, there is no gainsaying Whitman's jingoist support of the Mexican border campaign (how much more genteel was the tax-resisting Thoreau). The best that Kaplan can do is write: "When Polk's war message came over the telegraph from Washington, Whitman, a Democratic regular working for a Democratic paper in support of a Democratic president, took up the rant of the war party" (see *AS,* 38). Had Kaplan allowed himself a modicum of historical perspective, he would have seen that Whitman was a true believer, not a political opportunist. What is inconceivable to someone of Kaplan's persuasion is that in assessing both his own sexual orientation and America's role in the world, the good gray poet of American literature was closer to Roy Cohn than to Allen Ginsberg or Gore Vidal.

A Usable Past

In principle, Kenneth Lynn's objection to the genteel tradition is not that it espouses social and political views different from his own but that it allows ideology to distort the historical record. Lynn depicts the targets of his wrath as being every bit as meretricious as the historians in the Ministry of Truth in Orwell's *Nineteen Eighty-four.* (A case in point is Garry Wills, who tries to transform Jefferson's Declaration of Independence from an individualist to a communitarian document and thus, in Lynn's pungent phrase, "to supply the history of the Republic with as pink a dawn as possible" [*AS,* 10].) The most blatant example Lynn cites of falsifying the past is the bogus Civil War diary written by Mary Chesnut in the 1880s and hailed by historians who should have known better as an authentic, even prescient, depiction of Southern life before and during the war between the states.[3] If poor Mrs. Chesnut was simply hoping to make a buck, her uncritical admirers are trying to score ideological points.

The fact of the matter is that Mrs. Chesnut, who was a prominent Southern lady during the third quarter of the nineteenth century, did keep a diary in the 1860s. But the version she published two decades later was so heavily revised that it could be more properly called a novel posing as a diary. There is, of course, nothing wrong with Mrs. Chesnut or anyone else using the diary as a mode of fiction *as long as it was clearly marked as such.* But, to use John Hersey's phrase, the "legend on the license" was a fake. Thus, we get such improbable scenes as Jefferson Davis unburdening himself to the author during the darkest days of the Confederacy. (Given the need for high civilian and military morale in the South, Lynn finds it improbable that Davis would confess his insecurities to a notoriously talkative woman.) In addition, the view of slavery Mrs. Chesnut gives us in the published version of her "diary" is clearly revisionist. From what we know of the 1860s volume, Mrs. Chesnut saw slavery as a much more wicked institution close at hand. From the perspective of Reconstruction, however, she viewed it through magnolia-tinted glasses, which could see only happy darkies, paternalistic masters, and white mistresses every bit as saintly as Scarlett O'Hara's mother.

As suspect as Mrs. Chesnut's diary may be, an even more curious example of reconstructing the Southern past can be found in the work of Marxist historian Eugene D. Genovese. A specialist in antebellum Southern history, Genovese readily admits that his writing is animated by an implacable hatred of capitalism. Although this orientation places him on the far left wing of the political spectrum, he maintains close personal and professional ties with such arch-conservative defenders of the Old South as M. E. Bradford and William K. Scarborough and has published in that unapologetically neo-Confederate journal the *Southern Partisan*. Even more significant, Genovese has been so influenced by the pro-slavery polemicist George Fitzhugh that he writes, "I have come to think of [Fitzhugh] as an old friend. As my affection and admiration deepened, the task of rescuing him from detractors became something of a private mission" (quoted in *AS*, 206).

Behind the seeming schizophrenia of Genovese's position lurks the sort of consistency that says, "My enemy's enemy must be my friend." If capitalism is the most diabolicial economic system imaginable, then even antebellum slavery must have been better. By making the plantation system seem preferable to nineteenth-century capitalism, Genovese is better able to attack twentieth-century capitalism. In fact, Lynn suspects that he may have taken his cue from the following comment by Marx and Engels in the *Communist Manifesto:* "The bourgeoisie, wherever it has gotten the upper hand, has put an end to all feudal, patriarchal, idyllic relations. It has pitilessly torn asunder the . . . feudal ties that bound man to his 'natural superior' " (quoted in *AS*, 206).

It should be noted, however, that the unfavorable comparison of wage slavery in the North to chattel slavery in the South is not just the ingenious analogy of a contemporary ideologue. Such an ardent and popular opponent of Southern slavery as Harriet Beecher Stowe knew that the lot of a Northern or European factory worker could be worse than that of the most wretched field hand in Louisiana. To have one's children sold from under one's roof is heartbreaking. To see them stay at home and starve may be even worse. Such arguments are placed in the mouth of the kind-hearted plantation owner Augustine St. Clare, who easily outdebates his New England cousin Miss Ophelia.

Stowe, who was neither pro-slavery nor pro-Communist, used the charming and attractive figure of St. Clare to emphasize the universality of the moral issues with which she was dealing. Those who have never read *Uncle Tom's Cabin* often assume that it is an anti-Southern polemic, not realizing that it is equally harsh in its treatment of the North (Simon Legree, after all, is from New England). The historical conclusions of Eugene Genovese may be curious, but he is in interesting and respectable company. This fact should certainly come as no surprise to Kenneth S. Lynn, who has argued as effectively as any contemporary critic for the intellectual and aesthetic merits of *Uncle Tom's Cabin*.

The Party Line

When Lynn shifts his focus to the literary history of the twentieth century, one villain looms larger than all the others. In terms of sheer longevity, Malcolm Cowley, who was born in 1898 and died in 1989, not only outlasted the rest of the Lost Generation but lived to write and rewrite their story. More than any other individual, Cowley was responsible for establishing Faulkner's reputation in the years following World War II. As a critic of Hemingway, he has been instrumental in dispelling the macho myth the man known as "Papa" sought to project about himself and replacing it with a more sophisticated image of an existential loner living and writing a waking nightmare. (As we shall see in the next chapter, Lynn's most impressive contribution to literary biography is an attempt to explode that myth of Hemingway.) Cowley is most vulnerable, however, not in his reinterpretation of other writers but in what he says (or fails to say) about himself.

According to Lynn, Cowley's behavior during the 1930s, perhaps the most politicized decade in the history of American literature, is obscured by the selective memory of his account of that decade in his 1980 reminiscence *The Dream of the Golden Mountains*. (Equally regrettable is the failure of such eminent scholars as R. W. B. Lewis, Alfred

Kazin, and Daniel Aaron to set the record straight in their fawning reviews of Cowley's book.) As literary editor of the *New Republic* during the thirties, Cowley was one of the most influential critics in America. Unfortunately, his views on literature and practically everything else were shaped by naively pro-Communist literary sympathies. At a time when former Communists and fellow travelers were denouncing the Moscow show trials and the general brutality of Stalin's regime, Cowley maintained a see-no-evil attitude toward the Soviet Union. What made his credulity particularly reprehensible was the violence it did to his literary judgments.

His intemperate attacks on the anti-Stalinist *Partisan Review* may be written off as mere sectarian bickering. It is not quite so easy to excuse Cowley's role in what Lynn calls "the literary execution of John Dos Passos." Throughout the thirties Cowley praised the literary qualities of Dos Passos's politically correct *USA* trilogy; however, when those same qualities were evident in the antileftist novel *Adventures of a Young Man* (1939), they had been miraculously transformed into vices. In the opinion of James T. Farrell, Cowley's party-line denunciation of the new Dos Passos "reads like a warning to writers not to stray off the reservation of the Stalinist-controlled League of American Writers" (quoted in *AS,* 169). If, as Clare Booth Luce suggested, Henry Wallace was Stalin's Mortimer Snerd, Cowley was Uncle Joe's Colley Cibber.

As one might expect, Lynn's interpretation of the Lost Generation is considerably different from Cowley's. He argues, for example, that the alienation from bourgeois society and the general sense of spiritual disillusionment one identifies with the literary notables who came of age between 1915 and 1921 are not appreciably different from the attitudes of earlier and later generations of writers. Moreover, these same attitudes were shared by many nonliterary Americans of the twenties. What distinguishes the work of such disparate writers as Hemingway, Fitzgerald, Eliot, and O'Neill has more to do with personal genius than with generational affinity. Speaking of Cowley's *Exile's Return,* Lynn writes, "No other interpretation of American literature has more engaged the national mind, or more thoroughly stultified it, than the legend of the lost generation that Cowley wove from the warp of the Communist line and the woof of his own romanticism. One of the principal reasons why we still do not possess a satisfactory account of one of the most fascinating decades in American literary history is that Cowley's polarities leave no room for paradoxes, and without an appreciation of paradoxes there can be no understanding of the twenties" (*AS,* 95).

When Lynn is not training his sights on celebrities of Malcolm Cowley's stature, he uses his small artillery to go after conventional academics who he believes published when they should have perished. Although Lynn does not use the term, his description of the indefatigable Matthew J. Bruccoli—bio-bibliographer of Fitzgerald, Hemingway, and a host of lesser lights—reminds one of what Gore Vidal calls the "scholar-squirrel." Gathering his note cards and bibliography entries in much the same way that the lovable forest creature hoards nuts, the scholar-squirrel is committed to the notion that ye shall know the facts and the facts shall make you tenured. In the process, critical intelligence, biographical discrimination, and plain common sense are dismissed as "unprofessional." (When Hemingway writes in *A Moveable Feast* that Scott Fitzgerald came to him for reassurance concerning the adequacy of his sexual member, most knowledgeable readers figure that this is just Papa's pathetic attempt to convince the world of his own continuing virility; Bruccoli rounds up independent corroboration concerning the size of Fitzgerald's endowment.) It is a withering and caricatured indictment, but anyone who has endured the Chinese water torture called graduate school can recognize the kernel of truth in what Lynn is saying.

The penultimate entry in *The Air-Line to Seattle* is an attack on three scholars whom Lynn labels the "regressive historians" (as opposed to the "progressive" historians celebrated by Richard Hofstadter). This goodly company consists of Bernard Baylin, Eugene Genovese, and Leo Marx. My only reservation about the structure and placement of this essay is that the entire book does not conclude with a more detailed individual discussion of Marx. From the standpoint of metaphor alone, there could hardly be two more dissimilar attitudes toward American culture than those of Marx and Lynn. A quintessential figure of the sixties, Marx argued—in his classic book *The Machine in the Garden* (1964)—that the most significant and enduring motif in American literature has been the sudden and disquieting appearance of technology on the landscape. His true Eden was a secluded glade far from the airline to Seattle.

Radical dialecticians such as Herbert Marcuse and popularizers such as Charles Reich taught the counterculture of the sixties that "machines repressed instinctual drives, fostered psychic helplessness, and deserved to be depicted as horrid" (*AS,* 196). No wonder Leo Marx's reading of

American literature was well received by the more literate citizens of Woodstock Nation. It put him on the side of the angels and made many sensitive people ashamed to have flush toilets. To be fair, no one can gainsay the existence of a strong primitivist bias in American literature, least of all Kenneth S. Lynn, who is Johns Hopkins's Arthur O. Lovejoy Professor of History (Lovejoy and his colleague George Boas wrote a five-volume *Documentary History of Primitivism and Related Ideas*). The problem with Leo Marx is that, being a cultural Manichaean, he tries to account for far too much in terms of a split between beatific nature and satanic industrialism.

Like Thoreau's cabin at Walden, much of American literature is perched on the edge of the forest, where Adam can move freely between his second Eden and a New World Land of Nod. (It is no accident that the classicist Thoreau reserved his harshest judgment not for some jackbooted captain of industry but for a French Canadian woodchopper, who was *too much* a child of nature.) Hawthorne's arcadian repose might have been disturbed by the shriek of a locomotive whistle, but even the natural buzzing of an insect was enough to make that hypersensitive man lose his train of thought. The ethereal Emerson loved the convenience of riding the rails, and the nature-loving Sam Clemens took his pen name from steamboat lore. Indeed, the garden itself is an imposition of technology upon nature.[4] As Aldous Huxley noted, Wordsworth would not have been at home in the tropics.[5]

By adding a polemical dimension to his prose, Kenneth S. Lynn seems finally to have found a distinctive critical voice. For that reason, the essays in *The Air-Line to Seattle* are more interesting and memorable than Lynn's earlier work. Only someone who takes literature very seriously can manage to discuss it with such wit. As a critic, Lynn possesses both the virtues and the limitations of an expert counterpuncher. Instinctively spotting the weaknesses of an opponent's position, he piles up rhetorical points. It is great fun to watch, but after the seventh or eighth essay, you begin to wonder whether Lynn might be a kind of reverse Will Rogers, who never met another critic he did like (except for Joseph Epstein, to whom his book is dedicated). Still, the ride has been well worth the price of the ticket. With the airline arrived in Seattle, it is time to leave the good conversation in the smoking car, stretch your legs, and take a breath of fresh air. That interesting nuisance you've been listening to is reputed to be writing a book on Hemingway, and you can't wait to see the look on Malcolm Cowley's face.

Chapter Nine
Papa in Petticoats

The news of Hemingway's death came over the transistor radio I had taken to the pool that afternoon. It was July 1961—a little more than three weeks shy of my thirteenth birthday—and like so many others who believed too much of what they read, I was shocked that on that Sunday morning in Ketchum, Idaho, the greatest he-man of the age would put a shotgun to his head, and splatter his brains across the kitchen wall. Even then I realized how much more we needed to know about the tormented man and artist behind the public bluff. For the next quarter-century biographers and critics would provide us with a wealth of information and interpretation in an attempt to solve the Hemingway conundrum. Perhaps the most credible, and certainly the most controversial, of such attempts is Kenneth S. Lynn's *Hemingway*.

Life in the Woods

Lynn's views on Hemingway first sparked controversy in the literary world when his revisionist essay, "Hemingway's Private War," appeared in the July 1981 issue of *Commentary*. Although ostensibly reviewing Carlos Baker's edition of Hemingway's *Selected Letters*, Lynn is primarily interested in refuting an interpretation of "Big Two-Hearted River" that had been initiated by Edmund Wilson in 1939 and considerably embellished over the years by Malcolm Cowley, Philip Young, and others.[1] According to the Wilson-Cowley-Young thesis, Hemingway's protagonist Nick Adams is an emotionally disturbed World War I veteran trying to restore his psyche in nature. Lynn dismisses this theory on the grounds that there is no reference to the war in the text of the story and argues that any interpretation of Hemingway's fiction that is based on the notion of psychic wounding in war is really an example of special pleading by anti-American leftists.

If this had been all that Lynn was saying, he would not differ that much from the college sophomore who suspects that his pointy-headed lit prof is reading all sorts of trash into a story that any normal person can understand on its own terms. Lynn, however, is not content to read "Big Two-Hearted River" on its own terms but manages to read into it biographical information that tells us more about Hemingway's hatred of his mother than about his reaction to World War I. Like Lynn's essay on *Huckleberry Finn,* "Hemingway's Private War" gives us a new way to look at a familiar work of literature without convincingly refuting the existing critical consensus. Whether intentionally or not, Lynn seems to be setting up straw men and positing false dichotomies.

In order to prove that "Big Two-Hearted River" is about a war veteran, Wilson, Cowley, and Young are forced to cite evidence from outside the story itself. Some of this evidence is contained in letters from Hemingway to Cowley that the critic would later quote in a response to Lynn published in the Summer 1984 issue of the *Georgia Review.*[2] There is also Hemingway's published admission in *A Moveable Feast* that his story was "about coming back from the war [even though] there was no mention of the war in it."[3] Moreover, other Nick Adams stories show a wounded and disillusioned soldier eager to make a separate peace rather than fight for values in which he no longer believes. To make the case that Nick is running away from home, not war, Lynn is forced to cite other letters that show how much Hemingway hated his mother and other stories that depict Nick Adams's aversion to family life. That Hemingway might have seen the old fishing hole as a refuge from *both* the constraints of petticoat government and the absurdity of modern warfare is a possibility that seems to occur to neither Lynn nor Cowley in their polemical sniping at each other.

What is involved here, however, is not just a squabble over politics but a conflict of myths. When ordinary people think of the "Hemingway myth," they are apt to think of the public persona of Papa Hemingway. But that image began to die for literary folk even before the fatal Sunday in Ketchum. Today, it exists only to be exploited for commercial profit by the executives of Hemingway Ltd., a corporation that Frederick Crews tells us was "formed to market the label 'Hemingway' for use on tastefully chosen fishing rods, safari clothes, and (surely the ultimate triumph of greed over taste) shotguns."[4] Gore Vidal got it right when he referred to the Papa myth as "incredibly butch." No critic of Lynn's sophistication would waste his time debunking that myth. It is another, more insidious, Hemingway myth that Lynn seeks to explode. This is what Crews calls the "critic's legend," the notion that Hemingway was transformed by a traumatic war wound into a sensitive iconoclast who despised all institutions and causes, especially those associated with war. The macho bluster may have been for public consumption, but the critics prided themselves in knowing the troubled man behind the mask.

Lynn's startling thesis is that those critics were taken in just as surely as the public. Hardly of the antiwar party, Hemingway seems to have taken pride in his battle wounds and exaggerated their severity. The "separate peace" he has Frederic Henry declare in *A Farewell to Arms* is more a matter of expedience than ideology and is found in a novel published a decade after World War I, at a time when postwar disillusionment had become a literary fashion. What's more, by the time another decade had passed, the supposedly free-thinking pacifist was showboating on the fringes of the Spanish Civil War and swallowing Stalinist propaganda with a credulity matched only by Lillian Hellman or Malcolm Cowley himself.

If the author of *The Sun Also Rises, A Farewell to Arms,* and some of the most compelling short stories in the English language was finally more wounded than virile, the reasons go back much farther in life than his experiences in World War I. As Lynn shows us in his fascinating biography, the cryptic truth was there all along in Hemingway's most authentic fiction. By learning more about Hemingway's early years and studying manuscripts and papers previously inaccessible to scholars, revisionist critics such as Lynn believe that they now have the key for decoding the novelist's life and works. That key is Hemingway's lifelong, mostly sublimated, obsession with androgyny. When Lynn's *Hemingway* was published in the summer of 1977, newspapers across the nation carried a picture of the two-year-old Ernest dressed in a gown and bonnet and holding a bouquet of flowers. The original caption, supplied by the child's doting mother, read "summer girl." Upon seeing this picture a friend of mine remarked, "No wonder the poor son of a bitch blew his brains out."

A Wonderful Book

If running away from home and female tyranny has been a staple of American literature since "Rip Van Winkle," Hemingway seemed bent on running that theme into the ground. His first collection of short fiction, *In Our Time* (1925), continually derides conventional family life and heterosexual bonding. The truest companionship is among unattached males. And when that fails, there is only the solitary retreat into the wilderness as experienced by Nick Adams in "Big Two-Hearted

River." Three years later, Hemingway published a second collection of short stories, under the title *Men without Women*. It too advances the notion that mothers, wives, and girlfriends are generally bad news.

In the thirties Hemingway produced two of his most famous stories, "The Short Happy Life of Francis Macomber" and "The Snows of Kilimanjaro," both of which appear to present marriage in the worst possible light. Nor is the situation much improved in his two greatest novels. The protagonist of *The Sun Also Rises* (1926) has been emasculated by World War I, and his counterpart in *A Farewell to Arms* (1929) loses his beloved in childbirth. The later fiction, which is far too steeped in the Papa myth, despicts romance more optimistically only by imagining women to be exotic geisha types who live to please their men.

Although Hemingway's misogyny has usually been written off as male chauvinism and macho posturing, perceptive observers have long suspected that it was due to a more deep-seated sexual ambivalence. This suspicion was dramatically confirmed by the posthumous publication of a highly edited, but still revealing, edition of his unfinished novel *The Garden of Eden*. More explicitly than any of Hemingway's other works, this book deals with changes in sex roles, masturbation, lesbianism, voyeurism, and a whole range of nonphallic erotica. This book sheds a retrospective light on aspects of Hemingway's earlier fiction that critics have tended to minimize or ignore. It also invites us to take another look at the period in which Hemingway was beginning to form his own sense of sexual identity.

At first glance, the fact that Grace Hemingway dressed her infant son in girl's clothes hardly seems consequential. Sara Delano Roosevelt and other mothers of the late-nineteenth and early-twentieth centuries did much the same thing to their boys. What makes the Hemingway situation different is that Grace kept up the masquerade long after Ernest had ceased to be an infant. Also, it seems to have been part of a larger experiment to raise Ernest and his older sister Marcelline as unisex twins. Through changes in clothing and hair style, Grace would alternately turn the two into twin brothers, and twin sisters. By the time she was through, she had made her son into an androgynous creature who would perpetually try to prove a masculinity he was never confident he possessed. The results were disastrous for Hemingway's personality, particularly in his relations with women. The effect on his art was far more mixed.

Beyond his kinky sexual fixations, the Hemingway we encounter in

Lynn's biography possesses a quality that both the Papa myth and the critics' myth lack—an ability to identify imaginatively with characters of both genders. This is the positive side of androgyny and a capacity one would not think of attributing to any of the Hemingways we thought we knew. But the evidence was there all along in the work. As early as *In Our Time,* there are three stories in which the principal female character is presented more sympathetically than her male antagonist.

In "Up in Michigan" the sensitive waitress Liz Coates is sexually brutalized by a simian village blacksmith named Jim Gilmore.[5] "Cat in the Rain" features a neglected wife who identifies with an abandoned feline she sees outside her hotel window. (Although she complains that her short hair makes her look "like a boy," her husband will not let her grow it long.) And "Out of Season" (which is one of Hemingway's earliest pieces of published fiction) consists of an obliquely rendered argument between husband and wife. The husband is clearly a sexually incompetent wimp who, in the opinion of one critic, may be pressuring his wife into an abortion.[6] If this is so, it serves as a prelude to Hemingway's later story, "Hills Like White Elephants," which is unmistakably about a boorish young man's efforts to persuade his girlfriend to terminate her pregnancy.

If we follow Lynn's biographical inferences, stories such as these may be, among other things, a product of Hemingway's guilt over his ill treatment of his first wife Hadley. Consider, for example, the story "Indian Camp." This haunting tale of an Indian "brave" who quietly slits his throat while his wife is giving birth was written at the same time that Hadley was delivering the Hemingways' first child in a hospital in Toronto. When Ernest finally arrived at the hospital, after a long train ride from New York, Hadley described him as looking broken down "from fatigue and strain." In *The Air-Line to Seattle,* Lynn asks: "Did Hemingway on that long night [train ride], out of fear of being entrapped once again in family life, consider deserting his wife? Out of a sense of guilt at being absent from Hadley's side to help her through an ordeal which he himself had caused, did the train rider contemplate suicide?" Although we do not know the answers to these questions, we do know that Hemingway did eventually desert his wife and, as Carlos Baker's edition of his letters shows, "by the time that 'Indian Camp' and the rest of the *In Our Time* stories were published in October, 1925, the author was openly talking of killing himself" (*AS,* 125).

By reminding us of stories where Hemingway proves himself to be

anything but a simpleminded misogynist, Lynn raises the possibility
that the critical consensus about some of the author's "better-known"
work has been dead wrong. For example, in his reading of "The Short
Happy Life of Francis Macomber," Lynn joins the minority of critics
who have argued that over the years Mrs. Macomber has generally
gotten a bum rap.[7] Like so much of the conventional wisdom about
modern literature, this misinterpretation began with an influential
essay by Edmund Wilson.[8] According to Wilson, Mrs. Macomber
intentionally shoots her husband because she fears the newfound masculinity he has demonstrated by standing up to a wounded buffalo. (He
had previously proven himself a coward by bolting from a wounded
lion.) Although this conjecture is put forward in the story by the
Macombers' British hunting guide and was later endorsed by Hemingway himself in interviews, it is inconsistent with the facts of the
situation. Since the buffalo was about to gore her husband, Mrs. Macomber could have assured his death simply by doing nothing. The
most reasonable assumption is that when she shoots him, she is attempt-
ing to save his life, not take it.

Lynn reads this story as "a fable about the perils of self-overcoming."
"It is not wifely malevolence that brings Macomber down," Lynn concludes, "but his own dangerous aspiration to be recognized as intensely
masculine. . . . In making clear [Mrs. Macomber's] lack of culpability,
Hemingway demonstrated that his ability to portray real women with
real problems and to respond to their unhappiness with an overarching
sympathy had not vanished with the completion of 'Cat in the Rain' "
(H, 436).

If anything, Lynn's interpretation of *The Sun Also Rises* is more
original (some would say bizarre) than his reading of "Francis Macomber." For years critics have seen the sexually maimed Jake Barnes as
Hemingway's symbol of the spiritual sterility of modern civilization, a
sort of analogue to Eliot's Fisher King. While there may be some truth
to this analysis, it fails to explain why the macho Hemingway would
have made a castrato his spokesman and alter ego, especially since the
novel is close enough to a roman à clef to have enabled him to settle
scores with several personal enemies and literary rivals. Even the critics'
myth of Cowley and others takes us only so far. The unreasonable
wound is supposed to rob its victim of his idealism not his manhood.

Lynn argues that the key to *The Sun Also Rises* can be found in
Hemingway's friendship with a number of famous Parisian lesbians.
Although he detested male homosexuals, Hemingway was fascinated

by their female counterparts, including Natalie Barney, who lived at 20 rue Jacob, and Djuna Barnes of the Hotel Jacob. "From these two associations," Lynn writes, "Hemingway derived the name of a man who is passionately in love with a sexually aggressive woman with an androgynous first name and a mannish haircut, a man whose dilemma is that, like a lesbian, he cannot penetrate his loved one's body with his own" (*H,* 323). To complicate matters even further, Lynn argues that Jake's beloved, Lady Brett Ashley, is based not just on Lady Duff Twysden and other women of Hemingway's acquaintance but also on the author himself. Thus, the inability of Jake and Brett to consummate their love for each other is not primarily a synecdoche for life in the wasteland but the sign of a failure of self-love on the part of their creator.

Of all the Hemingway biographies published in the quarter century after Ketchum, Lynn's is the most daring and original. If subsequent scholarship demonstrates that some of his Freudian readings are a bit farfetched or that he has not always followed his evidence and his arguments to their logical conclusion, no one who has read Lynn's book will ever be able to see Hemingway in quite the same light again. Certainly, Lynn was working with advantages denied to earlier biographers, but he has made the most of his opportunities. More than any of his previous works, *Hemingway* reveals the breadth of Lynn's American Studies background and his talent for narrative writing. "What a book would be the real story of Hemingway," Gertrude Stein once said, "not those he writes but the confessions of the real Ernest Hemingway. It would be for another audience than the audience Hemingway now has but it would be very wonderful" (quoted in *H,* 170). Kenneth S. Lynn has finally written such a book. And it is indeed very wonderful.

Chapter Ten
Aristides the Just

One of the most astute literary critics of our time—J. D. Salinger's Holden Caulfield—asserts, "What really knocks me out is a book that, when you're all done reading it, you wish the author who wrote it was a terrific friend of yours and you could call him up on the phone whenever you felt like it."[1] Although this may not be true of all authors (I can't imagine wanting to phone John Milton or go out for a beer with Ralph Waldo Emerson), it is certainly the case with the familiar essayist. Like Willie Loman's mythical salesman, the guy who writes about everyday life had better be well liked. The political commentator and the literary critic can usually make it on the strength of logos and pathos; the Andy Rooneys and Russell Bakers of this world live or die on ethos. The reason is simple: no one wants to read the peeves and musings of someone who is not personally engaging.

When Joseph Epstein assumed the editorship of the *American Scholar* in 1974, he began writing a regular column of familiar essays under the pseudonym Aristides ("after Aristides the Just, the early fifth century Athenian leader who was finally ostracized by the citizens of Athens because they grew tired of always hearing him called the Just" [*FT*, vii]). This modern Aristides comes across as a whimsical fellow with a contagious interest in what Joseph Wood Krutch once called "those subjects which are neither obviously momentous nor merely silly" (quoted in *FT*, viii). Knowing how much mileage one can get out of self-deprecatory humor, he turns his wit more often inward than outward. When he is finding fault with the world, he seems more an amiable curmudgeon than a rancorous culture cop. He also astonishes his readers with an ability to write interestingly about virtually anything. Reading Epstein is like watching a brilliant improvisational comedian taking the most mundane premise beyond amusement into the realm of art.

Terra Cognita

There are probably fewer activities more inherently mundane than the consumption and burning of calories; however, human ingenuity can work infinite variations on these activities. For Joseph Epstein both appear to be largely spectator sports. Take the business of eating. Although one of Epstein's great culture heroes was the butterball journalist A. J. Liebling (whom he calls the "Minnesota Fats of American Prose"), our man Aristides has about him a lean and hungry look. Nevertheless, he regards food as "the sex of the middle-aged" and writes about it with obvious concupiscence. In fact, he thinks that the description of a meal (either delightfully magnificent or comically botched) is far more interesting than an account of a seduction. "Perhaps the reason for this," he writes, "is that eating is the more social function, sex the more personal, and as such eating shows people in a greater multiplicity of poses, moods, and characters than does sex" (*FT,* 181).

Epstein's essay "Foodstuff and Nonsense" is filled with both. He tells us of James Gordon Bennett, "heir to the old *New York Herald,* who one afternoon was unable to get his regular table at his favorite restaurant in Monte Carlo. To expedite matters he simply bought the place (reportedly for $40,000), removed the customers from his accustomed table, finished his lunch of mutton chops, and presented the waiter with the deed to the restaurant as a tip" (*FT,* 183–84). The list of those with whom Epstein would and would not like to eat speaks volumes. On the favored list are Robin Hood and his Merry Men ("To the tables, everybody, and stuff yourselves!"); Talleyrand before a revolution; the Brothers Goncourt on an evening when Sainte-Beuve appeared; Rousseau at a banquet in his honor; George Sand for breakfast in bed; H. L. Mencken in a restaurant; Hemingway at lunch; and Henry James anywhere but home. Those to avoid include the emperors Augustus and Julian the Apostate, the elder Tolstoy, Joseph Stalin, and anyone described as a gourmet cook.

Cyril Connolly once said that within every fat man there is a thin man struggling to get out. But for Joseph Epstein "the reverse condition obtains."[2] The fat man who struggles to get out of his relatively thin body looks upon gluttony in the same way that the man who reads *Playboy* looks upon fornication—with the fascination of the voyeur. "A Fat Man Struggles to Get Out" is a far more personal essay than "Foodstuff and Nonsense." (In recent years, Epstein's voice has grown

increasingly more personal.) Although he once again gives us some
marvellous trivia about eating, along with a hall of fame for both fat
and thin writers, the most effective (and affecting) moments in the
essay come when Epstein is remembering great gluttons he has known.
For example, the Falstaff of his youth was a 350-pound tub of mirth
who kept an old towel in his car, which he laid across his belly when
driving "to prevent the steering wheel from wearing away his trousers."
This jolly chap "was once described as eating corned-beef sandwiches as
if they were cornflakes," and in urging his dining companions to have
another piece of cheesecake, he summed up an entire philosophy of life
in five words: "you owe it to yourselves" (OMB, 189).

Like the compulsive dieter and health food nut, Epstein views the
conflict between gluttony and abstemiousness in almost Manichaean
terms. The difference is that he is spiritually on the side of the demons.
His feelings of inadequacy at not being able to eat an A. J. Liebling
under the table make for an amusing reversal of the condition most of
the rest of us find ourselves in. When recalling the halcyon time of his
youth, he conjures up the nights when he would not settle into sleep
without fixing himself "a little snack that might consist of, say, a dozen
or so cookies, a pint of butter-pecan ice cream, a gross or so of grapes,
and four fingers of salami." "Today, of course," he concedes, "this kind
of snack, attempted at my age, could only be construed as a suicide
attempt" (OMB, 182). Epstein's present fantasies of food tend to read
like Walter Mitty's night at the bordello, complete with his long-
suffering wife "driving up to an emergency room with me stretched
across the backseat, a cool compress across my brow, groaning and
pledging repentance" (OMB, 197). The fact that in reality he has nothing to repent of is lost as we laugh at Epstein laughing at his own mock
absurdity.

If the modern Aristides is not exactly digging his grave with a fork,
neither is he striving for eternal life through unseemly exercise. True,
he plays racquetball twice a week, frequently with Saul Bellow, but he
draws the line at running. As with gluttony, he also has role models for
sloth. The one from his youth was a fellow named Taxicab Rabinowitz,
so called because he traveled almost exclusively by cab. With his portly
body and the omnipresent Pall Mall dangling from his lip, the Cab was
"the very antithesis of all that is implied by the phrase 'in shape.' "
(" 'In shape?' I can easily hear Rabinowitz asking. 'In shape for what?' "
[FT, 149–50].)

In contrast, we have such cultural gurus as the runner Jim Fixx, who before his untimely death was disgustingly in shape. (Mr. Fixx, who was still alive at the time Epstein wrote about him, died at about the same time and at a younger age than the notorious hedonist Richard Burton.) When Fixx rhapsodizes about the joys of running on gravel past "three imperturbable skunks, a raccoon, a family of squirrels busily laying in a winter's supplies," and a pheasant noisily taking to the air, the imp in Epstein is stirred to life. "As he runs through his seaside park," Epstein writes, "I hope that he will one day perturb those three skunks sufficiently for them to loose their most noxious perfume upon him; that the raccoon will take a small bite out of his, Mr. Fixx's, running shoe; that the pheasant who now noisily takes to the air at the sound of Mr. Fixx's foot on gravel will instead smile at the sound of the same foot squishing in pheasant droppings" (*FT*, 156).

Epstein's interest in athletics is more as a spectator than a participant. He grew up in a culture where a lack of interest in sports would have led to social ostracism. And even though he now moves in circles where sports is not officially regarded as a topic of great metaphysical importance, he is constantly encountering intellectuals and writers who are closet sports fans. At least in masculine society, talk about sports can bridge the gap between the bookish and the nonbookish. (Epstein thinks it desirable to bridge that gap precisely because he feels less contempt for the ordinary working stiff than he does for many of his fellow culturati.) "Sports talk is the closest thing we have in this country to a lingua franca," Epstein notes, "though I wouldn't use that phrase in, say, a bowling alley or a pool hall" (*OMB*, 151).

Although academics are supposed to be appalled at the fact that uneducated athletes (some of whom left college before finishing, others of whom graduated barely literate, and still others of whom passed up the halls of ivy altogether) are paid fabulous sums of money for playing games, the sports fan (as in fanatic) Epstein is simply glad for the hours of pleasure they bring to him through the Sony television set in his den. After all, he knows enough about what passes for "education" on our nation's campuses to realize that when Magic Johnson and Isiah Thomas jumped to the NBA after their sophomore years, they really weren't missing all that much. Besides, if someone is going to make millions from the revenues generated by professional sports in this country, the athletes themselves are more deserving than the playboy industrialists who own the teams.

With the exception of professional wrestling, sports performance is one of the least fraudulent aspects of contemporary American culture.

Fame and prominence in the literary, academic, journalistic, and political worlds can be attained through "public relations, or social connections, or small corruptions, or fast talk"; but the gymnast needing a perfect ten, the basketball player standing at the free-throw line, and the golfer facing "a tricky twelve-foot, slightly uphill putt" (*OMB*, 153) have only their craft to fall back on.

Life in the Mind

When Epstein shifts his focus from the body to the mind, he runs the risk of moving into territory that is no longer familiar to the majority of readers. Although this is admittedly less of a risk for the editor of the *American Scholar* than it might be for someone writing in, say, *Car and Driver,* Epstein is careful to ground his abstract speculations in very concrete imagery. This is perhaps easiest when he is writing about humor. Jokes, when they are not too esoteric, can be readily grasped by people of normal intelligence. They combine the narrative mode with the pleasure of laughter. But they also go deeper than the immediate reaction in telling us revealing things about ourselves. While some pompous bores can write humorlessly about humor, Joseph Epstein possesses far too much wit and common sense to fall into that trap. His essays "Jokes and Their Relation to the Conscious" and "What's So Funny?" are superb combinations of those old standbys sweetness and light.

The title of the first of these pieces is obviously meant to remind the well-read of Freud's classic study *Jokes and Their Relation to the Unconscious.* Although Epstein has great respect for the sage of Vienna, his interests are more sociological than psychoanalytical. For example, he argues that even seemingly apolitical humor is often implicitly political to the extent that it appeals to either a conservative or a radical temperament. "A joke," he writes, "can be judged conservative or radical if, in its implications, it tends to reinforce the arrangements of society as it stands, or if it protests against current arrangements" (*FT,* 64). By such a definition, Lenny Bruce was a radical, even if most of his material was not explicitly political. Similarly, ethnic humor tends to be conservative, even xenophobic, in reinforcing stereotypes about groups outside the mainstream of society.

That so much ethnic humor is now considered déclassé in polite company can be attributed to the fact that ours is a fluid society in which previously spurned groups signal their newfound respectability by claiming an immunity from jest. What has replaced ethnic humor is the psychoanalytic joke, in which a Philip Roth or a Woody Allen makes fun of sexual foibles—his and ours. While such humor "has made possible many a hardy laugh, ultimately sex is the fringe beyond which it cannot get" (*FT*, 70). Regardless of its subject matter, however, "the great point about jokes is that they all have a point." This is what distinguishes them from so much contemporary literature, film, painting, and criticism. "If an analogy is wanted," Epstein concludes, "jokes may be likened to short stories of the traditional kind—not only in their brevity but in the range of their possible effects" (*FT*, 69).

When Joseph Epstein raises the question "What's so funny?," we can be certain that he has no shortage of answers in mind. To begin with the negative, his pantheon of the humorless includes Ralph Waldo Emerson, Douglas MacArthur, Walter Cronkite, D. H. Lawrence, William Wordsworth, Richard Wagner, the reigning Queen of England, Fidel Castro, and Poland's Wojciech Jaruzelski (a funny Communist is almost a contradiction in terms). Among those who are supposed to be funny but fail to amuse Epstein are Art Buchwald, P. G. Wodehouse, Peter De Vries, Ogden Nash, and (hold onto your hats) Mark Twain. Whom, then, does he consider funny? Among the movie comedians to whom he is partial are Chaplin, Keaton, and the Marx Brothers, but he is positively devoted to that master of revisionism with rancor W. C. Fields. The writers who most frequently have him slapping his knee include Franz Kafka, Marcel Proust, and (hold onto your hats again) Henry James. As Epstein notes, "The first condition of humor is its ununiversality. If music be a universal language, humor is a quite particular one" (*OMB*, 127).

As befits a neoconservative wit, Epstein is a connoisseur of the put-down. This taste goes back to his high school days, when adolescent acne was referred to as "tweed" and "whoever had the roughest case of it at any particular time was designated, after the Tammany Hall figure, 'Boss Tweed' " (*OMB*, 131). Later in life, he recalls "listening to a sonorous lecture on the subject of the importance of the humanities," when a friend sitting next to him said of the lecturer, "I'd like this guy better if his name were Moe" (*OMAB*, 128). Not surprisingly, his favorite bumper sticker reads, "If You are Jesus, Honk!" (*OMAB*, 134). Unfortunately, Professor Epstein's risibility is not shared by his literal-minded students. He once assigned his class a paper, which was to be at least five pages with margins no wider than his necktie. When a tardy student brought her paper to his office, she kept staring at his chest.

"'May I ask what it is you are looking at, Miss Simpson?' I asked. 'Your necktie, sir,' she answered. 'I wanted to make sure I got my margins right' " (*OMAB,* 139).

No prude, Epstein finds sex funny. "The best sex jokes," he writes, "demonstrate a tasteful perversity, such as the joke about the nonagenarian who reports to his physician that he notices himself beginning to slow down sexually. 'When did you first begin to notice this?' asks the physician, amazed that a nonagenarian is still sexually active at all. 'Last night,' the man says, 'and then again this morning' " (*OMAB,* 135). Like many people, Epstein is also not above enjoying a chuckle at the expense of homosexuals. He realizes, however, that such jokes, which might once have been regarded as morally objectionable, are shunned today mostly for fear of offending a sensitive minority group with considerable political clout. But since he edits his own magazine, Aristides is free to offend whomever he pleases.

Another group who will take scant comfort from his opinions are those who place their faith in what he calls "the therapeutic mode of perceiving the world." According to Epstein, "the therapeutic mode provides those who adopt it a way of dramatizing their lives. Its key metaphors are turmoil, crisis, struggle, and breakthrough: Oedipal turmoil, identity crisis, struggle between id and superego, conscious and unconscious, Eros and Thanatos"(*FT,* 105). Except for the rather limited genre of therapeutic humor, this excessively interior view of the world is a joke that isn't meant to be funny. It may well be the characteristic pomposity of our age. Epstein declares himself to be of the antitherapeutic party for several reasons, "but chief among them is my belief that the therapeutic mode does not now come anywhere near achieving its own pretensions to explaining the totality of human experience" (*FT,* 111).

Not only is it intellectually reductionist—"like a Chinese laundry of the mind, boiling out the stains and flattening life's interesting wrinkles" (*FT,* 113)—a faith in therapeutics can be pragmatically dangerous in suggesting that all problems, personal and social, are finally ones of emotional adjustment. True, psychotherapy has done much to help the genuinely mad, but as a theology it is a kind of low-church voodoo. "If modern psychology has in many instances made the neurotic well," Epstein wonders, "in how many others has it made the well neurotic?" (*FT,* 107). To reform the situation, one must first purge the liturgy, replacing the word *guilty* with *conscience* and *personality* with *character.* *Syndrome, latent,* and *complex* would also go, as would the therapeutic usages of *fulfillment* and *creative*. Purifying the dialect of the tribe may be the first step out of the waste land.

In one of the many delightful seances his whimsy conjures up, Epstein imagines a visit from Dr. Freud himself. The great man "sets down his umbrella, takes a seat on the couch across from my wing chair, and lights up a cigar" (*FT*, 117). After the conversation touches on sex surrogates ("in Vienna they had a different name for such women"), EST, and collateral nonsense performed in the name of the therapeutic, "Dr. Freud begins softly to sob. 'It did not have to be like this,' he says. 'The idea was to relieve misery, not to enact such pathetic clownishness.' " In his reverie, Epstein goes over to his visitor and pats him "gently on the shoulder, murmuring, 'There, there, Doctor, there, there.' " But try as he will, he cannot bring himself to say, "None of this is your fault" (*FT*, 118).

Life of the Mind

The scholar, according to Emerson, is man thinking. But even the sage of Concord admitted that thought cannot occur in a vacuum. Books are required, if only as a catalyst and inspiration. Few things are as revealing about the thinking man as the contents of his personal library. For that reason, Epstein's comments on the books he has acquired and those he has discarded over a lifetime of reading form a kind of confessional literature. Acquiring books can be impulsive (even compulsive), but getting rid of them is usually a deliberate and cold-blooded activity. Epstein was confronted with this fact when he was forced to trim his library so that there would be room in his home for furniture, people, and (most important) more books.

A part of Epstein admires those individuals ruthless enough to treat books as disposable commodities. He once knew a well-read engineer who would throw out even clothbound books that he liked as if they were yesterday's newspaper. (Epstein is the sort who would find it hard enough to toss the newspaper itself.) An internationally celebrated writer of his acquaintance finds his apartment flooded with unsolicited review copies and bound galleys from authors and publishers seeking blurbs. He would regularly offer Epstein his choice of the books most recently arrived. Once, when Epstein indicated no interest in any of the new arrivals, his friend picked up the entire pile and tossed them into the incinerator. "I gulped," Epstein recalls. "Bookburning, for God's sake! [His host] laughed, announcing, 'I am the Torquemada of the

thirteenth floor.' [Epstein's] immediate response was to run down fourteen flights of stairs to the basement and pull the books from the
flames" (*FT*, 73–74).

Trimming one's library is a very basic act of literary criticism.
Among those books that Epstein finds he can most easily dispense with
are those in the category of "Last Year's Novel of the Year—fiction of
purported seriousness with high commercial possibilities." He agrees
with the reviewer for the *Times Literary Supplement* who "not long ago
wistfully remarked that, for all the liveliness of American fiction, there
were still moments when he yearned for the fiction of J.D. Salinger:
'One [moment] might occur on reading page 235 of Pynchon's *Gravity's Rainbow* where the girl is defecating into the open mouth of
Brigadier Pudding and you realize there are 500 pages still to go' " (*FT*,
78).

A related category of dispensable books belong to what Epstein calls
the literature of the agitational culture—"works that appear on the
scene, make a great flap (and much money), and then merely lie there."
Examples include Philip Roth's *Our Gang* and Gay Talese's *Honor Thy
Father*, both of which were reviewed in the same week by the daily
press. Epstein recalls one reviewer saying of Roth's book that "as satire
it was of the quality of Swift" and of Talese's that "it surpassed Balzac."
Upon his reporting these findings to a friend, the friend commented,
"We sleep tonight—criticism stands guard" (*FT*, 81). Epstein sleeps
tonight without these and many other books in his home, having kept
only those that he is certain will interest him ten years from now. It is a
severe rule of thumb, he admits, and one which, "strictly adhered
to, . . . would not allow me to keep my own books and other scrib-
blings. The efficient life is hard" (*FT*, 86).

Epstein acquired his passion for books only after he had entered
college. But, as is the case with so many acquired tastes, he has spent
the rest of his life making up for lost time. Because he is determined to
do this at a leisurely pace (finding speed-reading to be as abhorrent a
concept as speed-eating or speed-lovemaking), much of his day is taken
up with reading. He recalls that when he was a distinctly unbookish
elementary school student, the library lady who visited his class told
him that books were his friends. He now thinks she was wrong. "Books
are not my friends; they have become more like family, except that I
probably spend more time with books than I do with my family."[3]

Epstein is a rare figure among modern intellectuals in being a prolific writer who is also reasonably well read. It may seem strange to the layman that reading and writing are rarely compatible activities. But it stands to reason that a person who spends most of his time reading or writing has little time left for the other activity. A productive professional writer whom Epstein knows once told him that he had time to read only those books and articles that related to the two books he was currently working on. Prolific writers tend to "use books, . . . scrounge around in them, . . . dig out from books what they need, but always with a purpose." The exceptions to this rule (Epstein mentions Coleridge, Matthew Arnold, Sainte-Beuve, Saintsbury, Edmund Wilson, and V. S. Pritchett; others might add Epstein himself to the list) are primarily essayists. "Perhaps they read too much to write full-blown books," Epstein surmises. "Like the man said, you can read 'em or write 'em, but you cannot do both" (*MMT,* 123).

Epstein's most recent, though probably not his final, statement on man reading is 'Joseph Epstein's Lifetime Reading Plan," a tongue-in-cheek essay inspired by a student's asking him for a list of books that would enable him to get the liberal education he missed in college. Although he is not averse to the Great Books approach to education, Epstein realizes that that approach can be oversold. Students who are no cleverer than he was as an undergraduate will find anywhere from 30 percent to 70 percent of what the great writers have to say sailing blithely over their heads (see *OMB,* 33). For Epstein the value of reading the great books lay not in absorbing their contents (that comes with greater intellectual maturity) but in the following: "it taught you who the important writers are; it gave you some notion of what is important about them, which is chiefly the questions they deal with; and it lent you a certain animal confidence, so that you were never afraid of taking on the most serious of books" (*OMB,* 34). How many present-day students derive even that much from their time in school?

If the Great Books approach has a major flaw, it is that it is based on the ideal of well-roundedness. As an antidote to this pernicious ideal, Epstein recommends a parlor game that he heard is played at some academic parties. In this game, everyone in the room confesses to not having read some great book he ought to have read. (With Epstein it is *The Brothers Karamazov.*) This game of one-downsmanship might begin with the novels of Norman Douglas, proceed through *The Autocrat of the Breakfast Table* and the poetry of Gerard Manley Hopkins, until only a few stalwart nonliterates are left. As the competition heats up, a full professor defiantly admits to having read no Yeats; another has not even read *The Faerie Queen*. The resident "female Marxist" not only hasn't read Chaucer, she is not even certain of the century in which he lived. But the coup de grace is administered by the head of the school's American Studies program, who "strides forth with obvious pride in his posture, to announce, I hate to break up these festivities, but I'm afraid that's just what I'm about to do. You ready for this? I have never read a play by Shakespeare—and that includes your bloody *Hamlet*" (*OMB*, 37).

The same impulse that leads Epstein to trim his library causes him to admire the concept behind a book entitled *Fifty Works of English and American Literature We Could Do Without*. "Sound advice on what not to read," he notes, "would be a boon to humankind, or so one might think. Every book one doesn't need to read, after all, represents one book more one will have time to read." (The problem with *Fifty Works* is that it includes too many of Epstein's personal favorites: "Many an icon is worth shattering; but *Fifty Works* is an attempt to blow up the church" [*OMB*, 40].) Because Epstein has never met an interesting polymath, he recommends that we not go to books to absorb as broad a range of knowledge as possible. Rather, he endorses the sentiment of Montaigne: "I seek in books only to give myself pleasure by honest amusement; or if I study, I seek only the learning that treats of the knowledge of myself and instructs me in how to die well and live well" (quoted in *OMB*, 38).

The Personal Voice

One of Epstein's principal virtues as an essayist is his versatility. Like a veteran character actor, he can play many different roles. In one piece he can read like Montaigne turned loose in the America of Andy Rooney, in another like Tom Wolfe in a blue blazer and Bass Weejuns, in yet another like Orwell as a Cubs fan. On occasion, however, we hear a more personal voice. Popular opinion notwithstanding, it is usually easier to write about great issues and ideas than about one's own experiences and feelings. The importance of public issues is taken for granted; fascination with one's life often seems limited to an audience of one. But Epstein is never more appealing than when he is waxing nostalgic or introspective. For those who share his dislikes, it is comforting to know that the smirking polemicist is also an honest-to-God human being. For those who want to go on hating him, that revelation is probably as disconcerting as being charmed by your ex-wife's current husband.

In reviewing his own less-than-sordid past, Epstein concedes that a happy childhood is a distinct disadvantage in the literary world. (Hemingway, who was something of an authority on both matters, thought that an unhappy childhood was the first requisite for success as a writer.) "The modern scenario calls for a childhood filled with frustration, rebellion, alienation. Childhood, in this script, is the time for being awkward, misunderstood, spiritually wounded. It is a fine time, too, for building up psychological gripes: father didn't show me enough love, mother showed me too much" (*MMT,* 220). (Putting a political twist on all of this, Epstein asks whether "their unhappy early years have given so many artists and intellectuals what one thinks of as their adversary disposition toward the society in which they live and toward life in general?" [*MMT,* 221–22].) But if childhood is a time of pain and misery, so too is old age. Then, there are always the traumas of adolescence and, later, what has come to be known as "mid-life crisis." Add to this those perils of early adulthood—loneliness, confusion, and conflict. "If all of this is so," Epstein surmises, "then it means . . . that we can figure on roughly thirty-five to forty minutes of enjoyment in a normal life span" (*MMT,* 222).

That Epstein has had more than his allotted thirty-five to forty minutes, not only as a child but as a grownup as well, is due at least in part to his sense of rootedness in a particular community. In this regard, he is less the cosmopolitan neoconservative sourpuss than a profoundly regional artist and thinker. As Allen Tate argues, it is the man who is cut off from the past, not the one who is loyal to his home turf, who is the true provincial. In contrast, Epstein maintains an enviable sense of continuity with both his cultural and personal past. The latter, he argues, is due largely to his living in the city where he grew up. As he tells it:

One of the consequences of living in the city of one's upbringing is that it throws one back upon one's youth more than if one lived elsewhere. Streets, buildings, even empty lots have interesting associations. I have gone to certain of the same restaurants for thirty years, to the same theaters and ball parks for forty years, man and boy. I have never used that phrase "man and boy" before, or quite comprehended its meaning. But as I travel about my old neighborhood, about the streets of my city, I realize that this is what I am, man and boy—and both simultaneously. *(MMT,* 224–25)

If Epstein is both man and boy in his identity as a Chicagoan, there are other respects in which he has put away childish things, or at least adolescent aspirations. As a high school student, young Mr. Epstein earnestly sought the popularity that comes with being known as a "good guy." In a sense, this role was his by default: "Since I was neither a first-rate athlete, nor a notably successful Lothario, nor even a half-serious student, all that was left on the buffet of roles for me to choose from was Good Guy or thug, and since I hadn't the wardrobe for a thug I went for Good Guy—and I went for it in a big way" *(OMB,* 161). Epstein prided himself at being able to fit in easily with vastly different groups of people and at collecting friends as others might stamps or baseball cards. It was only after he became a literary intellectual that he also began acquiring enemies. And the rest, as they say, is history.

As an adult Epstein has not given up on friendship; however, he has come to show more discrimination in choosing his friends. One of the advantages of middle age, he tells us, is that one can acquire friends several decades to either side of his own age. Being well supplied with mentors, protégés, and contemporaries, Epstein no longer needs to hoard friends the way he did in high school. It is probably also true that one who lives the life of the mind does not need the external ego reinforcement for which an insecure adolescent so yearns. Man thinking is often a man alone. When community exists, it is based not on anything so ephemeral as a ready smile and a pat on the back, but on shared values and what Epstein elsewhere calls shared antipathies. There is also a pleasing sense of cultural continuity that comes to one who has aged from promising young scholar to older role model. As Epstein notes, "I feel as if I am passing on the baton that had earlier been passed to me" *(OMB,* 173).

For all this talk of friendship, Epstein's essays are lacking in fully developed personality sketches. Cameo appearances by bizarre figures such as Taxicab Rabinowitz are generally means to an end rather than ends in themselves. One notable exception can be found in the essay "My Friend Martin," with which Epstein concludes *Once More around the Block.* Originally published in *Commentary* (it is the only one of his collected familiar essays that did not appear in the *American Scholar*), this piece tells of a recently deceased man whom Epstein had known over the years. Martin (we are never given his last name) was a New

York Jew who made himself into a rather eccentric cosmopolitan figure. One might say that like Jay Gatsby, he sprang from his Platonic conception of himself, except that he was not nearly as successful or as obviously doomed as Gatsby. "Sometimes I have thought that Martin was an artist," Epstein writes, "and that the sadness of his life was that he had no art to convey—except perhaps the creation that had become himself" (*OMB,* 296).

Epstein first met Martin when both were working for *Encyclopaedia Britannica* (Martin was later fired for going through the editor's files, motivated not by malice or calculation but by sheer curiosity). Like so many individuals who never achieve the riches and fame that seem to come so easily to the less gifted and the less intelligent, Martin appears to have been a charming underachiever. Epstein remembers him as someone who was enjoyable to be with and to remember afterwards. Among the many stories of Martin that he recalls, one took place during an afternoon in the late sixties. An antiwar rally was to take place on the plaza outside the building that housed *Encyclopaedia Britannica.* Those who planned to attend the rally wore black armbands and were excused from work. When an earnest young secretary asked Martin if he was going to the rally, he replied, "No, Naomi, afternoons such as this I generally spend at the graveside of Santayana" (*OMB,* 295).

After his forced departure from the encyclopedia (where he apparently did little work, anyway), Martin moved to London and failed to make much headway in the publishing business before dying of cancer. Although he was never well-known in his own lifetime and is now dead, Martin is made both familiar and living in Epstein's vivid tribute to him. We see him in his brown leather coat, with fur collar and fur lining—"the kind of coat some German general might have had made to order in anticipation of spending the winter on the Russian front." (Years later, when Epstein would call or meet him after having been out of touch, he would ask Martin how the coat was. " 'Holding up nicely,' he would say. 'It's kind of you to inquire' " [*OMB,* 293].) We hear him explaining how he never has trouble finding a parking place: "Always remember that there are two open parking spaces on every block in America: one where the fire hydrant is, the other at the bus stop" (*OMB,* 300). The accumulation of details may not convince us that we knew Martin but it makes us wish that we had.

If we can judge Epstein as blessed by the quality of his enemies, the same is probably true of the quality of his friends. His essay on Martin is a rare glimpse of such a friend. "Disappointed Martin may have been," Epstein writes, "yet—and here he was of a very select minority—he himself rarely disappointed. To be with him was always to be reminded of life's larger possibilities, which is the service performed by people who are original for the rest of us" (*OMB*, 308). In addition to being high praise for a friend, that description may tell us a good deal about what Joseph Epstein most values in life. In the many voices of his essays (particularly the familiar and personal ones), Epstein himself comes across as an original who rarely disappoints. As such, he passes the Holden Caulfield test with flying colors.

Chapter Eleven
Culture Cop

Those who enjoy the company of Aristides the Just are ill-prepared to deal with the critic Joseph Epstein. Familiarity breeds not so much contempt as a misleading sense of ease. Aristides comes across as a kind of bookish crank who is content to let the parade pass him by because he is having too much fun watching it. Then you loosen your tie, put your feet up, and are almost ready to call him "Joe," when he flashes his badge and starts reading you your rights. It's a case of outright entrapment. This regular guy is really a licensed culture cop, intent on cleaning out the literary underworld. That includes the *New York Review of Books,* critical theories from France and Germany, cultural trends from the sixties, overly generous book reviewers, most American English professors, and all living writers except for V. S. Naipaul. If officer Epstein has seen you consorting with any of these, you've got a heap of explainin' to do.

No More Mr. Nice Guy

On occasion, even the genial Aristides can, like the mild-mannered Clark Kent, jump into a phone booth and don his crimefighter's apparel. In the midst of his second collection of familiar essays, *The Middle of My Tether,* Epstein does precisely that in order to level the charge of vulgarity against American Culture. In a neoconservative twist on those insipid "happiness is . . ." cartoons, Epstein tells us that vulgarity is publicity, the Oscar awards, the Aspen Institute for Humanistic Studies, talk shows, Pulitzer Prizes, Barbara Walters, interviews with writers, Lauren Bacall, dialogue as an ideal, and (you guessed it) psychology. What all of these defendants have in common is a combination of shallowness and pretension.

Vulgarity is a condition that can exist only in a fluid social system. "The rise of the middle class, the spread of capitalism and democracy, opened all sorts of social doors; social classes commingled as never before; plutocracy made possible almost daily strides from stratum to stratum. Still, some people had to be placed outside the pale, some doors had to be locked—and the cry of vulgarity, properly intoned, became a most effective Close Sesame" (*MMT,* 131–32). By definition, vulgarity is the endemic vice of the bourgeoisie. Aristocrats are seldom vulgar—savages never. In the social world the nouveau riche define vulgarity; in the art world it is kitsch (although Epstein would probably argue that anyone who used such terms as nouveau riche and kitsch was himself a trifle vulgar).

Just as there are things that are supposed to be funny that fail to put Epstein rolling in the aisles, so too are there ostensible vulgarians who fail to offend him all that much. Taking another jaunt down memory lane he recalls his Uncle Jake, a corpulent bootlegger whose romantic tastes usually "ran to Hungarian women in their fifties with operatic bosoms." Jake would sit at the table eating soup from an oversized bowl that resembled a tureen. "He would eat hot soup and drink whiskey and sweat—my Uncle Jake did not, decidedly, do anything so delicate as perspire—and sometimes it seemed that the sweat rolled from his face right into his soup dish, so that, toward the end, he may well have been engaged in an act of liquid auto-cannibalism, consuming his own body fluids with a whiskey chaser" (*MMT,* 127). Because he was good-hearted, lacked pretension, and wouldn't have had the slightest idea what you were talking about if you called him vulgar, Uncle Jake was incapable of vulgarity. He is like the ingenuous Chicago politician "who, while escorting the then ruling British monarch through City Hall, supposedly introduced him to the assembled aldermen by saying, 'King, meet the boys' " (*MMT,* 139).

The bit of superciliousness that most sticks in Sanford Pinsker's craw can be found in another essay from *The Middle of My Tether.* Here, Epstein recalls his encounter with an earnest freshman at a college in Ohio. In a question-and-answer session following one of his lectures, the student asked Epstein if he did not engage in "dangerous generalizations." As evidence, she cited a relatively innocuous passage about the various professions into which different nationalities of immigrants gravitated on coming to America. Might such statements be offensive to the nationalities involved? Epstein thought not. "Still," his interrogator persisted, "what you wrote isn't true of *all* Greeks, Jews, Italians and Irish." Conceding the point, Epstein replied, "True enough. . . . Einstein didn't go into retailing but relativity. Fermi didn't go into flowers but fission. But there is enough general truth to my statements to hold up. At least I believe there is." Undaunted, the young champion of ethnic sensitivity said, "Even if there is, . . . I don't think you're entitled to say things like that." "And then it happened," Epstein writes: " 'Honey,' said I, 'if I can't say things like that, we may as well turn on the stereo and start dancing, because all conversation becomes impossible' " (*MMT,* 190).

What happened was that Epstein lost his patience with liberal naiveté and, as he ruefully admits, demonstrated his "ability to overpower an eighteen-year-old girl in argument" (*MMT,* 190). (Pinsker disingenuously pictures Epstein as gloating over this triumph.) Although I have no way of knowing if this is the case, I suspect that that student's freshman English teacher had cited Epstein's offending passage in class as an example of hasty, even dangerous, generalization. Epstein's account of this tête-à-tête merely serves as a lead-in to some reflections on the value of generalization to civilized discourse. But had he anticipated critics such as Pinsker and been inclined to deliver what the opening of his essay seems to promise, he would have said more about the sort of sensibility that teaches college freshpersons to be leery of generalization. Rather than fighting with a straw man (or woman), Epstein—in a sense—is the straw man.

Far from confessing to rancor or nastiness (the two main charges that Pinsker levels against him), Epstein will admit only to what Philip Rahv called "analytical exuberance." To be an intellectual means defending ideas that you believe in and challenging those you deem dangerous or meretricious. To hold otherwise is to deny the truth of Richard Weaver's aphorism, "ideas have consequences." Most controversialists, however, find it difficult to separate animosity for ideas from hatred for people who hold those ideas. (Of course, not everyone—certainly not Alexander Pope—would see that as even necessary.) As a result, paranoia is as endemic among intellectuals as, say, black lung among coal miners. " 'I don't know how it is in other professions,' says a character in George Gissing's *New Grub Street,* 'but I hope there is less envy, hatred and malice than in ours' " (*OMB,* 257).

A related but opposite problem is maintaining the requisite hatred and malice toward the objectionable ideas of people whom you personally like or pity. (One is reminded of Nick Carraway's affection for Jay Gatsby, a man "who represented everything for which I have an unaffected scorn.") Orwell was never able to attack Stephen Spender's ideas and poetry with quite so much analytical exuberance after the two met. (I have a friend who would never watch the late Woody Hayes on television for fear that the experience might somewhat diminish his hatred of the legendary coach.) Epstein recalls attending a conference where he saw the editor of a magazine that promoted "everything I found lamentable in public life." Before the encounter he was able to attack the editor's ideas without trepidation. But later, he found himself walking ten or fifteen yards behind the offending party. From that perspective Epstein noted that the editor had bad feet, walked funnily, and wore special shoes. Because "he lived with real discomfort, possibly persistent pain," he became more human for Epstein, who found he could "no longer dislike him with the same cheerful gusto." As William Dean Howells once noted, "Making enemies is easy, . . . but keeping them is not" (quoted in *OMB,* 260).

Epstein concedes a point that his enemies have long made ("See, we told you," one can hear them saying): "Shared antipathies can sometimes be the basis for friendship, especially when the antipathies give one the feeling of belonging to a select minority." As an example, he cites the experience of being in the antisegregationist minority while living in the south during the late fifties and early sixties. He has something of the same feeling today when he runs into someone who shares his views on fashionable literary criticism and social theories. Such an experience can even add flavor to lunch. "Tea and sympathy is nice," Epstein notes, "but tea and shared antipathy is even better" (*OMB,* 269). Does that mean that the rancorous crowd known as neoconservatives are nothing but a bunch of gleeful naysayers? Perhaps. But Epstein offers another way of putting the matter. "For myself," he writes, "it was only when I came to know what I hated that I came to love intensely those things that matter most to me in life" (*OMB,* 272).

Out of the Closet

As we have seen, Norman Podhoretz took confessional literature to a new low when he admitted to the secret passion, the lust that dare not speak its name. He was talking not about drug addiction, treason, or sexual deviancy, but about raw ambition—not the blind kind that one repents of after doing his time for insider trading, but the 20-20 variety that knows where it's going and doesn't give a damn if the rest of the world does too. When Kenneth S. Lynn wrote about the dream of success, it was with the circumspection of the young and proper literary scholar. Podhoretz sounded more like the drunk young kid who didn't care if he was throwing up in the subway as long as he could call the elders at *Partisan Review* by their first names. Thus, when Joseph Epstein decided to write about going for the main chance, his options were limited—the lit crit and confessional modes had both been done. So he split the difference, writing as Lynn had about the phenomenon of ambition in American culture but with the brassy self-confidence of Podhoretz. A writer for *Sports Illustrated* once described the New Orleans Superdome as looking like a Holiday Inn motel room blown up many times. *Ambition: the Secret Passion* reads like a Joseph Epstein essay blown up many times.

Epstein is barely into his book when he first tweaks the noses of all the pantywaist snobs in the literary establishment. "Perhaps," he says, "the one novel that no serious writer in America would care to write today is one about a man who sets out to succeed in life and does so through work, decisive action, and discretion, without stepping on anyone's neck, without causing his family suffering, without himself becoming stupid or inhumane" (*ASP,* 7). (One might as well imagine Phil Donahue doing a show on heterosexual monogamy.) Then, fewer than seventy pages later, he writes:

No major American literary figure has failed to get in his word on the subject of success, and most have not spoken kindly of it. James Fenimore Cooper, Nathaniel Hawthorne, Edgar Allan Poe, Herman Melville, William Dean Howells, Mark Twain, Robert Herrick, Frank Norris, Henry James—through the nineteenth century from Cooper's distrust of the self-made man to James's deliciously sneering reference to his countrymen's "grope of wealth"—viewed success in America in terms ranging from equivocation to condemnation. In the twentieth century, the terms have been closer to those of unrelieved contempt. Antisuccess has been perhaps the strongest strain in American literature of the past half century. (*ASP,* 75)

Epstein makes it clear that he will have none of this. The captains of industry had their flaws, but they also endowed museums, libraries, and universities, as well as created the material surplus that makes museums, libraries, and universities possible.[1] Accordingly, he pays his homage to the rich and famous by giving us capsule biographies of John D. Rockefeller, the Dupont and Guggenheim families, Dale Carnegie, the pathological anti-Semite and "car humanitarian" Henry Ford, Henry R. Luce, and Joseph P. Kennedy. Although he realizes these men were far from saints, he quotes approvingly Oliver Wendell

Holmes, Jr.'s comment (made in reference to Rockefeller): "I think we should do justice to those who do big things however little we want to dine with them" (quoted in *ASP,* 297).

It has been said that in life nothing succeeds like success, while in literature nothing succeeds like failure. Hamlet is a more interesting character than Fortinbras, and Hurstwood stirs our emotions far more than Carrie. As a literary character, God the Father can't hold a candle to Milton's Satan. However, unlike Lynn, Epstein says very little about success and failure in the storybook world. When he does deal with literature, it is the lives of writers that most interest him. Of course, in the case of Benjamin Franklin and Henry Adams, the most memorable work and the lives (or a selective interpretation of the lives) are one and the same. It is generally assumed that Franklin wrote the manual for success in America and Adams the manual for failure, but that is true only if one regards a life in the public arena as the sole measure of success. Adams's great-grandfather obviously thought that public controversy was something for one generation to endure so that succeeding generations could devote themselves to less mundane concerns. By that standard, Henry Adams was not a failure but the ultimate vindication of what his forebears had striven to accomplish. It was Adams's ironic flaw (one could hardly call it tragic) to define success in such a way as to doom himself to failure. As Carl Becker has noted, Henry Adams's "genius was at war with his ambition" (quoted in *ASP,* 31).

The only writers whose attitude toward money seems to meet with Epstein's wholehearted approval are Edith Wharton (who survived the fate of being a poor little rich girl to write about the American upper classes better than anyone before or since) and Wallace Stevens (who managed to be one of the twentieth century's premier poets while serving as a vice president of the Hartford Accident and Indemnity Company). Those who argue that inherited wealth or a life of commerce is inimical to art must either explain away the examples of Edith Wharton and Wallace Stevens or admit that the grapes they themselves disdain are not necessarily sour.

The list of other American writers whom Epstein discusses at length includes Mark Twain, Theodore Dreiser, and F. Scott Fitzgerald—all of whom had seen and written about the American dream from both sides. He also mentions the minor writers Ross Lockridge (author of *Raintree County*) and Thomas Heggen (author of *Mr. Roberts*), who found success so empty that they both took their own lives. (They fall into Epstein's special category of "failures at success.") Garry Wills once wrote, "Winners erect their own monuments, while losers ache with music."[2] (The anthem of American literature would have to be "Here's to the Losers.") Surely, the cult of Fitzgerald is due at least as much to the sad waste of his life as to the genuine achievement of his art. It is doubtful that Henry Adams would be as revered as he is today had his autobiography been called *Making It in the University*. And, as Epstein reminds us, no politician of the postwar era has stirred as much genuine passion among the culturati as the noble loser Adlai Stevenson.

In discussing Stevenson's career, Epstein argues that those who were "Madly for Adlai" (as the campaign slogan went) almost came to look upon losing as more refined than winning. Stevenson's defeats at the hands of the bourgeois Eisenhower were a confirmation of their belief that America was not good enough to deserve a president of such grace and sophistication. (Of course, the grace and sophistication were as important as the losing; otherwise we would hear intellectuals bemoaning the fact that the country was not good enough for Harold Stassen.) Epstein's interpretation is that Stevenson was constitutionally unable to admit to his political ambitions and thus became a victim of indecisiveness and equivocation.

It is not surprising that reviewers on what Orwell once called the "pansy left" took Epstein to task for praising success and lamenting failure. (James Wolcott, writing in the *New Republic*, even went so far as to call *Ambition* "Son of 'Making It.' "[3]) But what those reviewers seem not to realize is the degree to which Epstein has actually pulled his political punches. Not only does he fail to attack Henry Adams in the way that Podhoretz would do in *The Bloody Crossroads*, he passes up numerous opportunities to score points at the liberal Stevenson's expense.

Does Epstein believe that had Stevenson somehow managed to achieve his vulgar ambitions, his indecisiveness would have disappeared? A more hardnosed assessment might have held that Stevenson made losing seem superior to winning because he was simply better at it. If he seemed always to be hesitating when he should have jumped, his 1956 race against Eisenhower (complete with mudslinging references to Ike's health) was clearly a case of jumping when he should have hesitated. Had he sat out the presidential race in 1956 and rebuilt his power base in Illinois (perhaps by running for the Senate), Stevenson might have been in a commanding position to seek the presidency in 1960. As it was, he went into 1960 a two-time loser who refused to seek the nomination because he thought he deserved it unsolicited. As president, Stevenson would have had to succeed or fail at a much higher level of endeavor. But in either case, his mythos as the beautiful loser whose defeat confirmed the philistinism of the American public would have been a thing of the past.

Like Epstein's essays, *Ambition* is filled with what *Reader's Digest* would call amusing anecdotes and quotable quotes. (In fact, it is like Epstein's essays in using some of the same anecdotes and quotes— following the example of Uncle Jake in engaging in a kind of literary auto-cannibalism.) I am particularly fond of the following words of wisdom from Dale Carnegie's *Biographical Roundup:* "The main thing [in achieving success] is to have the courage to admit one's errors and to have the strength to correct them in the shortest possible time" (quoted in *ASP,* 54). Those words to live by come from Soviet yuppie Joseph Stalin. Closer to home, basketball great Oscar Robertson, "asked by a congressional investigating committee whether he thought he was worth the high annual salary he was paid, answered, fittingly enough, that the man who paid it to him must have figured he was, else he would not be getting it" (*ASP,* 138). A few pages earlier, Epstein uncritically cites Babe Paley, wife of the chairman of CBS, who observed that "one can never be too rich or too thin" (quoted in *ASP,* 134). (Of course, taken too literally, such an attitude can lead to the tragedy of anorexia. One need only contemplate the sad fate of Karen Carpenter to realize how witless Paley's witticism actually was.)

When Epstein speaks in his own right, he occasionally makes some very shrewd observations. For example, he notes that for a wealthy man the end of the class system "means the end of his ambition for his family, each of whose members, after his passing, will be on his or her own. . . . In such a world ambition becomes less public, more private; striving to secure position for one's children's children becomes rather preposterous. Ambition itself is thus deprived of much of its interest in the future" (*ASP,* 190, 191). (One has to go back to Edmund Burke's gushing over Marie Antoinette to find a more eloquent defense of privilege.) Epstein also argues that the class system is a needed buffer against the savagery of a pure meritocracy. "Status," he writes, "often functions as a cushion of sorts, taking some of the bumps out of life. If one comes into the world without great intelligence, beauty, or physical prowess, status offers compensations" (*ASP,* 271).

When Epstein speaks about attitudes on the university campus, he reveals a class myopia of his own. He tells us that students no longer look forward to going into a business career and making money. The reason for this is that commerce has been systematically downgraded in the humanities classes they take. They learn the following lessons: "Business . . . is hypocritical and sterile (see *Babbitt*). Ambition is unseemly and everywhere suspect (see *What Makes Sammy Run, The Great Gatsby,* and, for nonreaders, the movies *Citizen Kane* and *The Apprenticeship of Duddy Kravitz*). Middle-class life is essentially boring (see modern literature); upper-middle-class life, worse (see, these students say, their own families). Affluence is a sham, a greedy affair bringing no happiness (see Galbraith et al.)" (*ASP,* 131). Students may learn all of this at Northwestern and other elite schools, and professors shaped by the values of the sixties may try to teach it elsewhere, but with few exceptions the students aren't buying. I teach at a land grant university in the New South, which offers no courses in the classics but boasts of a thriving program in Language and International Trade.

Despite the sporadic excellences of *Ambition,* the book rambles and lacks focus. In the hands of someone as expert as Epstein, those qualities can give a familiar essay an appealingly rumpled look. In a full-dress book, however, not even Epstein can keep the baggy pants from looking tacky. To change the metaphor, one might ask what Epstein has lost in blowing up a Holiday Inn room of an essay into a Superdome of a book. (James Wolcott is convinced that he did it with a bicycle pump.) The answer, unfortunately, is the marvelous sound of a human voice speaking to us from the printed page. As an unabashed admirer of Epstein, I must reluctantly agree with James Wolcott that "ambition is what does *Ambition* in."[4] Finishing this book, I am reminded of the plea a disillusioned fan made to another famous Chicagoan: "Say it ain't so, Joe."

Walking the Beat

For anyone with an even moderately refined sensitivity to language, living in present-day America is akin to being locked in a room with a sadist who scratches his fingernail across a blackboard several hundred times a day. It is not clear who first noticed that the language was deteriorating, but the sacred text for most of the pop grammarians of our own time is George Orwell's "Politics and the English Language." As Orwell pointed out in his own plainspoken prose, language "becomes ugly and inaccurate because our thoughts are foolish, but the slovenliness of language makes it easier for us to have foolish thoughts."[5] If political partisans can argue about where Orwell would find himself on today's ideological spectrum, no advocate of the new illiteracy has had the gall to claim him for their own. Were he still alive, an aging but still cantankerous Orwell would undoubtedly be walking the beat with Joseph Epstein, culture cop.

Like Orwell, Epstein refuses to blame the unwashed masses for the deplorable state of the language (what John Simon calls "paradigms lost"). The damage has been done from the top down. (Epstein cannot "imagine any supposedly uneducated person using the word *supportive,* except possibly about his jockstrap" [*OMB,* 118].) "Bad language," Epstein writes, "is no longer picked up on the streets but in the classroom, where verbal gaseousness is part of the atmosphere. From the college classrooms it fans out into the media—and also filters down into grade and secondary schools—so that even if one is not able to go to college one still gets it all, through television and the press, by what is in effect a correspondence course" (*FT,* 22).

No doubt, universal schooling has exacerbated the situation. In an effort to preserve the superstition of mass education, teachers who should know better often pander to the lowest common denominator. Moreover, their own academic jargon frequently stands in the way of clear thought. What we have instead of concepts are "cepts"—"the clichéic distillation of complex thoughts." "Some days," writes Epstein, "listening to these cepts pinging off classroom walls, it seems as if the chief effect of the spread of education has been to allow more people to live, not more thoughtfully, but by somewhat more complicated clichés" (*MMT,* 47).

Some words and phrases (*life-style, midlife crisis,* and vegetation metaphors such as *growth* and *nurturing*) seem to be clichés from the moment of birth (Epstein calls them the "ephemeral verities"). Others become clichés the old-fashioned way—through overuse and misuse. The fact that certain ideas have become clichés is not to deny their original truth, only to suggest that they sometimes sacrifice nuance for glibness. "Finergrained writers—Montaigne, Pascal, Santayana—are not so easily summarized," Epstein observes. "Their thought cannot be grasped by the reins of a leading idea or two; rather like poets, they can scarcely be paraphrased. Marx and Freud are writers of great power in any case, but surely a large part of their popularity is owing to their supreme nomenclatural skill" (*MMT,* 52).

Clichés enable us to speak without thinking and certainly without seeing (I almost said visualizing). Consider, for example, the student who wrote in a paper for Epstein that "Madame Bovary's problem is that she cannot make love in the concrete." "How could he know," Epstein asks, "that the word 'concrete' is itself an abstraction, a by now quite stale metaphor, and one used in his unpracticed hand to hilarious effect"? (*Prejudices,* 353). As his teacher, Epstein might try to correct him, but the student might well argue that he has a right to his own language and cite the National Council of Teachers of English as his authority. Besides, when he sees some of the highest paid, most re-spected, and ostensibly best-educated figures in our society butchering the language, he will probably see little advantage in striving for grace and precision in his writing. We would have to go back at least to Herbert Hoover to find an American president even capable of writing his own speeches.

Being a language snob, which is what Epstein proudly calls himself, is clearly not an aspiration of the newly rich. To the extent that it is a mark of distinction at all it is a function more of social class than of economic status. "Today," Epstein hypothesizes, "when the ownership of a Mercedes, or even of a Chagall, is no longer a guarantee of distinc-tion, perhaps using 'hopefully' correctly can separate one from the general middle-class rabble" (*Prejudices,* 355). Among pop grammari-ans, the correct use of hopefully is what separates the true language snobs (Edwin Newman and John Simon) from such a rank latitudinar-ian as William Safire. *Hopefully* is finally more a matter of taste than of grammar, Epstein concedes. (After all, Safire argues, if we can use the adverbs *finally* and *basically* without a connecting verb, why not *hope-fully?*) But then, it is also taste that keeps us from eating peas with a knife. "My argument," Epstein concludes, "is that in a secular age, 'hopefully' has come to stand in for the old phrase 'God willing,' as in 'God willing, we shall not have another war in our lifetime,' and faulty grammar seems to me a poor substitute for religious feeling" (*Prejudices,* 365). (To paraphrase Hemingway's Brett Ashley, it's sort of what we have instead of God.) High church snobs (a redundancy if there ever was one) will probably want to replace *hopefully* with *Deo volente.*

Part of the pleasure of reading pop grammarians such as Newman, Simon, and Epstein is chuckling over the linguistic gaucheries they discover in public life. (Epstein is too polite ever to correct someone's language in private, but he regards "anyone who uses language publicly—a writer, politician, teacher, journalist—anyone who lives off language without caring about it . . . [as] fair game" [*FT,* 27].) One doesn't need to be a conservative (neo or otherwise) to look down his nose at Jimmy Carter's earnest prayer: "Let me live my life so that it will be meaningful." With Epstein, we ask rhetorically, "whatever can Carter have meant by meaningful? Hitler was meaningful, so was Gandhi, and Attila the Hun, and Jesus Christ, and Josef Stalin, and Saint Francis of Assisi. What Carter means only God knows, but since he is using the word in a prayer, perhaps that is sufficient" (*FT*, 21). Do euphemisms drive you up the wall (not "off the wall," which is another of Epstein's pet peeves)? Then chortle with Aristides when he hears the admonition "Due to mature theme viewer discretion advised." Never mind the improper use of "due to," what this means is "simulated fornication, extreme violence, and filthy language follow—get the kids the hell out of the room" (*OMB*, 114).

Language snobbery allows one to sneer not only at the swinish multitude but occasionally even at the immortals. While railing against the tautology "from whence," Epstein came across it in both Shakespeare and Edmund Burke (the snob who coined the phrase "swinish multitude"). "More recently still," he laments "I discovered T. S. Eliot—T. S. Bloody Eliot, for God's sake—misusing *presently* to mean 'now' or 'currently.' " "Shock and dismay is the language snob's lot, " he concludes. "Believe me, I don't enjoy feeling superior to Shakespeare, Burke, and Eliot, yet what is a man of serious standards to do?" (*OMB*, 113).

Perhaps remember that he who lives by the red pen dies by the red pen. One who scrutinizes *Once More around the Block* (the volume in which Epstein proclaims himself "Your Basic Language Snob") will find (on page 248) the Episcopal Church referred to as the "Episcopalian Church." Thus is a noun turned into an adjective when the proper adjective not only exists but is the root from which the noun was formed. Or what about the following sentence in the snooty essay itself: "As a snob, the people I like to lord it over are the quasi-semi-demi-ostensibly educated, B.A., M.S., Ph.D. and degrees beyond" (*OMB*, 108)? The dangling modifier would suggest that it is the lordees rather than the lorder who is the snob. But even an honest cop can occasionally misplace his Miranda card—or his Strunk and White. Even Homer nods.

Chapter Twelve
Correcting Taste

Like Norman Podhoretz, Joseph Epstein believes that the most talented writers in America today are either essayists by trade or novelists who do their best writing in the lower rent medium. (His honor role includes Tom Wolfe, Joan Didion, Edward Hoagland, Cynthia Ozick, Elizabeth Hardwick, Lewis Thomas, Gore Vidal, Susan Sontag, and Wendell Berry.) In analyzing the contemporary situation, he writes:

I grew up at a time when the novelist was the great cultural hero, and the novel, if it was written with power or subtlety (or both), seemed the most heroic cultural act. But, for a complex of reasons, the novel seems to be going through a bad patch right now. The essay, though it can never replace the novel, does appear to be taking up some of the slack. It is a form with distinguished predecessors and a rich tradition, and within its generous boundaries one can do almost anything one wishes; report anecdotes, tell jokes, make literary criticisms, polemicize, bring in odd scraps of scholarship, recount human idiosyncrasy in its full bountifulness, let the imagination roam free. (*Prejudices*, 411)

As we have seen, Epstein turns all of these tricks in his own writing. If George Will is correct in regarding him as America's premier essayist, then Epstein is by definition an important contemporary writer—sort of like the best player on the best team, if not necessarily the best over all.

The essay is at once a protean and restricted genre. Fiction writers and poets may tailor their style toward a particular journal, but they "are not as hostage as essayists to editors and the confinements of space and time set by their journals" (*Prejudices*, 405). Although just about all literary magazines have certain poets and fiction writers who appear frequently in their pages, stories and poems are rarely commissioned in the way that essays almost always are. The need to write on demand may make the essayist seem like something of a hack, in contrast to the more "creative" writer who plugs in his word processor only when the muse beckons. But there can be just as much grubby commercialism in song and story as in the discursive piece. (Fictionists and poets need to eat and pay the rent.) And if the end product is what is important, Matthew Arnold was right in saying that "excellent work in a lower kind counts in the long run above work that is short of excellence in a higher" (quoted in *Prejudices,* 398).

Judging from the qualities Epstein displays in his own writing and those he admires in the writing of others, it is clear that neither professional scholarship nor academic criticism has any place in the essay. When the essayist writes about books, he is doing so as an amateur enthusiast rather than a professional pedant. (This is true even though the essayist usually publishes in magazines that pay, whereas the pedant usually does not.) "The essayist might be found almost anywhere, " Epstein writes, "but the last place one is likely to find him is in the pages of the *PMLA.*" Epstein defines the essay as "a piece of writing that is anywhere from three to fifty pages long, that can be read twice, that provides some of the pleasures of style, and that leaves the impression of a strong or at least interesting character." Thus, "F. R. Leavis, though he might be writing at essay length, is always the critic, never the essayist. Max Beerbohm, even when he is writing criticism of the most ephemeral play, is perpetually the essayist" (*Prejudices,* 400). By the same token, Joseph Epstein gives the impression of being on leave from an age when one could write about books for love and money, not promotion and tenure.

His Craft and Sullen Art

Anyone interested in practical criticism, as opposed to the glossolalia of critical theory, would do well to commit long stretches of Epstein's essay "Reviewing and Being Reviewed" to memory. He brings to this topic the credibility of personal experience (ethos once again rears its charming head). But what is even more impressive, Epstein adds color to a black-and-white subject with vivid strokes of metaphor. Consider, for example, his reaction to being placed in the company of such immortal essayists as Montaigne, Pascal, Hazlitt, Lamb, Camus, Orwell, and John Leonard. Most writers would simply say that here is a classic instance of the picture where one element doesn't belong. Epstein goes several steps farther. "Indeed," he writes, "at the very mention of the name John Leonard it seemed that Montaigne threw his mantel across his shoulders and left the room, followed by Pascal delicately lifting the skirt of his vestments; Hazlitt said he had a previous appointment at the five courts, Lamb muttered something about his sister not being well, Orwell stubbed out his cigarette. Camus buckled the belt on his trenchcoat, and they were all gone, and so was any sense of pleasure I might have taken in the praise the rest of this review lavished on my book" (*Prejudices*, 46).

The point Epstein is making is that praise of the wrong kind can be as wounding as outright censure. It "can induce real discomfort, like a letter citing you for strength of character from, say, Spiro Agnew or Ted Kennedy" (*Prejudices*, 46). (Note the nice touch of bipartisanship.) While most of the rest of us would settle for fawning praise of even the most ignorant variety, Epstein demands that those reviewing his books be as discriminating a reviewer as he is. Instead, he finds that most reviews are long on opinions and short on analysis. The best that one can usually hope for are positive opinions phrased pithily enough to provide blurbs for the paperback edition of the book. Epstein advocates a good deal more.

The most basic obligations of Epstein's ideal reviewer are to the book he is reviewing and to his readers. He needs to report on what the book is saying, judge how well it was said, and determine whether it was worth saying. Beyond that (and here Epstein fully agrees with Podhoretz), the reviewer should use his review as an occasion to make his own statement about the issues the book raises. (When writing about literary works, Epstein prefers the essay-review because it enables him to place the latest book in the context of its author's entire career.) Like T. S. Eliot, Epstein believes that the highest function of criticism is to correct taste. Book reviewing offers the most frequent and visible opportunity to do that. Because the ideal reviewer believes that the shape and fate of culture is important, he regards book reviewing as nothing less than a moral obligation. "Judging books is of the utmost seriousness to him; misjudging a novel is of no less consequence than, say, misjudging a friendship" (*Prejudices*, 49).

The sort of misjudgment that Epstein finds most common in contemporary reviewing is a tendency to inflate the trivial. As a result, he sets out to trivialize the inflated. Although it is nice to be nice, indiscriminate praise does for literature what printing money does for the economy—it devalues the currency. Epstein believes that "books, unlike criminals, are best judged guilty until proven innocent" (*Prejudices*, 50). What is needed is not just a culture cop but a hanging judge who will hand out punishments to fit the crime. If, for example, Diane Johnson is caught puffing Joyce Carol Oates's reputation, the Lord

High Executioner would require her "to read, and show proof that she had read, all thirty-odd of Joyce Carol Oates's books." (As that was written in 1982, Oates's books are now many more than thirty odd.) If Mark Harris and Richard Stern are caught dedicating books to each other and then lauding each other's work in the *New Republic,* "they would be sentenced to slam, in conspicuous places, each other's next three books." As a kind of shock treatment, first-time and minor offenders "would be sentenced to read the collected reviews of John Leonard and to discover in each review the exact point at which that particular rhinestone reviewer disappears up his own metaphors" (*Prejudices,* 60).

Talk of the Town

The ads on cable television proclaim the *New Yorker* to be "the best magazine in the world. . . . Probably the best magazine that ever was." There is a sense in which the literary marketplace has validated that judgment. Ask any aspiring poet or fiction writer where he would most like to publish, and I suspect that the *New Yorker* would lead the list, if not by a country mile at least by a city block. (If you can make it there, you can make it anywhere.) So, if there was ever a huge reputation waiting to have the air let out, it is that of the *New Yorker* writers. True, some may deserve the adulation they have received. (If anything, Epstein believes, A. J. Liebling has been underrated.) But the Lord High Executioner does not regard S. J. Perelman, E. B. White, John Updike, and Ann Beattie to be among their number.

The difficulty Epstein has with Perelman (after reading over a thousand pages of the man's work) is that he knows too much about what a wretched human being the humorist was to take the requisite delight in his writing. Is the Lord High Executioner making a prejudicial ruling based on the biographical fallacy? Perhaps, but a funnyman needs his ethos as much as a prizefighter needs his reflexes. Other kinds of writers (Dionysian poets, heterosexual novelists) can survive and even capitalize on personal idiosyncrasy. "But from a humorist, alongside whom we are asked to laugh, a certain sanity, a certain decency, a certain balance is required. Even though the received wisdom in these matters instructs one to ignore the life and concentrate on the work, knowledge that such a man was fundamentally not nice does not lubricate one's laughter; quite the reverse, it can cause one to gag on the gags" (*Payments,* 355).

Perelman was an essentially bitter man who lacked a sure sense of identity. "He knew enough Yiddish to fool the gentiles—if not really enough to speak to the Jews" (*Payments,* 348). He neglected his family and badmouthed every institution he ever worked for (mostly in private, rarely raising his animus to the level of art). Like so many hacks with an artistic conscience, he "sold out" to Hollywood, took inordinate credit for the work he did there (particularly writing for the Marx Brothers), and wrote off the whole ambience as "cat vomit." Possessing a keen ear for urban speech and a sharp eye for the absurdities of everyday life, Perelman simply stretched his modest talent too thin. By the end of his life he was receiving more accolades than laughter. As a means to an end, humor can be a valuable, even essential, tool. As an end in itself, it is an incredibly demanding vocation. Few things are more embarrassing than watching a comedian "die," and Sidney Joseph Perelman did a lot of dying before he was finally relegated to the status of a national treasure.

Another national treasure from the pages of the best magazine that ever was is the highly esteemed Elwyn Brooks White. When he died, at the age of eighty-six, in October 1985, White was lionized in the nation's press as perhaps the premier prose stylist of our time. For over half a century, reporters who aspired to make an art of journalism had gone to school to E. B. White, first by reading his work in the *New Yorker,* and later by adopting his revision of William Strunk's *The Elements of Style* as a sacred text. As the long time chief editorial writer of the *New Yorker,* he did more than anyone else to establish the "tone" of that magazine. That tone, according to Epstein, "is an attempt at a compound of whimsy and common sense, modesty and decency, from which pretentiousness and heavy-handedness generally are excluded. The tone shimmers with an implied sensitivity, the chief implication being that we readers are ourselves highly sensitive characters— intelligent, good-humored, tasteful" (*Payments,* 302).

Behind the sunny persona that White projected, the Lord High Executioner discovers a confused and disturbed writer whose life and work were fraught with contradictions. He may have thought that he sounded "like Thomas Mann on the Concord and Merrimack," but Epstein believes that "it would be more accurate to say that E. B. White's essays sounded like Thoreau with hay fever and Norman Rockwell with a migraine" (*Payments,* 307–8). White "worried (in print) endlessly about the future, yet seemed only to love the past. He claimed not to have understood the meaning of life, yet was full of

advice for the living. E. B. White was a pessimistic utopian, a despairing optimist, a sour idealist, a man reputed to be a humanitarian who,
when one got right down to it, was made edgy by most human beings"
(*Payments,* 314).

The brooding essayist Epstein reveals in "E. B. White, Dark & Lite" is
certainly a more problematic figure than the one we thought we knew.
But the fact that he doesn't taste as good doesn't necessarily mean that he
is less filling. After all, when Lionel Trilling declared Frost to be a poet of
Sophoclean terror, the effect was to make the ostensible country philosopher into a much weightier literary figure. In a sense, Epstein does that
for E. B. White's venerable anthology piece "Once More to the Lake."
His analysis shows how the nostalgic, nature-loving White was also a
death-haunted elegist. (It stands to reason, after all, that nostalgia and
nature will remind any sensitive person of death.) In such an essay, the
prose master is almost a poet. Alas, such essays were few and far between.
Far too much of what E. B. White wrote was sententious propaganda for
world government, self-deprecating humor that was so mannered as to
be self-regarding, and a smug sensitivity that "can easily slide into
sentimentality" (*Payments* 316). "His was a career that strained after
significance; but despite all the honors he won, he himself was never
quite convinced he had achieved it" (*Payments,* 319). Neither is the Lord
High Executioner.

If the novel promises more than the essay, it also produces greater
disappointment when it fails to deliver. Such is the case, Epstein
argues, with the career of John Updike. "There are two jokes about
John Updike," Epstein tells us. "One is that he is an underacheever.
The other is that he is an overacheever" (*Prejudices,* 147). The superficial
confusion between Updike and John Cheever stems from their both
writing about suburban life and their both being associated with the
best magazine that ever was. But there the similarity ends. Updike
clearly has been the more versatile, productive, and ambitious of the
two. In terms of sheer prolixity, this book-a-year man has more than
fulfilled his early promise. The only thing Epstein sees standing in the
way of Updike's becoming a major novelist is the quality of his writing.

Echoing Podhoretz, the Lord High Executioner contends that Updike is too pyrotechnical a stylist. If having something to say can
improve one's style, the opposite is also true. "With Updike it appears
to be the case that the less he has to say the more he turns on style—
charm being intended to substitute for substance." ("The hero of *Marry
Me* cannot even urinate without Updike describing 'his diminishing arc

of relief' " [*Prejudices,* 150].) Updike's other great standby is graphic sex. Grown-up novelists, Epstein argues, are interested in sexual relations but allow the details to go on behind closed doors. By contrast, boy and girl novelists such as Updike, Norman Mailer, Philip Roth, Erica Jong, and Francine du Plessix Gray "are always lifting skirts, dropping trousers, adjusting ropes and pulleys, hooking up dry-cell batteries, bringing in zebras, passing out towels, what have you" (*Prejudices,* 154). Was John Updike once a promising novelist? If so, all that he has to show for that promise in a career now more than four decades old are "ornate sex and social clichés got up in velvet metaphors" (*Prejudices,* 157).

The generation of American writers after Updike has not been nearly so disappointing, if only because its literary ambitions have been so much smaller. This is the age of minimalism, and one of its most representative voices is that of the *New Yorker*'s own Ann Beattie. Epstein sees Beattie as being "from the sixties" in the same way that another writer might be from the south or from California. As products of the baby boom and postwar affluence, the generation that came of age during the sixties was both large and privileged. Because of certain educational and cultural advantages, these kids were led to believe that they were the advance guard for the millennium. They thought of themselves not only as promising but also as, "in some odd and never quite defined way, promised. . . . Because of their own intrinsic superiority, moral and intellectual, they felt they were promised a freer and richer and happier life than any known before here in America" (*Prejudices,* 162). When this turned out not to be the case, the resulting sense of disillusionment and ennui was profound.

The characters who populate Ann Beattie's fiction are upper middle-class survivors of the sixties (the "hippoisie") who have succumbed to a kind of moral and emotional lethargy. ("Things fall apart; the center, hell, in Ann Beattie's fiction not even the fringes seem to hold" [*Prejudices,* 164].) This attitude is evident not only in the lives of Beattie's characters but also in the very form of her fiction. "Chekhov instructed that if a gun appears on the wall in a scene in the first act of a play, before the play is over the gun will be fired. Not in Ann Beattie's stories; more likely the wall will disappear" (*Prejudices,* 164–65). For this reason, even Beattie's eye for detail and her ear for speech fail to involve her readers in her fiction. "While she knows a good deal about life's phenomena," Epstein writes, "she chooses to deny life's significance. In so doing she ends by denying significance to her own work, for literature is finally about the significance and not the phenomena of life. At this point in her career, Ann Beattie is the chief purveyor of her own generation's leading clichés—the L. L. Bean of what passes for sixties existentialism" (*Prejudices,* 170).

The Family Way

Having been born in 1937 and educated in the Midwest, Epstein was never a part of the New York intellectual scene in the way that Norman Podhoretz was. Although he did work for *Dissent* and is now a frequent contributor to *Commentary,* he has neither written for *Partisan Review* nor been an official member of The Family. Still, he has never questioned the importance of the New York intellectuals in shaping the literary and political culture of this country. Even when their impact has been for ill, members of The Family have exercised an almost comically disproportionate influence on what Epstein has called the verbal class. In the short run the pen may not be mightier than the sword, but its effects can be as lingering as the black death.

One of the youngest and most problematic members of The Family is the angry-and-funny-Jewish-novelist Philip Roth. One thinks of Roth in this way because his early work consists largely of his being angry and funny about being Jewish. (Making a coy allusion to the original title of *The Waste Land,* Epstein notes that Roth's gift for mimicry "allows him to do the Jews in a thousand voices" [*Prejudices,* 208].) This led to charges of self-hatred and anti-Semitism, which surfaced with Roth's first full-length work of fiction, *Goodbye Columbus,* in 1959, and reached a fever pitch with the publication of his runaway best-seller, *Portnoy's Complaint,* a decade later. But by that point, Roth's muse was beginning to move beyond ethnic humor and ethnic rage to encompass narcissism and what H. L. Mencken termed the "non-Euclidean" forms of sex. *Portnoy* was, as Epstein observes, a watershed novel. "If Berkeley was what happened to the university during the sixties, Andy Warhol what happened to contemporary art, *Portnoy's Complaint* was what happened to American Jewish fiction" (*Prejudices,* 211).

Although Epstein pays proper homage to Roth's talent, he is not amused with the turn that talent has taken. As Roth has become increasingly divorced from the real world of ordinary people, his powers of invention have become strained. It is perhaps fitting that the creator of Portnoy should have become so obsessed with sexual autobiography that he has turned novel writing into a kind of literary onanism. But it really is childish for him then to charge his readers with seeking voyeuristic kicks when they read his life into his work. "I think 'voyeuristic kick' is exactly the correct phrase," Epstein writes, "and my first response to it is that, if a writer doesn't wish to supply such kicks, perhaps he would do better not to undress before windows opening onto thoroughfares" (*Prejudices,* 214).

In yet another of his marvellously apt summary statements, Epstein compares finishing a Roth novel with the feeling of relief that a psychoanalyst must feel when knocking off for the day. "It's a small world, that of the patient—it has, really, only one person of importance in it. So, too, with Roth's novels which feel so terribly underpopulated, confined, claustral. One admires their sentences, picks up on their jokes, notes the craft that went into their making, and finishes reading them with a slight headache and a sour taste in the mouth" (*Prejudices,* 216).

A slightly older Family member who has been an even more ravenous publicity hound than Roth is Podhoretz's old buddy Norman Mailer. No more amused with Mailer than with Roth (unlike Lionel Trilling, Epstein was never really taken with the Norman invasion), the Lord High Executioner was more than ready to pronounce sentence by the time Mailer had published his long-awaited "Egyptian novel, " *Ancient Evenings.* Actually, "sentences" is more like it. "Along about page 421 of this more-than-700-page book," Epstein began composing reverse blurbs: "Insomnia sufferers, your cure is at hand." "Gives the argument for censorship a whole new lease on life." "Extremely repulsive, utterly loathsome" (*Prejudices,* 188). It is perhaps a tribute to Mailer's stature in the literary world that Epstein feels compelled to take eighteen book pages to demolish his entire career.

The thoroughness of the indictment is made all the more credible by the positive comments Epstein makes about a few of Mailer's books, especially *The Executioner's Song.* What Epstein genuinely likes about *The Executioner's Song* (Mailer's nonfiction novel about the final months in the life of condemned murderer Gary Gilmore) is that its style is so uncharacteristic of Norman Mailer, at least the Norman Mailer who has been writing since the mid-1950s. Instead, it reflects the influence of Mailer's earliest literary models, naturalists such as John Dos Passos and James T. Farrell. The egocentric rhetoric is gone. In its place is a seductively plain prose that brings to life a class of people radically different from the jet-set literati who hang out with Norman Mailer.

Epstein concludes that Mailer "is best when he is descriptive, when his imaginative sympathies are engaged. He is at his worst when he is being Norman Mailer, the modern thinker" (*Prejudices,* 201).

In his dissection of Mailer, the Lord High Executioner continually trivializes the inflated with well-timed colloquial asides. Consider this Mailerean pontification and Epstein's parenthetical response: " 'A totalitarian society makes enormous demands on the courage of men, and a partially totalitarian society makes even greater demands, for the general anxiety is greater' (tell it to Solzhenitsyn)" (*Prejudices,* 194). When he finally gets to the magnum opus itself, Epstein writes: "After forcing the spirit of his great-grandson to perform fellatio upon him—are you still with me?—he informs him (and us), lengthily about the theogony of the Egyptian gods: Ra, Amon, Maat, Osiris, Isis, Set, Horus, and, as a baseball announcer in my town has it, 'all that gang' " *Prejudices,* 202). On the next page, Epstein tells us that "too often the novel reads like something devised by Mel Brooks's Two Thousand Year Old Man—though he would have to be three thousand years old—but without the jokes" (*Prejudices,* 203).

Then there is Epstein's response to other critics who take Mailer's fascination with excrement a bit too seriously. He notes that "another admirer of the novel, George Stade, wrote in the *New Republic:* 'If you do not buy [Mailer's] notions of magic and the unconscious, of course, you will simply feel that Mailer is full of shit.' To answer a two-clause sentence in two parts: I don't, and therefore I do" (*Prejudices,* 205). Moving ever higher in the critical pantheon, the Lord High Executioner cites the most lionized of all contemporary pedagogues, Harold Bloom. The Author of *A Map of Misreading* "finds Ernest Hemingway in *Ancient Evenings,* for he reads Hemingway into the character of Ramses II and Mailer himself into that of Menenhetet I, adding that 'to have been bumbuggered by one's precursor is a sublime new variant on the sorrows of literary influence.' Clearly a critic's work is never done" (*Prejudices,* 206). It might be argued that the critic Joseph Epstein's work on *Ancient Evenings* was done when he summed up his view of the book's literary merit and its author's preoccupation with scatology by entitling his essay "Mailer Hits Bottom."

Cousins Philip and Norman may be the undisputed black sheep of the Family, but their immediate forebears included a few characters you might want to send on a long errand when company came to call. Epstein vividly remembers when he first saw a number of the uncles in the flesh. "One among them wore false teeth that, by comparison, made George Washington's dentist look like an artist. . . . Yet another looked like a Plymouth salesman down on his luck. When I was introduced to a literary critic whose work I then revered, my first instinct was to inform him that his shirt was sticking out of his trousers—except that it wasn't; it was merely the over-all effect of schlepperosity he embodied that led me to think it was. Another of these writers daintily crossed one leg over the other to reveal a sock into which was woven the figure of Donald Duck."[1] But when these slobs (none of whom is named) got behind the typewriter, they turned out work that was intellectually fastidious and stylistically elegant. They wrote for *Partisan Review,* which is Epstein's personal choice for the best magazine that ever was.

When *PR* was in its heyday, from the mid-1940s to the early 1950s, the best minds in The Family, both in America and Europe, practically invented what we now know as cultural criticism. However, too much intermarriage with the Woodstock crowd eventually contaminated the gene pool. The only thing connecting the *Partisan Review* of today with its fabled ancestor is the editorial presence of William Phillips. And therein, Epstein argues, much of the problem lies. "When the two principal editors of *PR* were Phillips and [Philip] Rahv," Epstein writes, "the magazine seemed to take on the character of Rahv; when the two principal editors were Phillips and [Richard] Poirier, it seemed to take on the character of Poirier. And now that Phillips is the sole principal editor of the magazine . . . , it seems to have scarcely any character at all " ("Polonius," 610).

Epstein made these remarks in a review of Phillips's autobiography, which he calls "Polonius Remembers the *Partisan Review.*" It is a book in which the Lord High Executioner discovers more waffling "than one is likely to find on a busy day at the International House of Pancakes" ("Polonius," 612). The waffle that seems to stick most in his craw, however, is Phillips's disowning of distinguished *PR* contributors who have moved from the trendy Left to the neoconservative Right. Recent advertisements for *Partisan Review* boast that the magazine has published such towering figures as Noam Chomsky, Morris Dickstein, Adrienne Rich, and Herbert Marcuse. But one will look in vain for the names of Sidney Hook, Norman Podhoretz, William Barrett, or Hilton Kramer. Just as Phillips has sought to minimize his own and his magazine's Communist past, he is careful not to portray it as a breeding ground for political and cultural reactionaries. "Or, as Polonius might put it, 'Neither a Communist nor an anti-Communist be' " ("Polonius," 615).

If You Can't Say Something Nice

I suspect that quite a few readers come away from a collection of Joseph Epstein's literary opinions convinced that the man subscribes to the Alice Roosevelt Longworth school of criticism. (Mrs. Longworth used to tell her dining companions, "If you can't say something nice, come sit by me.") One such reader—Louis D. Rubin, Jr.—even entitled a good-size review of *Plausible Prejudices* "Mr. Epstein Doesn't Like It." Although Mr. Rubin shares many of Mr. Epstein's specific antipathies, he is disturbed by the Lord High Executioner's seeming inability to recognize anything good on the present literary scene. In a particularly cutting remark, Rubin says of Epstein: "He disapproves of just about everything that has happened literarily since the death of Warren Gamaliel Harding [whenever someone uses Harding's full name, you know he's getting ready to lower the boom]. His manner is sometimes Menckenian; but his matter is more along the lines of the late Paul Elmer More."[2]

As an admirer of both Rubin and Epstein, I am prompted to do a William Phillips and argue that there is some truth to both sides of the argument. In his more recent book of criticism, *Partial Payments,* Epstein does say some nice things about a few writers who arrived on the scene after Harding departed from it (V. S. Naipaul, Marguerite Yourcenar, Jorge Luis Borges, Philip Larkin, and Barbara Pym, to name only those who are still living or only recently dead). Among *American novelists* who have gained fame since World War II, however, the only one who makes it into Epstein's pantheon is James Gould Cozzens.

Addressing the Lord High Executioner directly, Rubin writes: "If as seems clear you cannot find writing and writers worthy of your admiration in the places where you have been looking—the fashionable literary enclaves of the northeastern cities—then what you must do is look elsewhere."[3] Anyone who knows Rubin realizes that the elsewhere he has in mind is way down south in the land of cotton. It is perhaps significant that the only southern-born writer, living or dead, who merits an essay in either of Epstein's collections is the naturalized Manhattanite Tom Wolfe, whose writing Mr. Epstein doesn't like. Imagine a critic of sensitivity and taste who writes about John Irving and Ann Beattie while ignoring Walker Percy and Eudora Welty, and you imagine one dissatisfied customer. Writing in the provinces has its flaws, and a critic as discriminating as Epstein is likely to find them. But they are different from the flaws in the trendy books he has been reading. Variety may not ease discomfort but it can at least make the pain more interesting.

Chapter Thirteen
Positive Prejudices

If knowing what one hates is a way of learning what one loves, Joseph Epstein is a well-schooled literary critic. As Louis Rubin has pointed out, Epstein's dislikes are deeply felt and clearly articulated. However, of the thirty-six essays on individual writers to be found in *Plausible Prejudices* and *Partial Payments,* at least twenty-one are overwhelmingly positive. For every two writers he has sent to the scaffold, the Lord High Executioner has put nearly three back on the streets. Although he has probably found no subsequent writer as sublime as John R. Tunis, whose sports fiction for boys first stirred his passion for books, Epstein is more of an enthusiast for literature than a revisionist with rancor. His view of the critic's vocation is well summed up in the statement from G. C. Lichtenberg that serves as an epigraph to *Partial Payments:* "To read means to borrow; to create out of one's reading is paying off one's debts."

The Great Tradition

Was Matthew Arnold the first neoconservative critic? It is an intriguing question, even if it is one that Epstein does not raise directly in his essay "Matthew Arnold and the Resistance." If neoconservatism is primarily a philosophy of reaction (which is not the same as a reactionary philosophy), old-line preservationists such as Samuel Johnson are clearly paleoconservatives. Arnold, however, belongs to what Epstein thinks of as the Resistance. He believed that a nation's culture was a matter of utmost seriousness and that criticism existed to defend culture against vulgar taste and debased standards. Arnold was an unabashed elitist; however, his was an elitism neither of money nor family but of "the best that is known and thought in the world." If, as T. S. Eliot claimed, Arnold had turned culture into a religion, he was clearly one of its high priests.

Because Arnold spent almost his entire adult life as one of Her Majesty's school inspectors, he knew firsthand the squalid conditions in which the working classes lived and the wretched deficiencies in their education. In fact, as a critic of education he can be seen as a precursor of such contemporary neoconservatives as William Bennett and Allan Bloom. Moreover, Arnold's emphasis on high seriousness in literature was a rebuke to another cultural bane of his day—the excesses of romanticism. Although this was a pitfall from which his own early poetry was not immune, it is of the very essence of neoconservatism to be making amends for the follies of one's youth.

Because so much of what Arnold stood for is at odds with present-day academic criticism, he is a useful ally to appropriate. A critic who was deeply concerned with the condition of culture and the souls of men (albeit in a secular sense) would be appalled at the extent to which modern critical theory has separated the writer from the work and the work from reality, until—with the triumph of structuralism, semiotics, and deconstruction—"the work itself is denied any fixed reality whatsoever" (*Payments,* 27). Artistic standards and coherent critical thought are things of the past, and "a semiological study of Woody Woodpecker is the wave of the future" (*Payments,* 34). With a kind of wicked glee, Epstein imagines "Matthew Arnold reeling at a Modern Language Association meeting, in his hand a program announcing one goofy paper after another, while in the room the graduate students come and go, talking of Michel Foucault" (*Payments,* 36).

If Matthew Arnold has won Epstein's mind, his heart belongs to an American critic in the great tradition—Henry Louis Mencken. Like the young men Jake Barnes refers to in *The Sun Also Rises,* Epstein got many of his youthful likes and dislikes from reading Mencken. What is remarkable is that this was some thirty years after Hemingway wrote *The Sun Also Rises* and after Mencken himself was dead. What is even more remarkable is that Epstein's reaction to Mencken was quite similar to that of the young Richard Wright, who recalls sneaking a Mencken volume out of the Memphis library and being mesmerized by the way that Mencken used words as weapons. In his autobiography *Black Boy,* Wright recalls that "what amazed me was not what [Mencken] said, but how on earth anybody had the courage to say it" (quoted in *Payments,* 40). Even if Mencken can be neatly pigeonholed as a figure of the 1920s who spoke primarily to the young, what is one to make of the fact that young people as disparate as Joseph Epstein and Richard Wright were drawn to literature by his work?

The appeal, Epstein concludes, lay not in Mencken's opinions. By the time he had become an earnest young liberal, Epstein found

Mencken's conservatism politically objectionable. What he continued to like about the sage of Baltimore was his humor (which even at its most cynical always uplifted the spirit), the boundless energy of his prose ("Along with Ernest Hemingway, H. L. Mencken devised one of the few original and unmistakable American prose styles of the current century" [*Payments*, 42]), and something for which Epstein can find no more appropriate label than Mencken's point of view. As he has noted in many other places, Epstein agrees with V. S. Naipaul in regarding a person's point of view as something more than the sum total of his opinions.

What was Mencken's point of view? Epstein believes that it consisted of a tragic sense of life that made him a realist, a skepticism that made him the enemy of all who claimed to know the unknowable, and an essential sense of decency that made him the opposite of a hypocrite—a man who was better than he claimed to be. In his life, Mencken may have been the original cynic with a heart of gold. "Whenever Mencken registers what might be construed as an objectionable or cruel opinion," Epstein observes, "one can count on discovering acts of particular kindness that contradict that opinion. He attacks religion, then enters into friendships with nuns and ministers; he relentlessly mocks the pursuit of men by women, then, in middle life, himself marries a woman whose death within a few years is certain. . . . Although he did his best to hide it, the 'Holy Terror,' the 'Bad Boy of Baltimore,' as the press used to refer to him, appears to have been quite a good man" (*Payments*, 53).

Another of Epstein's great culture heroes is the critic and man of letters Edmund Wilson. Although he was certainly not the closet saint that Mencken turned out to be, Wilson has long since achieved a kind of secular sainthood among practicing critics. But as Epstein is quick to point out, this reverence has not carried over to the university. To the extent that Wilson is studied at all in the classroom, it is as an important minor figure in the literary history of the twenties (a friend and classmate of Fitzgerald and the like). Occasionally, his controversial essay on *The Turn of the Screw* will be cited as an example of Freudian criticism or his name will come up in connection with the politicizing of literature in the thirties. Otherwise, he is written off as an extremely learned reviewer and popularizer. In a way Wilson's fate is understandable. "His qualities are not teachable; they can merely be asserted: wide curiosity, utter seriousness, comprehensive reading, a shaping imagination, prose that without being at all idiosyncratic was nonetheless manly and personal" (*Prejudices,* 272).

Wilson's intellectual integrity and devotion to literature was so severe that he could be tactless and abrasive when dealing with his inferiors (which as a group included just about everybody). For example, to a professor who has just completed a study of his career, Wilson writes: "Though I doubt whether your book will ever get into a second printing, I may note that there are misprints on pages 18, 47, 49" (quoted in *Prejudices,* 275). Nevertheless, he could show genuine enthusiasm for work that interested him, whether or not it conformed to prevailing literary fashions. Lionel Trilling remembers with gratitude Wilson's encouragement of his book on Matthew Arnold, back in the thirties when everyone seemed swept up in radical politics and Arnold seemed hopelessly passé. These uplifting words of encouragement, Epstein notes, occurred when Trilling and Wilson ran into each other in the men's room of the New School for Social Research in New York— "impossible not to picture them, the past half-century's two most important American critics, trough to trough" (*Prejudices,* 276).

It is perhaps a tribute to Wilson's universality that his admirers come from both ends of the political spectrum. During the thirties, his flirtation with communism was as mindless as that of any intellectual dupe. Although he later recanted, Wilson once again became politically vocal in the sixties, denouncing America on the grounds that the cold war was largely a scheme to raise his income tax. Yet the essential Edmund Wilson managed to transcend occasional political looniness. Epstein agrees with Lynn in seeing the main text of *Patriotic Gore* as a moving, if unconscious, refutation of that book's crudely anti-American preface. If Wilson lacked much of a philosophical sense, he more than made up for it with a rich historical imagination. "When he was working well, which was most of the time, his criticism became strong narrative, blended with the dramatic play of ideas—and the result was literature, potent, compelling, built to endure" (*Prejudices,* 280).

Although it is important to read major writers such as Matthew Arnold, H. L. Mencken, and Edmund Wilson, they are often more useful as inspiration than as models. (People who actually try to write like Mencken, such as R. Emmett Tyrrell, editor of the *American Spectator,* quickly fall into unintentional self-parody.) Epstein believes that we can also learn from those writers who are less than major, those who stand somewhere in between the Olympians and the demigods of a season. These are what he calls special writers, "those we react to in a special, usually quite personal way, for we feel a kinship between their imaginations and our own" (*Prejudices*, 302). For Epstein, A. J. Liebling was such a writer. He was "urbane without cuteness, skeptical without sourness, and witty in a way that was at bottom serious" (*Prejudices*, 299).

Although Epstein's voice is very different from Liebling's, the stylistic virtuosity of the older writer is a quality we find in Epstein's own essays. In fact Epstein's description of Liebling's skill with the language could serve equally well for either word shark. "Like Minnesota Fats with a cue, so Liebling with an English sentence—there was nothing he couldn't make it do, including the work of three normal paragraphs. He could make a single sentence ride the crest of a classical allusion, dip down to capture a passing irony, pick up a startling analogy along the way, curl over the side for a comic touch, kiss off a serious observation, and, *plunk,* drop neatly into the pocket of a period to score a delicious original point" (*Prejudices*, 296). For Epstein's money, the best writing in the *New Yorker* came not from E. B. White, James Thurber, or Wolcott Gibbs, but from Joseph Mitchell, John Lardner, and, preeminently, Abbot Joseph Liebling. In fact, he would buy any copy of the magazine that carried a piece by Liebling even if nothing else in it interested him. Paying Liebling the highest form of personal tribute, Epstein writes: "I . . . have missed his prose more than that of any other writer who has died in my lifetime" (*Prejudices*, 302).

American Masters

A taste for both Henry James and Theodore Dreiser is a sure test of a reader's catholicity. By this measure, Joseph Epstein is something of an ultra-Montanist—if not more catholic than the Pope, at least less sectarian than Lionel Trilling (a James cultist) or Mike Gold (a party-line Dreiserian). The very different qualities that James and Dreiser represent test the limits of criticism; however, Epstein is the sort of inductive reader who believes that criticism must accommodate itself to literature rather than the other way around. In James, Epstein finds a species of writer that Dreiser was never accused of being—a great verbal athlete. (Dreiser was more like the klutz who is always chosen last in playground games.) By this Epstein means "someone who can really play the language, wringing a wide variety of effects from it, ranging over a vast field of moods, registering the most suitable modulations. The verbal athletes are the great natural writers: they have power over the language, and consciousness of this power, and joy in the consciousness" (*Payments,* 169).

Epstein notes that, as incredible as it may seem, Henry James wrote pretty much the way he talked. (By comparison, the "You-Tarzan-Me-Jane" prose style of Hemingway was pure artifice.) After Edith Wharton introduced James to Finley Peter Dunne, the creator of Mr. Dooley, Dunne commented, "What a pity it takes him so long to say anything. Everything he said was splendid but I felt like telling him all the time: 'Just 'pit it up right into Popper's hand' " (*Payments,* 164). Dunne notwithstanding, James's hesitations (Max Beerbohm called him one of the "great hesitators") were part of his personal charm and an absolutely essential means of conveying a sensibility that was so fine-grained it tended "toward shadings, subtleties, nuances, complexity" (*Payments,* 167).

In addition to James's much parodied but never successfully imitated style, Epstein is impressed with the man's personal and artistic integrity. When the editor of the *New York Tribune* claimed that James's regular cultural letter from Paris was going over the heads of his readers, James replied, "If my letters have been 'too good,' I am honestly afraid they are the poorest I can do, especially for the money" (quoted in *Payments,* 176). In his later years, when he was writing his greatest novels, James was plagued by critical indifference, public neglect, and the sort of physical and financial ills that would have sunk a lesser man; yet he never wavered in his devotion to art and his interest in life. (Epstein contrasts this heroic stoicism with the whining nihilism of James's pampered contemporary, Henry Adams.) After reading Leon Edel's four-volume edition of James's letters, Epstein concludes, "Henry James is one of those rare writers who does not seem more petty, abject, or repulsive the closer one looks into his life" (*Payments,* 184).

The same is most emphatically not true of Theodore Dreiser. In fact, petty, abject, and repulsive are precisely the words that come to mind when considering this utterly loathsome human being.

Through sharp dealing he kited up the price of his own manuscripts among collectors. He employed several literary and movie agents at the same time. He asked absolute fidelity from women, which he repaid with something akin to absolute infidelity [his *friend* Mencken said he enjoyed the sex life of a chimpanzee]. He hated capitalism and studied the stock market. The greater

the support publishers gave him the readier he was to betray them. . . . [He
was a] bore, crank, celery-juice drinker, and member of the select company of
morons who believed that Franklin Delano Roosevelt was part Jewish. (*Payments,* 277, 278)

He also wrote some of the most god-awful prose ever produced by a
supposedly major artist. And yet, in Epstein's opinion, Dreiser was one
thing more—America's greatest novelist.

The case for Dreiser's impact on literary history is easy to make. As
we have seen in Lynn's discussion of *Sister Carrie,* that novel scandalized
the keepers of public morality not so much because it depicted a woman
living in sin but because it showed her flourishing in the world rather
than departing from it. Dreiser's battle against censorship was perhaps
the one honorable activity of his life. It made possible a greater realism
in literature, especially in dealing with the two subjects most vulnerable to hypocrisy—sex and money. Epstein does not regret that that
battle was won, even if it has led to a situation in which "the
cunnilinguistic rhapsodies of John Updike and the sodomic violence of
Norman Mailer go directly to the best-seller tables" (*Payments,* 276).

It is true that Dreiser came along at a time when the Victorian
novel was dead or dying and the literary world (if not the censors) was
ready for what he had to offer. But others were writing at the same
time, and none of them effected the revolution that Dreiser did.
Epstein confesses that Dreiser's crude but undeniable power remains a
mystery to him and to criticism in general. Dreiser belongs to a select
group of world writers (Dostoyevski, Solzhenitsyn, Balzac) whose engagement with the world was so intense that their lack of stylistic
felicity seemed quite irrelevant. To Epstein's mind, novels are "the
instruments for investigating the connection between character and
destiny" (*Payments,* 263), and no American novelist before or since has
understood that as well as Dreiser. The fact that he could have been
such a sympathetic novelist and such an unsympathetic man is itself
the sort of cosmic irony that Dreiser would have understood and
appreciated. The best that Epstein can do is to suggest that "in some
artists—Flaubert, James—imagination is at the service of intelligence, while in others—Whitman, Tolstoy—intelligence is entirely at
the service of imagination. Dreiser is clearly among the others" (*Payments,* 278).

Although Epstein is contemptuous of any critical method that fails
to take a healthy interest in the lives of writers, he is also wary of the

damage that biographical politics can do to the critical enterprise. A case in point is that of Willa Cather. One of the finest regional novelists in American literature, Cather's place in the canon and the anthologies seems secure. If not quite so towering a figure as James and Dreiser or Hemingway and Fitzgerald, she was clearly at the head of the next rank. By the 1980s, however, Cather's importance was being redefined, not along literary lines, but in terms of her alleged sexual preferences. As Epstein puts it, she had been "appointed an honorary lesbian" (*Prejudices,* 303).

In his otherwise sound essay on Cather, whom he admires greatly, Epstein gets temporarily off track by arguing in a lawyerly fashion that it has never been proved beyond a reasonable doubt that Cather was a practicing lesbian. The standards of proof in literary biography, however, are closer to those of a civil than a criminal trial. Even if she was never caught in flagrante delicto, the weight of circumstantial evidence would lead most people to conclude that a woman who shared her entire adult life (and occasionally the same bedroom) with other women was of the Sapphic inclination. The scandal is not that this may have been so but that sexual politicians are now trying to use that fact for their own purposes.

Epstein sees this bit of special pleading as at least in part a consequence of the literary ethnocentricity of the sixties. If one is a black, then one is a black writer. If one is a Jew, then one is a Jewish writer. (To cross jurisdictional lines, as William Styron did in *The Confessions of Nat Turner* and *Sophie's Choice,* is simply asking for trouble.) But it is the essence of art to go beyond the givens of race, tribe, and gender. As Jane Rule argues, "What actually characterizes Willa Cather's mind is not a masculine sensibility at all but a capacity to transcend the conventions of what is masculine and what is feminine to see the more complex humanity of her characters" (quoted in *Prejudices,* 317). "To rediscover [Cather] now as a lesbian writer," Epstein concludes, "is the most efficient way to make a major novelist seem minor (*Prejudices,* 318).

If the liberal cultural trends of our day have made Willa Cather a more fashionable writer, much the opposite has happened to John Dos Passos. Along with Sinclair Lewis, Ernest Hemingway, and F. Scott Fitzgerald, Dos Passos was regarded as one of the four major American novelists of the 1920s. D. H. Lawrence said Dos Passos's *Manhattan Transfer* was "the best modern book about New York that I have ever read," and as late as 1938 Jean-Paul Sartre said flat out, "I regard Dos Passos as the greatest writer of our time" (quoted in *Prejudices,* 320).

The praise abruptly ceased after 1940, and long before Dos Passos's death in 1970, it had turned into virulent denunciation. What happened was that after his experience in the Spanish Civil War, the man whom Epstein calls "America's most unrelievedly political novelist" (*Prejudices,* 320) made an ideological U-turn from the Left to the Right.

Like Lynn, Epstein sees the reaction of the critical establishment to Dos Passos's political conversion as an example of ideological tendentiousness. But unlike Lynn, Epstein concedes that the older, leftist Dos Passos was the superior novelist. "The early Dos Passos, though every bit as doctrinaire as the later, was at least split in his novelistic preoccupations between anger at what he deemed the enemy and sympathy for the victims. . . . In the later Dos Passos, sympathy is drained, the interest in characters becomes chiefly an interest in their roles as targets for his contempt. The pamphleteer is in the saddle, and the novelist has all but disappeared" (*Prejudices,* 328). The lesson Epstein draws from this is not that Dos Passos should have remained a leftist but that doctrinaire politics of any stripe can be deadly to the sensibility of an artist. The most painful irony of all is that John Dos Passos, who set out to chronicle the life of his time, ended instead as "part of the sad story himself" (*Prejudices, 329*).

Jewels in the Crown

The phenomenon of literary expatriation presupposes that living in another country will be more hospitable to the artistic calling than staying at home. (This was particularly true for American writers during the 1920s, when a favorable exchange rate and the absence of Prohibition made it much cheaper to live the good life in Europe than in America.) In particular, the Anglophilic strain in American artists holds that in everything from the Rolls Royce to the Old Vic, the mother country is still a class act. This has probably been less true since World War II (Epstein thinks it unlikely that in today's world a Henry James or T. S. Eliot would be singing "Rule Britannia" at high tea); however, England and its waning empire is still capable of producing writers from whom Americans can learn a thing or two. The most recent additions to this company include Philip Larkin and V. S. Naipaul. Among earlier generations, there were W. Somerset Maugham and the inimitable Evelyn Waugh.[1]

To call Waugh inimitable is not to say that there haven't been plenty of artists who have tried to imitate him. Waugh's influence encompasses not only high art but also popular culture. (Epstein contends that "such British group efforts as 'Beyond the Fringe,' 'That Was the Week That Was,' and, on a cruder level, 'Monty Python's Flying Circus' are quite unthinkable without the precedent of Waugh" [*Payments*, 80].) It would be only a slight exaggeration to say that Waugh invented black comedy for the Anglo-American literary tradition. In what Epstein regards as "the single most penetrating sentence in all the criticism I have read of Waugh's work," V. S. Pritchett writes, "His early books spring from the liberating notion that human beings are mad; the war trilogy [*Sword of Honour*], a work of maturity, draws on the meatier notion that the horrible thing about human beings is that they are sane" (quoted in *Payments*, 95).

Analyzing Waugh's wonderful style captures only part of what made him such a distinctive writer. The other, and perhaps more essential, part is his sensibility as a human being. That is generally what his would-be imitators fail to master, either because they fail to grasp it or because it is so unfashionable that they hope they can do without it. Waugh could satirize the present so adeptly because he hated it so passionately. He was the perfect embodiment of Kenneth Minogue's definition of a reactionary: "someone with a clear and comprehensive vision of an ideal world we have lost." Waugh even refused to vote in general elections on the grounds that "the Conservative Party had never put back the clock a single second" (quoted in *Payments*, 85).

Perhaps Waugh's most notable rebellion against the modern world was his conversion to Roman Catholicism. Early in life, he concluded that there was no middle ground between Catholicism and chaos and chose the former as a stay against the latter. Although his religion failed to make him a very pleasant human being (he was definitely not the sort of writer Holden Caulfield would want to phone up on a whim), Waugh once said to his friend Nancy Mitford, "You have no idea how much nastier I would be if I were not a Catholic. Without supernatural aid I would hardly be a human being" (quoted in *Payments*, 87). What Waugh might have been without supernatural aid is a fascinating question. It is known that he would never show up at Cyril Connolly's house when Dylan Thomas was around. The reason, Waugh's biographer Christopher Sykes explains, is that Thomas wore checked suits like Waugh's, spoke in parody and fantasy like Waugh, was small and portly like Waugh, and often drank like Waugh. "In

Thomas, Evelyn Waugh saw a caricature of himself. 'He's exactly what I might have been,' Waugh told Sykes, 'if I had not become a Catholic' " (*Payments,* 88).

Although Epstein pays a kind of ritual homage to the great figures of high modernism (especially Proust), he seems to prefer writers such as Waugh, who were largely untouched by modernism, or those such as Philip Larkin, who were in active rebellion against it. To a large extent, W. Somerset Maugham fell into both categories. Born in 1874, he was three years younger than Proust and eight years older than Joyce. Thus, he was precisely the right age to have been caught up in the currents of literary modernism that swept Europe in the early decades of the twentieth century. Instead, he seems more a throwback to an earlier age. Without intending any disapproval, Epstein refers to Maugham's most popular work, *Of Human Bondage* (1915), as "the best nineteenth-century novel written well into the twentieth century" (*Payments,* 205). What Maugham lacked in technical innovation and pure imagination he made up for with common sense (one of Epstein's highest praise words) and incredible industry. His bibliography includes twenty-eight books of fiction, twelve of nonfiction, and thirty produced plays.

Although he had many admirers among writers and critics, Maugham has almost never been taught in the university and is consistently belittled by highbrow critics whenever they condescend to mention him at all. Epstein speculates that this was because Maugham was an affront to such critics and everything they believed in. Going against the grain of modernism and its celebration of difficulty, he preferred "instead to write as plainly as possible about complex things." The superstars of modernism always managed to keep the professional explicators gainfully employed. "In an idle fantasy," Epstein muses, "I sometimes think of these writers—Joyce and Eliot and Yeats and Kafka and the rest—mounted on motorcycles in a parade up the Champs Élysées, a critic or two sitting in a small sidecar attached to each cycle, beaming with pleasure at being allowed along for the ride." Maugham's crime was that he kept no sidecar. In what Epstein himself admits is a rather abrupt shift in metaphor, he imagines each of Maugham's books carrying "a small message, à la the surgeon general's warning on cigarette packages: "No explanation, explication, or exegesis required. Read on without prolegomenon" (*Payments,* 203).

Such a warning (one is reminded of Mark Twain's epigraph to *Adventures of Huckleberry Finn*) would also be appropriate for the collected poems of Philip Larkin. However, the premodernist traditionalism that

Larkin exemplifies is even more singular than that of Maugham, if only because Larkin was nearly fifty years Maugham's junior and wrote in verse. In fact, Larkin's career was the antithesis of what we have come to expect from twentieth-century poetry. To understand Epstein's admiration for Larkin it is helpful to understand his contempt for what has happened to poetry in our time. That contempt is aptly expressed in the title of his August 1988 *Commentary* essay "Who Killed Poetry?" Not surprisingly, Epstein's polemical answer to his own rhetorical question is "the poets themselves."

As with fiction, Epstein appreciates the contributions of the early modern poets—Eliot, Williams, Frost, Stevens, Cummings, Auden. He grew up practically worshiping them. At times, some of these poets may have been more difficult than was necessary, but they had an authentic vision. Although they certainly did not enjoy the mass popularity of a Longfellow or a Tennyson, educated people felt that it was important to read their work. Perhaps just as important is that the early modern poets were not primarily academics. Several were editors; Williams was a physician, Stevens an insurance executive, Eliot a banker.

Today, the vast majority of publishing poets make their living teaching creative writing in colleges and universities. In America alone, there are more than two hundred and fifty universities with creative writing programs, "which means that they not only train aspiring poets but hire men and women who have published poetry to teach them. Many of these men and women go from being students in one writing program to being teachers in another—without, you might say, their feet, metrical or anatomical, having touched the floor."[2] These poets read and comment on each other's work as it is published in magazines and by university presses that are heavily funded by private foundations and government endowments. What we have in effect is an insulated self-perpetuating clerisy maintained by a new form of aristocratic patronage. When poets became professionals, their poetry ceased to be of much interest outside the profession.

Philip Larkin belonged to an older tradition. He was a professional librarian who steered clear of the lecture platform and the creative writing workshop. (His friend Kingsley Amis once noted that everything that has gone wrong with the world since World War II can be summed up in the word "workshop.") Larkin believed that the artist should be concerned with both his material and his audience. While an excessive concern with audience can lead one to be a mere entertainer, most modern poets have made the opposite error and lost sight of their audience altogether. Larkin regarded this as "the aberration of modernism, that blighted all the arts." Against such aberration he extolled something he called "The Pleasure Principle."

Larkin held that "at bottom poetry, like all art, is inextricably bound up with giving pleasure, and if a poet loses his pleasure-seeking audience he has lost the only audience worth having, for which the dutiful mob that signs on every September is no substitute" (quoted in "Poetry," 17). Larkin saw a similar perversion running through modernist jazz, painting, and poetry (as represented by Parker, Picasso, and Pound). "I dislike such things," he wrote, "not because they are new, but because they are irresponsible exploitations of technique in contradiction of human life as we know it" (quoted in *Payments,* 144). Larkin's own poetry was very much concerned with human life as we know it. "T. S. Eliot, writing about Andrew Marvell, said that the poet possesses the ability to make the familiar strange and the strange familiar. But Larkin did something rather different: he made the familiar important" (*Payments,* 146).

Louis Rubin complains that in *Plausible Prejudices* all of the writers Epstein likes are not only older (he calls them "The Older Crowd") but also dead. The same is largely true of *Partial Payments,* where most of the tribute essays could easily double as obituaries. The exception that proves the rule is Epstein's laudatory discussion of V. S. Naipaul, the Anglo-Indian novelist who is described as "far and away the most talented, the most truthful, the most honorable writer of his generation" (*Payments,* 386). Should anyone think that that is damning with faint praise, Epstein compares Naipaul with Joseph Conrad, Henry James, Thomas Mann, Milan Kundera, and Aleksandr Solzhenitsyn. He believes that Naipaul's *A House for Mr. Biswas* (1961) is "as great a novel . . . as any written by a living novelist" (*Payments,* 369) and that Naipaul is "a being that not even Henry James, in all the richness of his imagination, could have anticipated" (*Payments,* 368).

Although Epstein pays homage to Naipaul as a stylist, he contends that "style, for Naipaul, has always meant not a way of arranging words in sentences but a way of seeing the world around one" (*Payments,* 379). Not surprisingly, the way that Naipaul sees the world is quite congenial to Epstein and quite infuriating to the literary Left. As a native of Trinidad, Naipaul's provenance is the third world; however, he is too much of a realist to align himself sentimentally with third world liberation movements. He knows only too well the barbarism usually associated with such movements. In fact, Naipaul may be the only living writer of stature who can speak of "barbarian peoples" without immediately being branded a racist. But, as Epstein is quick to point out, it is not "only, or even chiefly, the dark-skinned who are barbarians in Naipaul's work" (*Payments*, 374). His novels are so devastating in their depiction of white revolutionary camp followers that when, at the conclusion of *Guerrillas*, one "is gruesomely raped and murdered by a failed black revolutionary at the end of his spiritual tether" the reader finds this act, "if not warranted, understandable." As a result, Epstein calls this "perhaps the most terrifying single scene of violence in a serious contemporary novel" (*Payments*, 375).

It is in *Guerrillas* that a Naipaul character observes that a great many opinions do not necessarily add up to a point of view. What Epstein most reveres about Naipaul is that his various opinions add up to a compelling point of view—a conservatism that is more tragic than polemical. In delineating Naipaul's "almost excruciating sense of the perilousness of civilization," Epstein writes, "he cannot resist underscoring that near a golf course laid out in the administrative city of Yamoussoukro in the Ivory Coast, crocodiles are kept and fed live chickens. The power of day, in the places Naipaul visits, is perpetually battling the power of night. The bush is silently growing back, the sands shifting, the wild grass popping through the crevices in the cement, all inexorably mocking the notion that modernization is tantamount to civilization" (*Payments*, 377). It is with such nightmare images that the conservative imagination writes the history of our times.

Chapter Fourteen
In Defense of Rancor

If ideas have consequences, what are the cultural consequences of neoconservative criticism? To ask that question, of course, begs the larger question of whether there is such a thing as neoconservative criticism. Podhoretz, Lynn, and Epstein are certainly engaging and provocative writers, as are the lesser lights who cover the literary scene for *Commentary,* the *American Scholar,* and the *New Criterion.*[1] But it is not self-evident that their many opinions add up to a point of view that is distinctively neoconservative. We think we know what a political neoconservative is, but the term has not been around long enough in literary circles to take on a definite meaning. Still, I think Sanford Pinsker was on to something when he identified a new species of criticism on the cultural landscape. And, without endorsing the conclusions he draws, I think he was also on to something when he characterized this species of criticism as "revisionism with rancor."

Making much the same point as Pinsker, Mark Schechner wrote in his review of Joseph Epstein's *Ambition:*

> The prose of embattlement, which is vital to the mythos of neoconservatism, serves nicely to mask the self-congratulation of the top dog. More self-assured conservatives, who didn't arrive at the metaphysics of self-interest by tortuous paths from the City University of New York or its equivalents (for Epstein it seems to have been the anti-poverty program in Arkansas), have no need for the excesses of the adversary or counter-cultures to justify their principles, which would be quite the same no matter what barbarities were in vogue in Berkeley or at *The New York Review of Books.*[2]

After we discount the Marxist polemics, the kernel of truth here is that for many readers the literary critics commonly identified as neoconservatives seem always to be on the attack.

Strictly speaking, this is an unfair judgment. As we have seen, Joseph Epstein's two books of literary essays hand out a third again as much praise as censure. For Podhoretz's *The Bloody Crossroads,* the mix is no worse than even. It is true that Lynn's *The Air-Line to Seattle* is a

148

pretty sour tome, but his biographies of Howells and Hemingway display a sensitive appreciation of their subjects. It could be that the neoconservatives are simply more convincing as pit bulls than as lap dogs. I suspect, though, that it is neither tone nor politics that keeps many sensitive readers from giving more than two cheers for the neoconservative critics. The problem is that in the contemporary books they choose to discuss, there always seems to be a hidden agenda. With Podhoretz it is fighting communism; with Lynn it is reclaiming the American literary canon; with Epstein it is debunking whatever happens to be the current literary fashion. These are all worthy goals; however, there are contemporary books worth reading that will further none of them. Must a living writer wave a red flag at the neoconservatives in order to get their attention?

In comparison to the many virtues of the neoconservative critics, these shortcomings may seem like mere nit-picking. Were Podhoretz, Lynn, and Epstein not on the scene, today's general level of critical prose would be even more deadly. Nor would I want to see critics of a conservative sensibility retreat to aestheticism and leave the social and political dimensions of literature for only leftists to comment on. Nevertheless, I think the neoconservatives do a disservice to their own cause when they choose to write almost exclusively about the fashionable literature of the day, even when their criticism is exactly on target. The problem is that in writing so incessantly about such figures as John Irving and Robert Stone or Malcolm Cowley and Leo Marx, Epstein and Lynn only confirm the notion that these are the important writers and critics of our time. (Except for his feud with Gore Vidal, Podhoretz usually doesn't waste his time with the second rate.) To believe this is to believe that an admittedly gloomy literary scene is nearly hopeless. In the midst of all the garbage that is being published today, some promising literature and scholarship can be found if one looks west of the Hudson and south of the New Jersey Turnpike.

In his review of *Plausible Prejudices,* William H. Pritchard paid Joseph Epstein a pointed compliment by writing, "Although [Epstein] asserts that criticism is in decline, it cannot be in decline merely, when provocative critics like himself are on the scene."[3] The positive value of the revisionism-with-rancor crowd is precisely this: they serve as models of what critical prose is capable of being. At the most basic level that simply means writing well. Like Somerset Maugham, the neoconservatives are strong on clarity, simplicity, and euphony. It is an irony worth noting that so many academic critics fail in their pedagogical function because they are either unable or unwilling to make complex ideas clear and simple. Perhaps they have gone soft from having to pitch their message to a captive audience. What a pleasure it is to turn away from the murky prose of the academic journals to open an issue of *Commentary* or the *American Scholar.* Like all good writers of critical prose, the neoconservatives assume an audience that is highly intelligent but easily bored.

To use a fairly mundane metaphor, winning and keeping an audience is like selling a product. (Style may not be character but it sure as hell is ethos.) To sell that product, one must first believe in it. For a critic that means believing in himself and in his own point of view. One of the reasons academic criticism is frequently so boring is that it spends too much time hedging and waffling. A critic who is not sufficiently intelligent and well-read to be justifiably confident of his own judgment should look for another line of work. The neoconservatives are sometimes wrong but never in doubt. (That can infuriate those who disagree with them, but at least the infuriators know that the infuriatees have been listening.) Another thing the neoconservatives know that your typical scholar-squirrel has forgotten is that criticism involves both explication and evaluation. No matter how ingenious it is, an explication that makes a work of literature more obscure rather than less so is worthless. The critic who explicates, however brilliantly, and fails to judge has left his job only half done. In an age of aesthetic relativism, it is so much safer to deconstruct texts than to correct taste.

Of the three figures considered in this book, Norman Podhoretz probably has the keenest analytical ability. The brand of cultural commentary Lionel Trilling espoused may be the dominant influence on his critical method, but when Podhoretz writes about literature as literature, one is reminded that he also studied under Frank Raymond Leavis. Podhoretz combines explication and discrimination to show *how* a particular work either succeeds or fails. His taste and judgment are not always reliable (witness his nearly wholesale dismissal of Southern literature), but his opinions invariably strike one as more than just plausible prejudices. He made many cogent observations about the contemporary literary scene when he was reviewing books regularly in the fifties. If he should ever leave the "bloody crossroads" to explore those byways where literature and politics do not meet, he could certainly turn the trick again. It may be that Podhoretz is F. R. Leavis's most gifted living disciple, along with being a much more engaging writer than the master himself.

Kenneth S. Lynn is the most venturesome member of the trio. It is relatively easy to be original when one is reviewing the latest books before the ink is dry. Lynn's turf, however, is the American literary canon. When writing about figures as well known as Mark Twain and Hemingway, one has basically two paths to originality: apply some arcane critical theory to otherwise familiar works or argue that the existing critical consensus is all wet. Lynn has taken the latter route, arguing that we like the right authors for the wrong reasons (or, as in the case of Emerson, the wrong ones for the wrong reasons). Huck Finn wasn't a nineteenth-century hippie but an incipient mama's boy eager to return to the Widow Douglas. Hemingway was neither a he-man nor an existentialist loner, but a happy warrior who imagined himself a lesbian. What is remarkable is that Lynn writes with such learning and chutzpah that he makes even the most seemingly outlandish theories sound plausible. Unlike Podhoretz and Epstein, he has proven himself capable of writing the big book that is more than just a blown-up essay. In the process, he has helped to restore the sagging reputation of Howells (a hazard of old fortunes?) and to change the direction of Hemingway studies.

As a stylist, Joseph Epstein runs with some pretty fast company. Those who wish to praise his familiar essays are always comparing him with Hazlitt, Lamb, Orwell, Montaigne, Pascal, and John Leonard (as Senator Claghorn would say, "That was a joke, son"). Even Sanford Pinsker can't help liking the laid-back Epstein, saying that "he can toss off a familiar essay with the panache we generally associate with English, rather than American, writers."[4] Even though Epstein gets tougher and crankier when he is writing about literature than when he is being Calvin Trillin in academic tweed, he is a consistently witty guy. He has the knack of writing about very serious subjects in an engagingly informal way. His wit, metaphorical whimsy, colloquialisms, contractions, and examples from popular culture make his prose seem natural and unaffected. Epstein is probably the least stuffy literary critic writing today. Given his critical stance, he just about has to be. He is not primarily a political thinker like Podhoretz or a literary historian like Lynn, but an old-fashioned moralist. I cannot think of a single one of his critical essays where moral considerations are not an essential part of the judgment he renders. But because of his considerable stylistic charm, Epstein can make you believe that the moral evaluation of literature is the most fun you can have with your clothes on.

That still leaves the question of whether the neoconservative critics are operating on philosophical assumptions that make them distinctive. We know that they are not leftists, but is there a paleoconservative brand of criticism with which they are at odds? That would be the case if there is a school of criticism that grounds its antipathy to the Left in religious rather than rationalist principles and envisions the good life in agrarian rather than industrial terms. Although not confined to any particular region or nationality, such a tradition has always been strong in the American South. The Agrarian manifesto *I'll Take My Stand* raises the Luddite sensibility Podhoretz so detested in F. R. Leavis to the level of a metaphysical principle. As a movement for social reform, Agrarianism is simply a footnote in the history of American eccentricity. As an essentially poetic means of apprehending the proper relationship of God, man, art, and society, it remains a powerful myth. As Leslie Fiedler has noted, "The manifestos of the Agrarians tell the kind of lie which illuminates the truth of the fiction of Faulkner and Warren and Bishop, even as the Marxist manifestos tell the kind of lie which illuminates the truth of the novels of Nathanael West and Henry Roth."[5]

To use Fiedler's terminology, the truth of the Agrarian lie continues to illuminate much Southern literature, as well as the kind of criticism one finds in the *Sewanee* and *Southern* reviews and such broadly based magazines as the *Southern Partisan* and *Chronicles of Culture.* When Russell Kirk, M. E. Bradford, Joseph Sobran, Clyde Wilson, J. O. Tate, and other admirers of Richard Weaver write for *National Review,* the Agrarian strain of paleoconservative criticism ceases to be just a regional oddity. Over against this tradition, we have the twice-born Marxists who would have written for *Partisan Review* in the thirties had they been of age then. If the neoconservatives are the lost sheep of the Marxist fold, the third- and fourth-generation Agrarians have never strayed far from their spiritual home.

Following in the footsteps of Joyce's Stephen Dedalus, many twentieth-century literary folk see art as what we have instead of God. Is this true of neoconservatives? It is certainly possible for a neoconservative to be devoutly religious, but it is hardly necessary. M. E. Bradford calls his review of *The Bloody Crossroads* "The Vocation of Norman Podhoretz"[6] and reminds us that in addition to studying under Trilling and Leavis, Podhoretz had once been a student at the Jewish Theological Seminary. One can detect in his anticommunism a transferred sense of religious fervor and vocation (a bloody crossroads instead of a bloody cross?). When T. S. Eliot set out to correct taste, it was always with reference to a transcendent source of meaning. The same was true of C. S. Lewis and Jacques Maritain. One would not make the same claim of Podhoretz, Epstein, and Lynn.

It is ironic that the single greatest hero of the neoconservatives is probably Aleksandr Solzhenitsyn, a man whose vision is paleoconservative if not downright paleolithic. He is an ardent Russian Orthodox Christian with a precapitalist view of society. The tendency among Western intellectuals has been to admire his courageous battle against Soviet tyranny while condescending to the very beliefs that made that battle possible. To his credit, Podhoretz does not take that easy way out. Instead, he argues that "whether or not one believes in God, and whether or not one believes that Solzhenitsyn is an instrument of the divine will, *his* belief has produced those 'clear effects' to which William James pointed as the 'pragmatic' test of a genuine religious experience" (*BC*, 201). And later, Podhoretz concedes that Solzhenitsyn achieves a kind of superhuman selflessness in *The Gulag Archipelago*, where he fulfills his prophetic vocation by becoming a vessel for powers beyond the mere craft of writing. No critic who regarded art as an adequate substitute for faith would have made such an admission.

The usefulness of any form of literary criticism lies in what it says about the means of art. Its ultimate seriousness lies in what it conceives to be the ends of art. The neoconservative critics know a good deal about artistic means and even demonstrate a mastery of those means in their writing. What is more important, the rancor of their revisionism is based on the belief that literature is not its own excuse for being. What we choose to revere in forms of expression says quite a bit about who and what we are. When the neoconservatives attack the tawdry and meretricious, it is because they think that people ought to be better than tawdry and meretricious. They may write like smart alecks and wise guys, but they are profoundly serious in their intentions. Some think the neoconservatives could look a bit harder and farther for signs of health in our culture. Still others would say that the only true way to leave the Finland Station is to seek the Heavenly City. But the healthy don't need a doctor, and those who cast out demons are already on the side of the angels.

Notes and References

Chapter One

1. See Sanford Pinsker, "Revisionism with Rancor: The Threat of the Neoconservative Critics," *Georgia Review* 38 (Summer 1984): 243.

2. Writing in the fall 1979 issue of *Commonsense*, a publication of the Republican National Committee, Jeane Kirkpatrick explained why she and fellow neoconservatives were not yet ready to join the Republican party. According to Kirkpatrick, the GOP had not articulated "any inclusive vision of the public good that reflects concern for the well-being of the whole community" (quoted in *Current Biography Yearbook, 1981,* ed. Charles Moritz [New York: H. W. Wilson, 1981], 257).

3. Stephen J. Tonsor, "Why I Too am Not a Neoconservative," *National Review,* 20 June 1986, 55.

4. Dan Himmelfarb, "Conservative Splits," *Commentary,* May 1988, 56.

5. Ibid., 56.

6. Ibid., 56.

7. See M. E. Bradford, "The Lincoln Legacy: A Long View," *Remembering Who We Are: Observations of a Southern Conservative* (Athens: University of Georgia Press, 1985), 143–56.

8. Norman Podhoretz, *Breaking Ranks: A Political Memoir* (New York: Harper & Row, 1979); hereafter cited in the text as *BR.*

9. Norman Podhoretz, *The Bloody Crossroads: Where Literature and Politics Meet* (New York: Simon & Schuster, 1986); hereafter cited in the text as *BC.*

10. Joseph Epstein, *Plausible Prejudices: Essays on American Writing* (New York: Norton, 1985), and *Partial Payments: Essays on Writers and Their Lives* (New York: Norton, 1989); hereafter cited in the text as *Prejudices* and *Payments,* respectively.

11. This essay was republished in Lewis A. Coser and Irving Howe, eds., *The New Conservatives* (New York: Quadrangle, 1974), 9–28.

12. Joseph Epstein, "The Rise of the Verbal Class," *Harper's,* March 1984, 80. For a fuller discussion of the evolution of Epstein's political views, see his contribution to "Liberalism and the Jews," *Commentary,* January 1980, 34–37.

Chapter Two

1. Norman Podhoretz, *Making It* (New York: Random House, 1967), 37; hereafter cited in text as *M.I.*

2. The closest Podhoretz came to such an experience was when he attended a political dinner in the sixties, where he first heard the United States compared to Nazi Germany. He regards that evening as the opening phase of his break with the Left: "[W]hat finally alienated me from the radical movement of the '60s was its hatred of America." See his contribution to *Second Thoughts: Former Radicals Look Back at the Sixties,* ed. Peter Collier and David Horowitz (Lanham, Md.: Madison Books, 1989), 193.

3. Norman Podhoretz, *Doings and Undoings: The Fifties and After in American Writing* (New York: Farrar, Straus & Giroux, 1964), 248; hereafter cited in the text as *DU.*

4. Given the fact that most American blacks already have some white blood in their veins, this would hardly seem an ideal solution. As Ralph Ellison pointed out to Podhoretz, the only result of increased miscegenation in American society "would be to increase the number of 'colored' children" (*BR*, 132).

5. Norman Podhoretz, *The Present Danger: Do We Have the Will to Reverse the Decline in American Power* (New York: Simon & Schuster, 1980); hereafter cited in the text as *PD.*

Chapter Three

1. Gore Vidal, "The Empire Lovers Strike Back," *Nation,* 22 March 1986, 350.

2. When Joseph Sobran, a conservative syndicated columnist and an editor of *National Review,* made apparently anti-Semitic statements, William Buckley disassociated himself and his magazine from those sentiments. For Podhoretz's account of the Vidal and Sobran controversies, see "The Hate That Dare Not Speak Its Name," *Commentary,* November 1986, 21–32.

Chapter Four

1. For Podhoretz's discussion of the philosophical attitudes expressed in contemporary fiction, see his essay "The New Nihilism and the Novel" (*DU,* 159–78).

Chapter Five

1. Joseph Epstein contends that "everyone has opinions—some correct, some incorrect—but not everyone has a point of view: a standpoint, a perspective, from which to view the world going on about him" (*Familiar Territory:*

Observations on American Life [New York: Oxford University Press, 1979], vii; hereafter cited in the text as *FT*).

2. See Conor Cruise O'Brien, Trop de Zele," *New York Review of Books,* 9 October 1986, 11–12, 14.

3. Saul Bellow, *Mr. Sammler's Planet* (New York: Viking, 1970), 42.

4. Orwell did publish in *Commentary* during the 1940s, when the magazine still shared the liberal anti-Communist consensus of the Western world.

5. Conor Cruise O'Brien contends that "the only intellectual who clearly exercised a significant influence in bringing about the defeat of Jimmy Carter and the election of Ronald Reagan was that eminent paleoconservative scholar, Imam Khomeini" (O'Brien, 12).

Chapter Six

1. Joseph Epstein, ed., *Masters: Portraits of Great Teachers* (New York: Basic Books, 1981); hereafter cited in the text as *Masters.*

2. Joseph Epstein, *Ambition: The Secret Passion* (New York: Dutton, 1980); hereafter cited in the text as *ASP.*

3. Kenneth S. Lynn, *The Dream of Success: A Study of the Modern American Imagination* (Boston: Little, Brown, 1955); hereafter cited in the text as *DS.*

4. Kenneth S. Lynn, *The Air-Line to Seattle* (Chicago: University of Chicago Press, 1983); hereafter cited in the text as *AS.*

5. Kenneth S. Lynn, *Visions of America: Eleven Literary Historical Essays* (Westport, Conn.: Greenwood Press, 1973); hereafter cited in the text as VA.

Chapter Seven

1. Kenneth S. Lynn, *Hemingway* (New York: Simon & Schuster, 1987); hereafter cited in the text as *H.*

2. Kenneth S. Lynn, *Mark Twain and Southwestern Humor* (Boston: Little, Brown, 1959), and *William Dean Howells: An American Life* (New York: Harcourt, Brace, Jovanovich, 1971); hereafter cited in the text as *MT* and *WDH,* respectively.

3. On the occasion of the centennial of *Huckleberry Finn,* Norman Mailer "reviewed" the book as if it were coming out today, citing as "influences" such writers as Sinclair Lewis, John Dos Passos, and John Steinbeck, and such novels as *The Adventures of Augie March, The Catcher in the Rye, Deliverance,* and *Why Are We in Vietnam?* See Norman Mailer, "Huckleberry Finn, Alive at 100," *New York Times Book Review,* 9 December 1984, 1, 36–37.

4. Although it was also the birthplace of poet James Wright, Martins Ferry and the surrounding region are best known for producing sports greats such as John Havlicek, Joe and Phil Niekro, Lou and Alex Groza, and Bill Mazeroski. In the early 1980s, when writer Peter Davis wanted to study the

most typical American town he could find, he settled on Hamilton, Ohio. See Davis's *Hometown* (New York: Simon & Schuster, 1982).

5. John Seelye, "The Rise of William Dean Howells," *New Republic*, 3 July 1971, 23.

Chapter Eight

1. Cleanth Brooks, R. W. B. Lewis, and Robert Penn Warren, "Ralph Waldo Emerson," *American Literature: The Makers and the Making*, vol. 1 (New York: Saint Martin's Press, 1973), 670.

2. Harold Bloom, "Mr. America," *New York Review of Books*, 22 November 1984, 19.

3. According to Lynn, the principal culprit was C. Vann Woodward, the liberal Southern historian who edited the most nearly definitive edition of Mrs. Chesnut's "diary" in 1981.

4. For a fuller discussion of this concept, see Frederick Turner, "Cultivating the American Garden," *Harper's*, August 1985, 45–52.

5. See Aldous Huxley, "Wordsworth in the Tropics," *Do What You Will* (London: Chatto & Windus, 1929), 113–29.

Chapter Nine

1. See Edmund Wilson, *The Wound and the Bow* (New York: Oxford University Press, 1947), 214–15; Malcolm Cowley, "Nightmare and Ritual in Hemingway," in *Hemingway: A Collection of Critical Essays*, ed. Robert P. Weeks (Englewood Cliffs, N.J.: Prentice-Hall, 1962), 40–55; and Philip Young, *Ernest Hemingway: A Reconsideration*, 2d ed. (University Park: Pennsylvania State University Press, 1966), 43–48.

2. See Malcolm Cowley, "Hemingway's Wound—and Its Consequences for American Literature," *Georgia Review*, 38 (Summer 1984): 223–39.

3. Ernest Hemingway, *A Moveable Feast* (New York: Scribner's, 1970), 76.

4. Frederick Crews, "Pressure under Grace," *New York Review of Books*, 13 August 1987, 30.

5. Hemingway had wanted to include "Up in Michigan" in the original edition of *In Our Time* (1925) but dropped it when his publisher, Horace Liveright, objected to its frank depiction of sexual intercourse. From 1938 on, this story has preceded the other selections from *In Our Time* in editions of Hemingway's collected stories.

6. See Kenneth G. Johnston, "Hemingway's 'Out of Season' and the Psychology of Errors," *Critical Essays on Hemingway's "In Our Time,"* ed. Michael S. Reynolds (Boston: G.K. Hall, 1983), 227–34.

7. See, for example, Virgil Hutton, "The Short Happy Life of Ma-

comber," *The Short Stories of Ernest Hemingway: Critical Essays,* ed. Jackson J. Benson (Durham, N.C.: Duke University Press), 239–50.

8. See Edmund Wilson, "Ernest Hemingway: Bourdon Gauge of Morale," *The Portable Edmund Wilson,* ed. Lewis M. Dabney (New York: Viking, 1983), 115–24.

Chapter Ten

1. J. D. Salinger, *The Catcher in the Rye* (New York: Bantam, 1964), 18.

2. Joseph Epstein, *Once More around the Block: Familiar Essays* (New York: Norton, 1987), 181; hereafter cited in the text as *OMB*.

3. Joseph Epstein, *The Middle of My Tether* (New York: Norton, 1983), 113; hereafter cited in the text as *MMT*.

Chapter Eleven

1. This argument is essentially an industrial age variation on John Adams's famous observation, "I must study politics and war that my sons have the liberty to study mathematics and philosophy. My sons ought to study mathematics and philosophy . . . in order to give their children a right to study painting, poetry, music, architecture, statuary, tapestry, and porcelain" (quoted in *ASP,* 171).

2. Garry Wills, *Bare Ruined Choirs* (Garden City, N.Y.: Doubleday, 1972), 5.

3. James Wolcott, "Son of 'Making It,' " *New Republic,* 24 January 1981, 34–36.

4. Ibid., 36.

5. George Orwell, "Politics and the English Language," *Shooting an Elephant and Other Essays* (New York: Harcourt Brace, 1950), 77.

Chapter Twelve

1. Joseph Epstein, "Polonius Remembers the *Partisan Review,*" *Sewanee Review* 92 (Fall 1984): 607; hereafter cited in the text as "Polonius."

2. Louis D. Rubin, Jr., "Mr. Epstein Doesn't Like It," *Sewanee Review* 94 (Winter 1986): 114.

3. Ibid., 117.

Chapter Thirteen

1. Epstein also likes the novelist Barbara Pym and the essayist Max Beerbohm but can manage only "One Cheer for E. M. Forster." His discussions of all three of these figures can be found in *Payments.*

2. Joseph Epstein, "Who Killed Poetry?" *Commentary,* August 1988, 14; hereafter cited in the text as "Poetry."

Chapter Fourteen

1. A neoconservative cultural journal founded by the art critic Hilton Kramer.
2. Mark Schechner, "The Ford in Our Past," *Nation,* 17 January 1981, 56.
3. Quoted on the dustjacket of *Payments.*
4. Pinsker, "Revisionism with Rancor," 250.
5. Leslie Fiedler, *The Collected Essays of Leslie Fiedler,* vol. 2 (New York: Stein and Day, 1971), 258–59.
6. M. E. Bradford, "The Vocation of Norman Podhoretz," *The Reactionary Imperative: Essays Literary and Political* (Peru, Ill.: Sherwood Sugden, 1990), 27–38.

Selected Bibliography

PRIMARY WORKS

Norman Podhoretz

Books

The Bloody Crossroads: Where Literature and Politics Meet. New York: Simon & Schuster, 1986.
Breaking Ranks: A Political Memoir. New York: Harper & Row, 1979.
Doings and Undoings: The Fifties and After in American Writing. New York: Farrar, Straus & Giroux, 1964.
Making It. New York: Random House, 1967.
The Present Danger: Do We Have the Will to Reverse the Decline in American Power? New York: Simon & Schuster, 1980.
Why We Were in Vietnam. New York: Simon & Schuster, 1982.

Books Edited

The Commentary Reader: Two Decades of Articles and Stories. New York: Atheneum, 1966.

Other Essays Cited

"The Hate That Dare Not Speak Its Name." *Commentary,* November 1986, 21–32.
Contribution to *Second Thoughts: Former Radicals Look Back at the Sixties,* edited by Peter Collier and David Horowitz, 189–95. Lanham, Md.: Madison Books, 1989.

Kenneth S. Lynn

Books

The Air-Line to Seattle: Studies in Literary and Historical Writing about America. Chicago: University of Chicago Press, 1983.
A Divided People. Westport, Conn.: Greenwood Press, 1977.
The Dream of Success: A Study of the Modern American Imagination. Boston: Little, Brown, 1955.

Hemingway. New York: Simon & Schuster, 1987.
Mark Twain and Southwestern Humor. Boston: Little, Brown, 1959.
Visions of America: Eleven Literary Historical Essays. Westport, Conn.: Green-
    wood Press, 1973.
William Dean Howells: An American Life. New York: Harcourt, Brace, Jo-
    vanovich, 1971.

Books Edited

The Comic Tradition in America: An Anthology. Garden City, N.Y.: Doubleday,
    1958.
The Professions in America. Boston: Houghton Mifflin, 1965.
"The Scarlet Letter": Text, Sources, Criticism. New York: Harcourt, Brace, and
    World, 1961.

Other Essays Cited

"F. O. Matthiessen." In Epstein, *Masters*, 103–18.

Joseph Epstein

Books

Ambition: The Secret Passion. New York: Dutton, 1980.
Divorced in America: Marriage in an Age of Possibility. New York: Dutton, 1974.
Familiar Territory: Observations on American Life. New York: Oxford University
    Press, 1979.
The Middle of My Tether: Familiar Essays. New York: Norton, 1983.
Once More around the Block: Familiar Essays. New York: Norton, 1987.
Partial Payments: Essays on Writers and Their Lives. New York: Norton, 1989.
Plausible Prejudices: Essays on American Writing. New York: Norton, 1985.

Books Edited

Masters: Portraits of Great Teachers. New York: Basic Books, 1981.

Other Essays Cited

Contribution to "Liberalism and the Jews: A Symposium." *Commentary*, Janu-
    ary 1980, 32–34.
"The New Conservatism: Intellectuals in Retreat." *The New Conservatives: A
    Critique from the Left*, edited by Lewis A. Coser and Irving Howe, 9–28.
    New York: Quadrangle, 1974.
"Polonius Remembers the *Partisan Review*." Review of *A Partisan View* by
    William Philips. *Sewanee Review* 40 (Fall 1984): 604–17.
"The Rise of the Verbal Class." *Harper's*, March 1984, 73–80, 82.
"Who Killed Poetry?" *Commentary*, August 1988, 13–20.

Short Fiction

"The Count and the Princess." *Hudson Review* 35 (Spring 1982): 47–68. Reprinted in *Best American Short Stories 1983,* edited by Anne Tyler and Shannon Ravenel, 117–40. Boston: Houghton Mifflin, 1983.

"The Goldin Boys." *Commentary,* October 1989, 46–55.

"Kaplan's Big Deal." *Commentary,* June 1989, 42–53.

"Low Anxiety." *Commentary,* January 1989, 47–54.

"No Pulitzer for Pinsker." *Commentary,* March 1988, 59–68.

"Race Relations." *Harper's,* March 1979, 105–10, 112–13.

"Schlifkin on My Books." *Hudson Review* 38 (Spring 1985): 63–78.

SECONDARY WORKS

General

Conant, Oliver. "Culture and the Neoconservatives." *Dissent* 34 (Spring 1987): 241–45. "The usual neoconservative tone of unrelieved scorn, and even more the idea they entertain of themselves as a sort of saving remnant . . . must arise from a growing sense that they have so far failed . . . to make much of an impact upon . . . the educated public."

Kazin, Alfred. "Saving My Soul at the Plaza." *New York Review of Books,* 31 March 1983, 38–42. A generally derisive account of the conference on "Our Country and Our Culture" sponsored by the Committee for the Free World at New York's Plaza Hotel. Podhoretz and Epstein were both featured speakers.

Pinsker, Sanford. "Revisionism with Rancor: The Threat of the Neoconservative Critics." *Georgia Review* 38 (Summer 1984): 243–61. The first essay to identify the neoconservatives as a specific school of literary critics. A harsh and supercilious attack.

Steinfels, Peter. *The Neoconservatives: The Men Who Are Changing America's Politics.* New York: Simon & Schuster, 1979. An early critical assessment of neoconservatism as a political phenomenon. Focuses on Irving Kristol, Daniel Patrick Moynihan, and Daniel Bell.

On Norman Podhoretz

Adler, Renata. "Polemic and the New Reviewers." In *The Young American Writers,* edited by Richard Kostelanetz, 3–24. New York: Funk and Wagnalls, 1967. Cites *Doings and Undoings,* along with contemporaneous books by Arthur Mizener and Irving Howe, as examples of a polemical trend in recent book reviewing.

Beichman, Arnold. "Their Present Danger." *National Review.* 3 September 1982, 1088–89. A survey of the negative critical response to *Why We Were in Vietnam.*

Bradford, M. E. "The Vocation of Norman Podhoretz." In *The Reactionary Imperative: Essays Literary and Political,* 27–38. Peru, Ill.: Sherwood Sugden, 1990. In *The Bloody Crossroads,* Podhoretz "has sustained his interest in literature and in one way of dealing with it—to our great profit and advantage."

Enright, D. J. "Articles of Use." In *Conspirators and Poets,* 19–26. London: Chatto & Windus, 1966. Says of *Doings and Undoings:* "What Mr. Podhoretz is undertaking here is an elaborate and sophisticated version of 'the greatest novel I have read this week.' "

Epstein, Joseph. "Remaking It." Review of *Breaking Ranks. New York Times Book Review,* 21 October 1979, 3, 50–51. Podhoretz "provides a vivid history of the political life of intellectuals during a time when intellectual integrity has been subject to a cruel strain."

Garrett, George. "My Silk Purse and Yours: *Making It,* Starring Norman Podhoretz." In *The Sounder Few,* edited by R. H. W. Dillard, George Garrett, and John Rees Moore, 327–42. Athens: University of Georgia Press, 1971. Says of *Making It:* "The truth of this book, disguised as it is from the protagonist, is poetic, a statement of the eternal paradox of man's goals in the only world he knows for sure, the one he lives in and will die in."

Hakola, Stewart. "Norman Podhoretz." In *Contemporary Authors: New Revision Series,* vol. 7, edited by Ann Evory et al., 392–96. Detroit: Gale Research, 1982. A bio-bibliographical sketch of Podhoretz's career up through 1982.

Hart, Jeffrey. "The Good Fight." Review of *The Bloody Crossroads. National Review,* 4 July 1986, 36–37. "Trilling and Leavis are indeed presences here, and behind them the major tradition of humane criticism that stretches back from Edmund Wilson through Arnold and Hazlitt."

Hentoff, Nat. "Cool, Like Blocked." Review of *Doings and Undoings. Nation,* 3 March 1964, 298–300. "The book merits attention . . . for what it tells about the problems of the sophisticated American liberal in his thirties."

Hills, Rust. "The Dirty Little Secret of Norman Podhoretz." *Esquire,* April 1968, 92, 164, 166, 168–72, 174–78. Published shortly after the appearance of *Making It,* this essay argues that Podhoretz expresses outrageous opinions simply to attract attention. Accompanied by nine David Levine caricatures.

Hitchens, Christopher. "An Exchange on Orwell." *Harper's,* February 1983, 56–58. Podhoretz "only really likes Orwell for his flaws, and cannot read him or discuss him as a whole."

———. "No End of a Lesson." Review of *Why We Were in Vietnam. Nation,* 3 April 1982, 403–4. "Podhoretz's world view is . . . so neurotic and unstable that he regards any challenge of any kind, from any quarter, as a personal threat."

Kramer, Hilton. Review of *Breaking Ranks*. *New Republic*, 17 November 1979, 32–35. "This is a combative book, vivid in its account of people, ideas, and events, and unusually candid in its criticism of celebrated individuals—both living and dead—who have rarely, if ever, been subjected to such shrewd and searching analysis."

Lekachman, Robert. "Mean to Me." Review of *Breaking Ranks*. *Nation*, 10 November 1979, 469–70. Compares *Breaking Ranks* to *Making It*. "The first book's discussion of people was indiscreet and mean-spirited. The tone of the second is almost unbelievably vindictive."

Mailer, Norman. "Up the Family Tree." In *Existential Errands*, 171–97. Boston: Little, Brown, 1972. Originally published in *Partisan Review*, this essay begins by attacking those who trashed *Making It* but concludes by joining them. Effectively ended the friendship of Mailer and Podhoretz.

Marshall, Charles Burton. "Lucky No Longer." Review of *Why We Were in Vietnam*. *National Review*, 2 April 1982, 363–64. "Podhoretz traces [the Vietnam War's] vexing course from the standpoint . . . of the interplay of ideas in the nation's public life."

O'Brien, Conor Cruise. "Trop de Zele." Review of *The Bloody Crossroads*. *New York Review of Books*, 9 October 1986, 11–12, 14. "Mr. Podhoretz is neither Henry Kissinger nor Henry Adams. And he is not so much an authority on 'the bloody crossroads' as another of the romantic and power-infatuated victims with whom that crossroads is bestrewn."

Ozick, Cynthia. "Hypnotized by Totalitarian Poesy." Review of *The Bloody Crossroads*. *New York Times Book Review*, 18 May 1986, 11–12. Praises Podhoretz for attacking "the reluctance of many Western intellectuals to [realize that, even in theory, communism] leads as ineluctably to the gulag as Nazism led ineluctably to the death camps."

Ross, Jean W. "*CA* Interview [with Norman Podhoretz]." In *Contemporary Authors: New Revision Series*, vol. 7, edited by Ann Evory et al., 396–98. Text of a telephone interview with Podhoretz conducted on 1 June 1981. Published in tandem with Stewart Hakola's bio-bibliographical essay.

Schlesinger, Arthur, Jr. "Make War Not It." Review of *Why We Were in Vietnam*. *Harper's*, March 1982, 71–73. "In their sentimental conception of foreign policy, in their conviction that the duty of a state in its international relations is to subordinate interests to ideals, [Podhoretz and the New Left] are really mirror images."

Sheed, Wilfrid. *The Morning After: Selected Essays and Reviews*, 283–92. New York: Farrar, Straus & Giroux, 1971. Sees *Making It* as "a book of no literary distinction whatever, pockmarked by clichés and little mock modesties and a woefully pedestrian tone."

Teachout, Terry. Review of *The Bloody Crossroads*. *American Spectator*, August

1986, 38. Podhoretz's "field of interest is worthy, his discriminations central, his arguments stated with the greatest possible clarity."

Ulam, Adam B. "To the Brink." Review of *The Present Danger* and Solzhenitsyn's *The Mortal Danger*. *National Review*, 14 November 1980, 1402–3. "Mr. Podhoretz is particularly perceptive in analyzing the various psychological components of the 'culture of appeasement,' as he calls it."

Van Den Haag, Ernest. "Breaking Bones." Review of *Breaking Ranks*. *National Review*, 8 February 1980, 163–64. "Anyone interested in the intellectual life, in those who live it, in the never-ending battle of fact and fashion, should read *Breaking Ranks*."

Vidal, Gore. "The Empire Lovers Strike Back." *Nation*, 22 March 1986, 350–51. A virulently anti-Zionist attack on Podhoretz and Decter as Israeli fifth columnists. Prompted Podhoretz to accuse Vidal of anti-Semitism.

On Kenneth S. Lynn

Baender, Paul. Review of *Mark Twain and Southwestern Humor*. *Modern Philology* 57 (1960): 285–86. "The book has little other than cautionary value for the professional scholar and critic."

Bell, Gene H. Review of *Visions of America*. *Science and Society* 40 (Spring 1976): 86–88. "As the Alexandrian world of academic literary criticism breaks up into ever-narrower sects . . . , each one selling its methodological solipsism as the latest in grand theory, Kenneth Lynn's understated exercises come as a breath of fresh air."

Chaffin, Tom. "Love-It-or-Leave-It Lit. Crit." Review of *The Air-Line to Seattle*. *Nation*, 9 July 1983, 55–57. Thinks that Lynn would be more effective "if he were more willing to grant other writers their complexities and less willing to sacrifice irony for ideological stridency."

Cowley, Malcolm. "Hemingway's Wound—and Its Consequences for American Literature." *Georgia Review* 38 (Summer 1984): 223–39. Cowley's response to Lynn's attack on him in "Hemingway's Private War." Uses previously unpublished letters to argue for the importance of Hemingway's war wounds to his writing.

Cox, James M. "Getting the Best of Ernest." Review of *Hemingway*. *Sewanee Review* 96 (Summer 1988): 511–16. "Lynn pugnaciously exposes the weaknesses of earlier commentators. The result is a more dramatic life of Hemingway than we have yet had, and the biographer himself plays no small part in the drama."

Crews, Frederick. "Pressure under Grace." Review of *Hemingway*. *New York Review of Books*, 13 August 1987, 30–37. Lynn has "provided a model of the way biographically informed criticism can catch the pulse of works about which everything appeared to have been said."

DeMott, Benjamin. "Papa's Mama Trouble." Review of *Hemingway*. *Atlantic*,

July 1987, 91–92. "Lynn's achievement as biographer is that he sets up a field of coherent relationships among previously difficult to read phenomena."

Heath, William G., Jr. Review of *Visions of America. New England Quarterly* 47 (June 1974): 309–11. "Lynn's methodology involves the tools of the biographer, historian, and psychologist, as well as the critic."

Johnson, Diane. "Mama and Papa." Review of *Hemingway. New York Times Book Review,* 19 July 1987, 3, 25. "The overwhelming impression is a sympathetic and detailed one of a writer trapped . . . in a more conspicuous life than he could manage."

Kazin, Alfred. "A Farewell to Art." Review of *Hemingway. New Republic,* 13 July 1987, 27–29. "Of all the many portraits of Hemingway I have encountered, Kenneth Lynn's obsessively Freudian attempt to show Hemingway as an unconscious homosexual is the most relentlessly researched and the most condescending."

Marx, Leo. "Offerings to the Bitch-Goddess." Review of *The Dream of Success. New Republic,* 9 May 1955, 20–22. Lynn "is a clinician more interested in the etiology of disease than in the patients or their pathetic tales."

Pinsker, Sanford. "Hemingway and His Biographical Wounds." Review of four Hemingway biographies. *Gettysburg Review* 1 (Winter 1988): 137–45. "The effect [of Lynn's biography] is to see Hemingway as a man split between *chutzpah* and *pudeur,* between brazenness and sexual shame."

Popkin, Henry. "American Myth." Review of *The Dream of Success. Commonweal,* 29 July 1955, 429. This book "belongs more to the history of mass culture than to the history of ideas."

Randolph, Vance. "A Treasury to Draw Upon." Review of *Mark Twain and Southwestern Humor. New York Times Book Review,* 28 February 1960, 6, 42. This study is "a fresh and exciting evaluation of the whole matter of Mark Twain scholarship."

Seelye, John. "The Rise of William Dean Howells." Review of *William Dean Howells: An American Life. New Republic,* 3 July 1971, 23–26. "Lynn's perspective brings out the Christ in the man we always thought was jesting Pilate."

Shaw, Peter. "After the Genteel Tradition." Review of *The Air-Line to Seattle. American Scholar* 52 (Autumn 1983): 546, 548, 550. "If Lynn has not singlehandedly solved the enigma of scholarly and intellectual decline, he stands out as one of the finest critics, and undoubtedly the most vigorous and wide-ranging one, to have called it to public attention."

Tate, J. O. "Ideologue's Bane." Review of *The Air-Line to Seattle. National Review,* 5 August 1983, 948–50. "Because of their unity of purpose and perception, these essays . . . make for an unusually satisfying collection."

Thompson, John. "A Hundred Years of Howells." Review of *William Dean Howells: An American Life. Harper's,* June 1971, 94–98. Lynn "places

Howells . . . firmly in the past, gives him in addition to his literary mission his own timeless and therefore historically irrelevant humanity."

On Joseph Epstein

Bloom, James. Review of *Partial Payments. New York Times Book Review*, 12 March 1989, 23. "Instead of informing and illuminating—which he often does well—Mr. Epstein frequently wastes time maligning his own Classic Comics images of modern psychology, Saab-driving Marxists and the Beatles."

Bromwich, David. "A Regular Joe." Review of *Once More around the Block. New Republic*, 8 June 1987, 45–48. "Epstein measures himself too much against the dazzling winners of this world and compares himself too comfortably to those he thinks it safe to regard as losers."

Conarroe, Joel. "From Aristotle to Zelda." Review of *Once More around the Block. New York Times Book Review*, 7 June 1987, 13. "The subject of these pieces, whatever the announced topic, is Joseph Epstein. . . . To read him is to sit in the company of a bookish, witty, abrasive individual with a liberal education and conservative views."

Core, George. "Procrustes' Bed." *Sewanee Review* 93 (Fall 1985): xci–xcv. Discusses *The Middle of My Tether* along with other recent books of essays. Calls Epstein "one of the brainiest and best-read writers now publishing regularly."

———. "Procrustes' Bed." *Sewanee Review* 96 (Fall 1988): lxxxviii–lxxxix. Says of *Once More around the Block* "it is gratifying when a writer whose work you admire doesn't level out and get stuck on a plateau, no matter how high that plateau."

DeMott, Benjamin. "Animadversions and Amusements." Review of *Familiar Territory. New York Times Book Review*, 4 November 1979, 12, 47. "In snippets and sometimes for as long as half a column, Mr. Epstein . . . establishes that, at his best, he is a critic with real force of mind."

Fenyvesi, Charles. Review of *Familiar Territory. New Republic*, 10 November 1979, 37–38. "These are times that call for tracts rather than essays—purposeful jogging rather than a stroll. Epstein and his fellow essay writers are elegantly out of fashion."

Iannone, Carol. "Payment in Full." Review of *Partial Payments. National Review*, 21 April 1989, 46–47. Argues that "the grounds on which [Epstein] discusses literature are so fertile that even if you dissent from individual judgments, you can savor what's behind them."

Jacoby, Russell, "Is Aristides Just?" Review of *The Middle of My Tether. Nation*, 19 November 1983, 489–91. "Epstein writes essays that crackle with wit and insight; he is an observer with a gift for detail and language. Yet . . . conservatism and self-satisfaction threaten to dull his sensibilities."

Johnston, George Sim. Review of *Plausible Prejudices. American Spectator*, June

1985, 42–43. "Epstein is a man with an argument, and the point he drives home again and again is that much of our literature has been reduced to a flea market of received ideas."

Larkin, Philip. "On familiar ground." Review of *The Middle of My Tether. Times Literary Supplement,* 13 January 1984, 29. Says Epstein's "subjects are tossed up, turned around, stuck with quotations, abandoned and returned to, playfully inverted, and finally set back on their feet, as is the reader, a little breathless but quite unharmed."

Lilla, Mark. Review of *The Middle of My Tether. American Spectator,* January 1984, 39–40. "Epstein knits and purls his anecdotes, selectively dropping the appropriate aphorism (by Santayana, La Rochefoucauld, Montaigne, Karl Kraus, Yogi Berra), concluding with his serious punch line buried in a clever little joke."

Miller, Stephen. "The Fuel of Achievement." Review of *Ambition. Commentary,* April 1981, 79–82. "*Ambition* is a book both admirably free of cant and marked by what I would call critical generosity."

Petrimoulx, Paulette. "Joseph Epstein." *Contemporary Authors,* vol. 119, edited by Hal May, 97–100. Detroit: Gale Research, 1987. A biobibliographical survey of Epstein's career up through *Plausible Prejudices.*

Pritchard, William H. "Kind to the Dead, Hard on the Living." Review of *Plausible Prejudices. New York Times Book Review,* 24 February 1985, 8. "Although [Epstein] asserts that criticism is in decline, it cannot be in decline merely, when provocative critics like himself are on the scene."

Rubin, Louis D., Jr. "Mr. Epstein Doesn't Like It." Review of *Plausible Prejudices. Sewanee Review* 94 (Winter 1986): 111–17. Epstein's "manner is sometimes Menckenian, but his matter is more along the lines of the late Paul Elmer More."

Schechner, Mark. "The Ford in Our Past." Review of *Ambition. Nation,* 17 January 1981, 53–56. "*Ambition* is a little *McGuffey's Reader* for intellectuals, consisting of stirring vignettes from the lives of the great [and] illuminating quotes from the successful and famous."

Stevens, Rodney. Review of *Plausible Prejudices. Studies in Short Fiction* 23 (Fall 1986): 472–73. Epstein's observations "spur us—with their wit, erudition, and perspicuity—to reassess (or to reaffirm) our notions of what makes a story or essay truly first-rate."

Teachout, Terry. "In the Company of Liebling and Mencken." Review of *Once More around the Block. Wall Street Journal,* 26 June 1987, 17. "Mr. Epstein's way with the familiar essay . . . has much in common with that of Messrs. Beerbohm, Liebling and Mencken."

Wolcott, James. "Son of 'Making It.' " Review of *Ambition. New Republic,* 24 January 1981, 34–36. "With *Ambition,* Joseph Epstein has taken the bicycle pump out of the garage and blown up an essay-length topic into an air-bloated tome of nearly 300 pages."

Index

The Author

Mark Royden Winchell is known to Twayne readers for his books on Joan Didion, William F. Buckley, Jr., and Leslie Fiedler. He has also published critical studies of Horace McCoy and John Gregory Dunne in the Boise State University Western Writers Series. His book *Talmadge: A Political Legacy, A Politician's Life* (written in collaboration with Herman E. Talmadge) was voted Georgia Biography of the Year for 1987 by the Dixie Council of Authors and Journalists.

Winchell received his Ph.D. from Vanderbilt University in 1978. He is currently professor of English at Clemson University and managing editor of the *South Carolina Review*. He lives with his wife, composition scholar Donna Haisty Winchell, and a menagerie of stuffed animals.

The Editor

Frank Day is a professor of English at Clemson University. He is the
author of *Sir William Empson: An Annotated Bibliography* and *Arthur
Koestler: A Guide to Research*. He was a Fulbright Lecturer in American
Literature in Romania (1980–81) and in Bangladesh (1986–87).